to Mike Caslin

War and Empire

" MY COUNTRY RIGHT OR WRONG
BUT
WITH ITS WRONGS TO RIGHT! "

Paul Atwood
April 21, 2010

WAR AND EMPIRE

The American Way of Life

Paul L. Atwood

www.plutobooks.com

First published 2010 by Pluto Press
345 Archway Road, London N6 5AA and
175 Fifth Avenue, New York, NY 10010

www.plutobooks.com

Distributed in the United States of America exclusively by
Palgrave Macmillan, a division of St. Martin's Press LLC,
175 Fifth Avenue, New York, NY 10010

British Library Cataloguing in Publication Data
A catalogue record for this book is available from the British Library

ISBN   978 0 7453 2765 5   Hardback
ISBN   978 0 7453 2764 8   Paperback

Library of Congress Cataloging in Publication Data applied for

10   9   8   7   6   5   4   3   2   1

Designed and produced for Pluto Press by
Chase Publishing Services Ltd, 33 Livonia Road, Sidmouth, EX10 9JB, England
Typeset from disk by Stanford DTP Services, Northampton, England
Printed and bound in the European Union by
CPI Antony Rowe, Chippenham and Eastbourne

For Adrian and Amelia

Contents

Acknowledgements   xi
Preface   xii

1 **Introduction: American Ideology versus American Realities**   1

2 **By the Sword We Seek Peace**   17
Microbes: The ally of rape, torture and conquest?   18
Spaniards discover civilizations far more advanced
    than their own – except for 'guns, germs and steel'   22
Faced with economic and social disruption at home,
    the British join the game of empire   26
The Virgin Queen's colony   30
A blood-soaked city on a hill   34
Property and profit as the sign of God's favor   36
The 'Spawn of Satan'   38
The first all-out war   39

3 **French, Indians, Rebellion and Repression**   43
The first global war prefigures more global war   43
Americans who wanted war now refuse to pay for it   49
Those who made the greatest sacrifices are betrayed   52
The new American elite taxes and forecloses on those
    without representation   54

4 **An Empire for Liberty?**   59
Creating an enemy to thwart the Bill of Rights   59
Many trails of tears   62
Land hunger provokes an unnecessary war   64
Laying claim to the hemisphere   66
'Anglo-Saxonism' and the march to the Pacific   69
To the halls of Montezuma   71

5 **From Ashes to Empire**   75
Not fighting to free slaves   75
The compromise of 1877: Selling the freedmen out   78

Massacres in the west   79
Industrialism renewed and the ascension of finance   81
Cycles of boom and bust produce political instability   83
Class war intensifies   84
To contain the revolt of the masses and restore
    profitability, the plutocrats opt for empire   86
The Monroe Doctrine enforced   89
The ideology of expansion   91

6   War with Spain, then Another and Another   97
    As a pretext for war, Spain is declared a threat to
        American security   97
    The press reveals its racism and lust for empire   100
    Cubans on verge of winning independence on their
        own alarm Washington   101

7   World War I: Making the World Safe for American
    Capital Investment   104
    Germany's potential dominance in Europe a threat to
        the Open Door   106
    The standard interpretation of American entry is
        superficial   107
    Britain violates American neutrality but Wilson does
        nothing   110
    Though its blockade damages the American economy
        the House of Morgan invests in Britain   111
    Wilson's neutrality a charade   112
    Wilson positions himself to be global messiah   114
    Bolsheviks take Russia out of the war and pose a new
        threat to the Open Door   116
    American entry tips the balance though Germany is
        not militarily defeated   117
    Wilson's peace plan fails but the US becomes the
        global finance capital   119
    A war against democracy at home   119
    A world made safe only for more war   121

8   Pearl Harbor: The Spark but not the Cause   124
    Day of infamy – or deception?   126
    Japan's empire threatens western colonialism   127
    Admiral Richardson warns FDR that his measures
        threaten war   128

American military officials long understood that
    Pearl Harbor was vulnerable to surprise attack   129
Electronic intercepts and radio direction finders
    indicate Japan's intent   130
Philippines left vulnerable by General MacArthur   133
Neither Germany nor Japan capable of attacking the
    continental US   134
If the Axis posed no military threat to the US what
    was the real worry?   138
America and the Holocaust: Not rescuing Jews   143
The atomic bombings: To save lives or to intimidate
    communists?   145
Downfall   147

9   **Cold War: The Clash of Ideology or of Empires?**   151
Soviets indispensable to defeat of Hitler   152
Yesterday's essential ally becomes the new threat   154
The atomic arms race begins   157
Soviets withdraw voluntarily from conquered areas   157
Capitalism and communism vie for the loyalties of
    the defeated empires' colonies   159
The threat of a closed world remains: Germany
    becomes a new axis   161
Control of oil becomes the linchpin of American policy   163
The 'Martial Plan'   165
The future of Germany further polarizes the Cold War   168
Building the permanent war economy   169
Losing China to the Chinese   171

10 **Cold War/Hot War: Savage Wars of Peace?**   174
Creating the warfare state   175
Korea   178
Vietnam   188
The Middle East and the Cold War   200

11 **War on Terror**   215
A new American century?   215
Giving the Soviet Union its Vietnam War   216
Terrorists as 'freedom fighters'   218
Terrorizing Iraqi civilians   219
Abandoning Afghanistan to warlords and the rise of
    the Taliban and Al Qaeda   220

Demonizing Iraq for the events of 9/11 to foster
    hysteria at home   221
The real reasons the US invaded Iraq   223
The prize   224
Co-opting the Russian and Chinese backyards   225

12 Conclusion   229

Notes   240
Bibliography   257
Index   265

Acknowledgements

In addition to my editors at Pluto Press, especially Roger van Zwanenberg, Robert Webb and Rebecca Wise, I would like to recognize the following people who gave me direct assistance in the writing or conception of this book, or who gave me insight, inspiration or encouragement along the way:

Christine Atwood, Andrew Bacevich, the late Irving Bartlett, Kevin Bowen, Mary Anne Ferguson, Harold 'Shep' Gurwitz, Linda Rhine, Lois Rudnick, Winston Warfield, Marilyn Young and Howard Zinn.

Preface

For a quarter century I have been teaching courses at the University of Massachusetts-Boston on American wars of the twentieth century with emphasis upon social, political and economic consequences to the United States and the even more bitter costs to those nations on the receiving end of American firepower. Any assumptions I had initially about basic knowledge on the part of students were shattered early on. Even back in the 1980s, only a decade after the war in Vietnam ended, many students did not know whether the US had sided with the North or South. Many had no idea who Ho Chi Minh was. I encountered one student who had come to believe that the pernicious communists had employed 'Asian Orange' herbicides on American troops in an attempt to poison them. Many students, and presumably the larger public, remain unaware of what occurred at Pearl Harbor during World War II, or of what nations comprised the Axis. Nor could many name even one of the US presidents during that conflict! More than a few believed the US had fought the communists. World War I and the Korean War are *terra incognita* to say nothing of the Spanish–American, Mexican and all other wars. All this in a major university! Matters seem to be getting worse.

Gore Vidal mocks the country of his birth as 'the United States of Amnesia', knowing full well that none of this is an accident. Many years ago, shortly after undergraduate studies and just as the innovative educational experiments of the 1960s were undermined by the conservative reaction, I worked as a substitute high school teacher in a Boston suburb and attempted to bring in materials outside of the prescribed curriculum to make sense of matters in the assigned text that were incomprehensible otherwise. I was told in no uncertain terms that I would teach that curriculum or I would be gone. I was shortly gone. Commercial television, pop music and Hollywood have widely replaced reading as a source of 'information' and those who control such channels ensure that the menu of choice involves very little that can explicate for viewers the world they have inherited, much less provide any analysis or discussion about what alternatives might be possible. The culture of narcissism ensures a certain kind of moral blindness to the very real crises that emerge throughout the world and the suffering these impose on victims. The internet provides some hope but there is much quackery there and studies have shown that a majority of users visit pornography, sports or betting sites in any case.

So the conundrum remains: given the function of the mass media as purveyors of consumerist propaganda, how can we inject more relevant analysis of the past into the culture in order more clearly to illuminate our present and journey therefore into a better future?

Most young people remain aghast at the attacks that took 3,000 American lives on 9/11 but have no idea that the US has killed quite literally, directly or indirectly, millions of civilians across the planet since the 1940s, let alone the body count in the national territory since 1607. When informed that their nation has troops in 140 of the 191 nations globally most students shrug. If such is the case, they seem to imply, there must be a justifiable reason, and anyway what can be done about it? To the extent that students know anything of past wars these and the current wars in Iraq and Afghanistan are rationalized by the usual rhetoric. If queried to answer with any detail about *why* the US entered any of its wars the all-too-usual answer, often punctuated by a quizzical look, is 'freedom?' or 'national security?' Despite the absolute centrality of war to the creation and evolution of the United States, the nation's public schools, and for that matter universities and colleges, do a miserable job of educating the young about these crucial matters. More to my dismay, for almost two decades I have hosted annual workshops for high school teachers and discovered that alarming ignorance about American warfare also characterizes too many charged with that instruction.

As I tried to understand this state of affairs I thought about my own grade school introduction to the past, in the shadow of World War II, and remembered the highly jingoistic mis-education about that war drummed into my head, long ago concluding that it was the sort of triumphalist version that victors always write. But at least I had essential facts upon which to build when I began to delve deeper. That is not so today. In almost all states today history is taught 'to the test', i.e. to standardized prescriptions about what great names, events and dates students need to memorize in order to pass an examination that is the pre-requisite of graduation. With few exceptions students revile their history curricula, condemning them as insufferably boring and a 'turn-off'. Students who pass such high stakes tests most often instantly forget what little of substance they have been 'taught'. The inevitable result is widespread ignorance and an equal aversion to any more history, or its close relatives – politics, economics and sociology.

Some might say that this is really an advantage for teachers since we don't have to overcome entrenched mythologies, but the real problem is that while the details of many hyper-nationalistic legends have largely been lost to today's youth, the highly idealized belief system they were intended to buttress remains as deeply rooted as ever, according to which the American way of war is really the way of peace and the defense of liberty. The American people are essentially peace-loving and go to war only when the misdeeds of others force their hand. That is the incessant credo propagated in most of the mass media and increasingly unchallenged in academia.

Henry Giroux, an American professor driven to a Canadian university because he challenged the corporatization of the American university, has said that:

Universities, in general, especially following the events of 9/11, were under assault by Christian nationalists, reactionary neoconservatives and market fundamentalists for allegedly representing the weak link in the war on terrorism. Right-wing students were encouraged to spy on the classes of progressive professors...Put differently, corporate and Pentagon money was now funding research projects and increasingly knowledge was being militarized in the service of developing weapons of destruction, surveillance and death. Couple this assault with the fact that faculty were becoming irrelevant as an oppositional force... and many simply no longer had the conviction to uphold the university as a democratic public sphere.

If colleges and universities are inexorably being drawn into the orbit of the warfare state should we really be surprised that the realities of that state's agenda should be hidden or overlaid with mendacity?

This slim volume is a modest attempt to provide a framework for young readers to understand the confusing, and perhaps disturbing, historical process in which they find themselves and who wish to begin formulating an alternative interpretation of the American past by which to measure the present. Given the limits of space I make no claim to be comprehensive. That would require a volume many times this length. I've chosen the key conflicts that have shaped the American present with a view toward elucidating their causes and consequences. The study of history is not a sterile exercise wherein we implant our heads in the sands of the past. Imperfect as it is, history is the only roadmap we possess to see the landscape of the present. As a useful guide to the future we ignore its milestones at great hazard.

As I write, the United States and the world are in an economic crisis of such depth not seen since the 1930s. If we examine the Gilded Age or the Roaring Twenties, and the economic collapses they engendered, we encounter the same moral and financial corruption so much in evidence today, and, most perilously, the wars chosen by elites to resolve *their* problems and discipline the masses. Our roadmap shows us that we've been on this treacherous terrain before; we need not repeat past tragedy by enacting cruel farce yet again. If this text accomplishes nothing else I hope it reveals that every war in the American past was at bottom a matter of choice, not, as our national ideology proclaims, a necessity. War has never made the world safe for peace but only for more war.

1
Introduction: American Ideology versus American Realities

How many Americans have ever paused to consider that the United States has never bombed any nation that could bomb us back? Ponder the 'Good War'. Neither Germany nor Japan was remotely capable of devastating American cities during World War II, as the US assuredly desolated theirs. If they had possessed such capacity we would never have bombed them for the same reason we never bombarded the Soviets. Since neither of the Axis allies wished war with the US (for the simple reason that they didn't believe they could win), and neither could cross the ocean to attack our cities, neither constituted a genuine military threat to the US. In Chapter 7 we shall examine the real danger officials perceived, and how the administration of Franklin Roosevelt manipulated events such that both Germany and Japan would view America as the primary threat to their imperial aims, and therefore opt for war as their only possible insurance, thereby enabling the US to enter a war the public had decidedly not wanted. But would Roosevelt have *chosen* war, as he surely did, had he believed that a majority of our cities would lie in ruins? Of all belligerents the United States lost the fewest lives by far. Would decision-makers have been willing to accept civilian casualties on a scale like Dresden, Tokyo, Hiroshima, or even London during the Blitz? The strategic goal of American elites in World War II was to expand their global power and reach, taking advantage of the ruin and decline all the other combatants would suffer, enemies and allies alike. The US waged war in such a way as to rise in the global hierarchy, not to sink, and it rose to the top.

Certainly there were American casualties in all wars but never on the scale faced by the losing side. None of this is to dishonor those who gave or risked their lives. Most believed what their officials told them about the threat to the nation. In all cases officials who opted for war believed material gains would far outweigh the loss of life since the war makers would not be risking their own, or in most cases, their kin's.

Or consider how the US approached its communist enemies of a generation ago and ask the same questions. Though the US falsely blamed both the Soviet Union and China for the wars in Korea and Vietnam, and for resistance to the US throughout the so-called 'Third World', American bombs were never unleashed on either of them, though American ordnance lay waste to Korea and Indochina. The reason is quite elementary. The communist giants had nukes and could incinerate us. We ravage only those who lie all but helpless before us.

I challenge any who disagree with the foregoing to name a single American war, with the exceptions of the Revolution and War of 1812, in neither of which Britain brought its full might to bear, where the opponent came close to matching the wealth, resources, and military power the US threw against it. Could any of the following have despoiled our own territory? Iraq? Afghanistan? Serbia? Panama? Nicaragua, Vietnam? Cambodia? Laos? Dominican Republic? Korea? Spain? The Philippines? The Sioux? The Cheyenne? Mexico? The Cherokee? Both Germany and Japan were the strongest enemies the US ever faced in battle, but let us note whose cities were reduced to rubble at the close of that war, and whose were not. The US emerged from World War II with the fewest casualties, its continental territory unscathed, and richer and more powerful by far.

I'm not aware of any scholarship that attempts to quantify the number of civilians killed by the US in its many wars. The figure must be in the millions though many policy-makers, military strategists and arm-chair generals would undoubtedly claim that most such civilians were victims of the misfortunes of war – 'collateral damage' is the current newspeak on the subject. But in many cases the killing of helpless civilians was deliberate. Tokyo, Hiroshima, Nagasaki? General Curtis LeMay insisted there were no such thing as civilians in Japan but one of his principal lieutenants, later Secretary of Defense, Robert McNamara, has admitted that had the US lost the war *he* would have been tried as a war criminal. Pyongyang? Hanoi, Haiphong? 'Free fire zones' across South Vietnam, killing and maiming the very people we were supposed to be saving? Cambodia, Laos, Belgrade, 'Shock and Awe' Baghdad, Falujah? And we mustn't forget the many hundreds of thousands killed by Washington's clients who received advanced American weapons and who were given tacit permission for wholesale murder in places like Indonesia, Chile, Argentina, Guatemala, El Salvador, Nicaragua, Congo, Angola, Lebanon and Palestine, even Iraq when Saddam

Hussein was our man in Baghdad. For a people outraged at the murder of our civilians on 9/11 we are morally anesthetized when it comes to admitting the crimes our own actions, votes and tax dollars have wrought.

A survey of the American past indicates beyond any doubt, and only with the exception of the British during the earliest years of the Republic, that the US has consistently waged warfare always by choice and only against foes that could not win. The romantic fantasy surrounding the Revolutionary War and War of 1812 ignores the fact that the British did not project their full power because they were tied up with more powerful foes in Europe. If they had dispatched their best troops instead of numerous mercenaries the outcome would have been quite different. Washington, Jefferson, Franklin et al. would have swung from the gallows. Since that era the US government, and American public opinion, has always claimed, in all wars, that it was the enemy that initiated hostilities, to which the inherently peaceful American people were honor bound to respond in order to defend ourselves, to restore justice, and overcome 'evildoers'. But this is simply false. Enemy attack of one kind or another was always the justification for war, but in all cases the preconditions, indeed pretexts, for war were set in motion prior to actual combat. American wars have always been matters of choice, not necessity.

Today, less than a generation after the Cold War ended, the United States is at war again, in Iraq and Afghanistan, and is threatening to attack Iran and Pakistan. Of the 191 states comprising the United Nations, the US has military bases in 140 of them. American arms patrol all the seas and skies, including outer space. The Pentagon declares flatly that its strategic agenda is to achieve nothing less than 'full-spectrum dominance' over any potential foe of the future. While many American officials wring their hands about nuclear weapons proliferation, those same public 'servants' believe that the US is justified in constantly upgrading its own nuclear arsenal and missile systems, dismissing the real fear that others have about this. Nor is much made of the hypocrisy of condemning violations of nuclear proliferation in Korea, Pakistan or Iran, while condoning, and even aiding, them in Israel or India.

Much media commentary about the policies of the Bush Administration insists that all this is a perverse departure from the traditional American values and ideals that are claimed to have been in play since the founding of the Republic. But that is a self-serving fantasy fortifying our national conceit that we are a people apart, exceptional and singled out by God or Destiny to redeem humanity. The template for current policies and war was set even before the Founders rose in rebellion against their government. While many of them used powerful rhetoric to exclaim about natural rights and liberty, they only meant such to apply to 'natural aristocrats', like themselves. Their primary goal was to replace their masters in London, to reap the riches of the American continent themselves, thence, as the motto on the dollar proclaims, to establish 'a New Order of the Ages'.

The American enterprise began in savage violence against the peoples Europeans encountered on this continent. The US itself was brought forth by martial exploits glorified and celebrated every Fourth of July, and its vast territory was wrested from others by pretext, aggression, extreme brutality, genocide and 'ethnic cleansing'. Since the US emerged from World War II as the most potent nation in history we have slaughtered millions, directly or not, the vast majority being helpless civilians. In the requisite patriotic storyline, we congratulate ourselves as apostles of peace, compromise and conciliation, and insist that our grossly uneven campaigns are evidence of national heroism mounted against evil.

Mass public acceptance of hypocrisy on this scale requires a deeply-rooted rationale for explaining to ourselves why we can commit naked aggression and not have to experience the guilt or shame which we insist others should feel when they act similarly. In sum, Americans possess a highly adaptive ideology that provides ready-made justifications for our actions, and reproaches for those who oppose us. At bottom the American ideology claims to adhere to a morality that defends self-determination universally for all. But that assertion is honored mainly in its breach.

Humans tend to take their idea systems for granted, descended as if from heaven, not paying much attention to how they have developed, what purpose they serve, who transmits ideas in whose interest, or how they've been acculturated to accept them as given. In all cases, the predominant ideas that circulate, that are *allowed* to circulate, are the ideas of the dominant members of any given society, and they justify or rationalize the privileges, advantages and interests the system gives them. So long as any given system works well enough for most of the population a level of stability sustains the status quo.

Americans pretend not to be subservient to set dogma, believing ourselves to be utterly pragmatic and utilitarian; that is to say, non-ideological. We even contend to be anti-ideological when we oppose the claims of communists or jihadists, yet refuse to believe that we ourselves are captives of an idea system that colors our every perception and renders us incapable of seeing the world as it really is, much less seeing ourselves as others see us. That belief system has developed and evolved over the 400 years since Britain erupted from its slim borders. Inheriting ideas and methods from British empire-building, the US eventually surpassed its parent in scope and method.

The American idea system, which justifies and explains the economic and political system, has evolved incrementally, with each stage building upon earlier suppositions derived originally from Britain itself. No radical break occurred as was the case with the French, Russian or Chinese Revolutions. Both the American and British polities evolved along a similar trajectory. From the beginning in the US a self-selected and tiny elite spoke of 'We the people' and 'democracy' but actually feared popular rule, and created two-tiered political institutions designed to thwart it, much like their model, the British Parliament. The system of profit known as capitalism has always been claimed as the only engine of economic and political activity that can rationally meet human needs. Though the communist world was condemned for its 'slave system', we breezily dismiss the fact that the American system at its inception was built on the backs of the dispossessed and enslaved, or people in other conditions of servitude, and is today proclaimed as the culmination of human political evolution. More than 150 years ago, during America's bloodiest war, Abraham Lincoln declared that the US was 'the last, best hope of mankind'. More recently, Secretary of State Madeleine Albright averred that 'we are the indispensable nation'. For some time now humans in most 'advanced' civilizations have regarded themselves as the crown of creation. Today Americans believe they are the apex of human social evolution.

At every stage of American development key ideas circulated widely to rationalize the circumstances and policies of the day. Actions, often brutal, revealed true motivations. At the dawn of British colonization, Protestant and Puritan religious ideas portrayed a 'New Canaan', a new land endowed to a new 'Chosen People'. The early republic advanced ideas already prevalent in England, borrowed in part from the study of ancient Roman texts, about the rights of citizens and balanced government, although ancient certainties that only an aristocracy should rule were also retained. By the mid-1800s religious ideology merged with what was claimed to be 'scientific' racism in the doctrine of 'Manifest Destiny', avowing that the rapid spread of Anglo-American civilization across the entire continent was evidence of God's approval and blessing upon the United States. By the turn of the twentieth century, with massive demographic shifts and industrialization utterly transforming the social landscape, the national ideology proclaimed that the American way of organizing society was the most advanced the planet had ever witnessed, and called for the world to open its doors to American capital. At the start of both World Wars I and II, as economic collapse threatened the very foundation of the American system, the nation promoted itself as the savior of democracy, pitted against the forces of aggression and militarism, utterly discounting the means by which the US has always wielded its power.

We shield ourselves from such unpleasant truths by imagining we have created this most materially prosperous society by virtue of our own industry, creative genius, work ethic and our exceptionally humane national character. We fantasize that if nations or peoples remain 'undeveloped' and mired in poverty, it can only be because they are slothful, or uneducated, lacking in drive or ambition, or otherwise benighted. Others see more clearly. As an African student of mine once put it, angering American students in the process, 'With what are we to develop? We have been plundered of our very people and resources for five centuries for the sake of *your* development!'

The reality is that the United States has become an empire, an empire different in certain respects from others. But just as all empires before it, the American model seeks to enrich itself by exploiting the peoples over whom it rules.

In 1789 upon leaving Independence Hall in Philadelphia, Benjamin Franklin, who had presided over the Constitutional Convention, was asked what the 55 men inside had accomplished. His answer was terse and succinct: 'A republic if you can keep it!'

Like the other Founders, Franklin was well aware of the slim history of self-governing peoples. In all cases, institutions of representative government, from ancient Greece to Rome to the Italian republics of the Renaissance, had decayed owing to corruption and had devolved into dictatorship. Old Ben was not optimistic about the chances for the newest republic. Rome had once been a functioning republic with popular institutions to safeguard the rights of citizens, but for a full century before an emperor assumed the throne these had been collapsing as the hunger for more land and treasure and the armies to procure these became the principal preoccupation, first of the ruling classes, then of the plebs. Even the imperial dictatorship was circumspect enough to retain the outward symbols of representative government like the Senate and tribunes of the people, in order to foster the illusion that civil rights were still intact. But Rome was increasingly ruled by the sword and by imperial fiat.

The same fate is now befalling the United States. Every president since World War II has engrossed the powers and perquisites of the office. Congress is but a debating society doling out treasure to its corporate benefactors, chiefly banks, insurance giants, oil corporations and military contractors. Bit by bit the Bill of Rights erodes before our eyes with measures like the Patriot Act eroding privacy rights and the prohibition against unwarranted searches. American 'popular' culture (manufactured from above) is little more than videonic 'bread and circuses', the imperial Roman practice of distributing food to the masses when unemployment rose too steeply, and allowing them entry into the chariot races and gladiatorial combat in the arenas, in order to let off frustration that might have led to riots. If ordinary Americans oppose the current wars they do so for the most part only tepidly because we are a people, like others, who prefer the guise of fantasy to reality. We have the most bloated civilization and lifestyle ever seen on planet earth and we know, if only by keeping this forbidden knowledge just below our consciousness, how we got to this state, and whom we had to kill. And we do not want our globalized cornucopia to cease providing its fruits. If the resources we need to sustain our conspicuous consumption happen to be in other people's countries, if their labor is cheaper in order to provide the goods, then history obliges us to do what the Romans did. And we do.

The United States was born amidst war, slavery and genocide at the dawn of the Age of Empire. The American system of production and allocation required unpaid or cheap labor and began with outright plunder and annexation of other peoples' land. That system has evolved to deal with domestic inequality, mal-distribution of wealth and political instability by continually enlarging the pie, at the expense of others. Though elites remain firmly in control of power and own or control the vast bulk of resources, enough surplus is generated so that, with significant exceptions, the American system has been able to include vast sections of the middle and working classes in its material bounty and rewards, but always because others had to die or be dispossessed. As long as the American economy does not allow extreme poverty and unemployment to rise above a certain threshold and affect the largely white middle class, it has generally had at least the passive support of a majority, except when the inherent defects lead to recession or depression. But the prism of ideology has always filtered out much in the larger spectrum of reality. We refuse to believe that the American way of life is, and always has been, the way of war, conquest and empire. We refuse to believe that many Americans enjoy bloated, wasteful lives by wreaking havoc upon others, and because we have promoted our own model of industrial development as the zenith of human progress we have inspired or induced other nations to follow the example, thus inflicting mayhem upon the very biosphere itself. We could, if we were honest, dub ourselves the culture of spoliation.

To be sure there are some who will say that throughout the human condition it has always been thus. History would seem to agree. But we Americans are in profound denial of the extent to which we are *not* exceptions to this arc of history. Thus, any serious hope or prospect for peace in the twenty-first century must frankly confront the indisputably bloody history and present policies of the most potent armed entity ever to bestride the planet. And then, or else, we must begin to live up to the ideals and professed values we claim and teach small children.

Most are taught that the American Revolution was necessary to right the intolerable injustices the British had visited upon their colonial subjects. Yet analysis of the financial interests of the principal Founders indicates clearly that they stood to gain far more by being rulers than the ruled. Their rhetoric of freedom certainly was not applied to the majority of Americans, including most white men who were not allowed to vote. The Declaration of Independence decried the 'slavery' that British rule had imposed upon the likes of Washington, Jefferson and many others but manifestly excluded the real slaves. No sooner had the infant US come into existence than it set out immediately to replace the former mother country as the ascendant power in the entire western hemisphere, more than once attempting to wrest Canada too. It waged war against the Spanish and the French to acquire the lands they claimed, and then against the indigenous peoples over whom the empires alleged to reign. In the most rapid territorial expansion in history the US transited the continent 'from sea to shining sea', piling up a mountain of corpses along the way and trailing millions of slaves in their wake.

By the middle of the nineteenth century the southern slavocracy's desire to exploit more land for the profits generated by unpaid labor dovetailed with the northern industrial-financial elite's longing for the ports of Los Angeles and San Diego. The problem was that these lands belonged to the newly independent nation of Mexico. So the dark art of pretext was employed, as it would be so many times again, and Mexico was charged with violating American territory, whereas exactly the reverse had occurred. The result was that Mexico lost almost half of its land and the US augmented itself by about one-fourth.

Now a Pacific power, the US lost no time in crossing the vast ocean to open what was hoped would be the Great China Market. Bases would be needed and in due time Samoa and Hawaii were annexed, the latter by force. The hermit island-nation of Japan could serve nicely as ports for American warships and merchant vessels, but the local *daimyos*, or warlords, wanted to be left alone and isolated. This would not do. So American warships were dispatched to teach them the error of their ways. The result was Japan's awakening to the fact that much of Asia was being conquered by westerners. Putting aside their differences Japan's rulers unified and centralized authority in their emperor and entered the contest of empire themselves, hoping to beat the west at its own game, a move that would bring on the tragic Pacific War of the mid-twentieth century.

Back in the US, acquisition of the Mexican territories spurred the onset of Civil War and while the competing elements of the American ruling classes sorted out their differences to the tune of 620,000 dead, the nation would await the further development of its financial, industrial and military thrust.

By the late 1800s, with most native tribes subdued or eradicated, with growing wealth produced by the internal combustion engine, electricity and the poorly paid labor of immigrant millions, the US was set to emerge as one of the new arrivals on the stage of empire, hungry to displace the competition. As matters turned out, in addition to Japan there was another latecomer hungry for its own place in the sun – Germany. The martial landscape of the coming twentieth century was looming into focus.

In 1898 another pretext was employed for war, this time against tottering Spain. In the midst of the worst depression in history up to that time, the American polity was being rent asunder. The unprecedented wealth resulting from industrialization remained in the hands of a tiny elite of 'plutocrats' while huddled masses endured terrible privations. Popular demands for a radical redistribution of wealth terrified the plutocrats and *nouveau riche*. Their solution was to openly embrace empire and seek new sources of wealth overseas, thereby enlarging the economic pie and dispensing larger crumbs to the bottom of American society while retaining control at the top. Though members of the patrician classes like Teddy Roosevelt declared that the object of war was to liberate the peoples of Puerto Rico, Guam, Cuba and the Philippines, they were more worried about the threat of revolution at home and the means to avoid it.

In short order, with a crushing victory over Spain, the Caribbean Sea became, as the Romans used to say, *mare nostrum*, 'our sea'. All four island-nations became *de facto* American colonies, exploited as bases for the American navy and for their resources, their people now serving American masters. Cuba's constitution was written in Washington and came with the proviso that the US could intervene militarily on the island any time American interests were said to be at risk. The American base at Guantanamo Bay was signed over in perpetuity for insurance. The Philippines had been promised outright independence but Manila Bay put the US at 'the doorstep to Asia' and no imperial advantage such as this could be surrendered no matter what had been guaranteed. When Filipinos rose in rebellion against the army that had claimed to free them, the US had its first counter-insurgency jungle war and waged it with utmost brutality and racism, killing upwards of 200,000 civilians, the greatest number in one conflict up to that time. The Philippine War could have served as the template for the war in Vietnam but by the 1950s Americans had long since forgotten that the US had conquered the Philippines 40 years before the Japanese tried to in World War II.

With the riches of Asia looming, which of the new empires would dominate?

At this critical stage the US enunciated its plans for the future and on first sight these seemed benign and equitable as well. The Open Door policy asserted the right of all empires to access the wealth of China on equal terms. But since the US economy could already out-compete its capitalist rivals, and would begin with a clear-cut advantage, American competitors understood that the US could potentially close the doors to them. Japan especially took notice. Washington was asserting the fundamental rules of a new game, applicable to the entire world, even if the US was not yet powerful enough to enforce them. But the message was clear. Henceforth, the markets and resources of the world would remain open to American penetration. From that moment on the US would rely increasingly on its arms to enforce what would be its overarching policy.

Meanwhile, the shores of the new American lake had to be pacified. American marines landed in Mexico, Nicaragua, Honduras, Haiti and the Dominican Republic and those nations were brought to heel. Colombia was refusing to allow a new inter-oceanic canal through its province of Panama to enable the American navy and merchant fleet to pass easily between the Atlantic and Pacific. Roosevelt's solution was simple. He told Washington's handpicked Panamanian rebels to declare independence and then dispatched the navy and marines to prevent Colombia from doing anything about it. Some in Congress objected to this naked land grab but, said Teddy, 'I took the Panama Canal, let Congress debate!' Only a few years later Woodrow Wilson would justify a new war against Mexico with the words 'I will teach them to elect good men.'

Now an imperial power of the first rank with an economy larger than the next three rivals combined, the United States stood ready to challenge for supremacy. In Europe the older empires Britain, France and Russia now also faced a unified and highly militarized Germany. With the outbreak of World War I Europe was about to self-destruct.

President Wilson ran for re-election in 1916 claiming he would keep the country out of the war but his policies flatly contradicted that assertion. Wilson proclaimed neutrality yet, on terms essentially dictated from Wall Street, the US had been steadily building up a vested and one-sided interest in the war's outcome. Unless the Allies won the war, the money loaned and invested in them would never be repaid, and if Germany came to dominate central Europe that vital market might be closed to American business, at least on American terms. Worse, that nation might rise as a powerful economic competitor in the very markets of the world desired by American enterprise.

Germany sought to strike at Britain's economic lifeline with the US and began sinking British merchant vessels, inflicting enormous losses. When in desperation Germany announced it would sink all ships attempting to enter British waters, including American ones, and then did so, Wilson and the war hawks had their reason to enter the war and to attempt to shape the order that would follow.

The entry of the US immediately altered the battleground and forced Germany to seek a cease-fire, hoping to gain at least half of its war aims. But it was internally divided and too weak. The British and French were able, despite Wilson's efforts, to impose draconian peace terms that ravaged Germany's economy even further, ultimately setting the stage for the rise of the Nazis.

Wilson's proclaimed agenda for a 'peace without victory' and to 'make the world safe for democracy' came to nothing. The war destroyed the Russian crown and brought on communism. The colonies of Britain and France sensed their growing weakness and they desperately sought to maintain their eroding imperial positions. In Germany, Adolph Hitler came to power vowing to return the nation to glory and to exact revenge against the victors, the communists – and the Jews. In Asia Japan rejected the American Open Door and occupied Manchuria. All the 'Great War' had accomplished was to make the world safe for more carnage. The brief truce unraveled and the world descended again into the maelstrom of war.

American culture perceives World War II as the 'Good War'. Accordingly, the US, again with the greatest reluctance, took up the sword righteously to rout those who had treacherously stabbed us in the back, and thereby prevented the evildoers from achieving their totalitarian aims. As the other empires descended into war the American people insisted that their government stay out. But there is no disputing the fact that prior to December 7, 1941 President Roosevelt secretly ordered the US Navy into the Battle of the Atlantic as a *de facto* ally of Britain and engaged in a real shooting war with Germany. As Japan expanded its occupation of China, Roosevelt allowed American fighter pilots to resign from the Army Air Corps and fly for China in aircraft supplied by the US. Roosevelt provoked both nations. As the commander of the US Pacific fleet revealed, FDR hoped that 'Sooner or later the Japanese would commit an overt act against the United States and the nation would be willing to enter the war.' Thus Congress' Neutrality Act, the expressed will of the people, had been rendered null and void. Ten days before Pearl Harbor, on FDR's orders, the US State Department issued an ultimatum to Japan to withdraw from China and Indochina with the full knowledge that Japan would no more capitulate than Washington would have, had Tokyo demanded the return of California to Mexico. FDR desired war and knowingly made Japan an offer it could only refuse.

Contrary to what many university freshmen believe, the US did not enter World War II to save Jews or rescue the defenseless. Nor did Germany and Japan have the remotest possibility of invading, much less conquering, the United States or of bombing it from afar. Both nations were creating their own self-contained spheres in regions the US wished to penetrate, much as the US had been doing in the western hemisphere. Both nations' imperial aims in vital areas of world trade promised to shut out American capital and business, at least on the Open Door terms that were the essence of the US strategy. Both nations, if successful, would build giant economic powerhouses competing with the US. Given the nature of capitalism there would be no escape from depression and domestic instability at home other than to defeat the competitors and then to open access to resources and consumers by force.

The US faced much the same problem as it had in the late nineteenth century. The inability of the American public to absorb what the economy produced was a major factor in the Great Depression. The surplus had to be sold abroad. This time opening new sources of consumption would not be as easy as in the 1890s. Now the US faced the 'nightmare of a closed world'. To avoid a radically diminished standard of living, and a profound change in the political structure at home, ruling elements of the American oligarchy maneuvered to remake the global order entirely and conform it to American corporate interests. This would require entering the war at the right time, under the right circumstances. World War I had cost 110,000 dead; this time the ruling elite would have to sacrifice 405,000 lives, not to mention the millions of enemy civilians killed.

The notion that the primary motive of the FDR Administration was humanitarian is belied by its deliberate inaction on the Nazi extermination of Europe's Jews and by the fact that victory against Hitler was impossible without an alliance with Soviet communism, a system every bit as murderous as the Nazi regime, and one equally committed to thwarting American capitalism, if by different means. At the war's end the Red Army occupied half the territory the US wished to free from Hitler and cut off from capitalist penetration. While far less powerful than the US, the Soviet Union was still potent enough to obstruct the American grand agenda. The wartime marriage of convenience unraveled, devolving into the most deadly arms race in history, more than once bringing the planet to the brink of nuclear war.

Unscathed by World War II, the US emerged the most powerful and wealthiest nation in history. As such, it alone could spell the terms by which both its allies and enemies could be reconstructed and re-integrated into the new world order desired in Washington and on Wall Street. The long-range goal of a world open to American business enterprise on American terms seemed at last in sight. There were two great obstacles, however. On the one hand, the colonies that American allies and enemies had exploited now sensed the weakness of their European imperial overlords. They would soon be in full revolt. In another of history's ironies the very defeat of Germany and Japan enabled two even greater powers – the USSR and China – to rush into the vacuum and obstruct American goals. The world American rulers wished to reconstruct on their terms was not cooperating.

As millions of soldiers returned to the US, a resumption of mass unemployment loomed and those who had directed wartime production called for a 'permanent war economy'. For that a *permanent enemy* would be required. Thus yesterday's ally became the new foe. All opposition to the American grand strategy was ascribed to the communists (though that was untrue) and on the basis of this they were proclaimed the new threat. American society was militarized as never before, increasingly ruled by what President Dwight Eisenhower would call the 'military-industrial complex'. The Cold War that replaced the carnage of World War II lasted almost half a century, and witnessed numerous hot wars across the planet, from Korea, to the Middle East, to Vietnam, Southeast Asia and Afghanistan, and back to the Middle East. In addition to outright war the newly established National Security Council and Central Intelligence Agency ensured there would always be new foes to fight as they fostered the very anti-Americanism they claimed to oppose by engaging in illegal, covert operations across the planet, overthrowing governments, assassinating leaders who opposed their agenda and undermining entire economies. In this new Orwellian world millions of human beings died while the corporations that fed from the dollars provided by the warfare state racked up trillions in profit, all in the name of national security.

By outspending the communists in the arms race the US hoped to force the USSR to choose between the proverbial 'guns and butter': either to provide material prosperity for its citizens, or to devote the bulk of productive capacity to the arms race. Thus unable to meet its promises of a materially rich and classless society, communism would collapse from within. This was a profoundly dangerous gambit and during the Cuban Missile Crisis of 1962 brought the planet to the brink of Armageddon.

Even as the 'Evil Empire' of the Soviet Union collapsed in the late 1980s, there would be no end to enemies. Even as they outspent almost all other nations combined on national defense and deployed their armed forces to two-thirds of all the nations on earth, American leaders insisted the US was a lone island of righteousness encircled by geo-political sharks. The USSR's demise was hastened by the trap the US had laid by arming Afghan militants and then drawing Soviet forces into a no-win war in Afghanistan. By playing a major role in the utter destruction of that poor nation the US was thus setting itself up for what the CIA terms 'blowback'. Having recruited many thousands of Islamic jihadists from the entire Muslim world to wage holy war on the evil empire, the US soon saw the weapons it had provided those clients turned upon itself. As the twenty-first century dawned the US would find itself bogged down in an impasse in Afghanistan.

No sooner had the American ploy to fell the communist giant succeeded than Saddam Hussein, who had been assisted to power in Iraq by the US in the first place, was regaled as the re-incarnation of Hitler. Earlier he had proved valuable by killing at least half a million Persians when Iran had broken away from the American imperial yoke and raised the specter of Islamic revolution in the Middle East. Yet, when Saddam stepped outside the role created for him by invading Kuwait, putting the US supply of oil, its cost and the value of the dollar at risk, American forces almost effortlessly crushed him, while allowing him to remain in power so that a convenient demon could always be invoked.

Even before the attacks of 9/11 the so-called neo-conservatives who had ascended to power in the George W. Bush Administration had issued their manifesto 'Rebuilding America's Defenses'. The document emphasized the extraordinary opportunity the US now had with the collapse of the USSR and called for nothing less than American dominance in every conceivable sphere of life – economic, political, military and cultural – but bemoaned the probability that the plan could not become operational without a 'catalyzing event like a new Pearl Harbor'.

Then the attacks on the World Trade Center and Pentagon became precisely that catalyzing event.

Although American arms and a vise-like embargo had nullified Saddam since 1991, he was nevertheless held culpable for the horrifying attacks in the US on 9/11. The claim by the Bush Administration that Iraq had abetted the attacks and had nuclear weapons it could launch at the US were fabrications designed to win popular support for the invasion of Mesopotamia, the takeover of the world's second greatest reservoir of petroleum, and the opportunity to build permanent American bases from which to project military power throughout the Middle East.

The 'New American Century' envisioned by the neo-conservatives, and accommodated by neo-liberals, therefore depends on maintaining control of the critical fuel necessary to power the American economy and its massive military machine that now straddles the globe. Yet the very exhortations we delivered to former enemies to follow our example have brought forth bitter fruit. They *have* followed our example. China and Russia are now fellow travelers and as such compete with the US for the very resources and markets that we had previously sought to deny them. In the inevitable irony of history China now deposits its surplus production on the US and holds a substantial portion of the US national debt. Our new capitalist comrades are now more competitive than before. It is past the time when humans understand that such a 'zero-sum game' or beggar-my-neighbor system inexorably leads to violence, and given the advancement of super-destructive weapons, the arc of history has brought the entire species to a crisis. We now assuredly have the means to make ourselves extinct. Unless Americans begin to re-orient the employment of our power away from hypocrisy and toward genuine international cooperation and compromise we will be met inexorably by resistance that will take new, unparalleled and destructive forms. We cannot continue to ignore the exacting toll this mutual competition has taken on the environment and the diminution of un-renewable resources that will, in turn, lead to yet more conflict. The circumstances are ripe for a mere accident or minor spark to ignite another, perhaps final, global holocaust. The times and the future of humanity itself call for an unparalleled commitment to global mutual cooperation, compromise and assistance.

2
By the Sword We Seek Peace

Thus was God pleased to smite our enemies and to give us their land for an inheritance...the Lord was as it were pleased to say unto us, the Land of Canaan will I give unto thee though but few and strangers in it.

Captain John Mason, 1637 (Drinnon, 1990)

The Great Seal of the Commonwealth of Massachusetts depicts a native dressed in traditional Algonquian clothing, holding a bow and an arrow with its point turned downward, an obvious symbol of that peoples' ignominious defeat. This image remains from the seal of the original Massachusetts Bay Colony, which as early as the 1640s adopted the likeness and depicted the Indian pleading 'Come on over and help us'. The state motto accompanying the seal is in Latin and is translated as 'By the sword we seek peace, but peace only under liberty'. These are curious insignia of statehood since natives made mighty efforts to prevent Massachusetts from becoming a British possession at their expense in the first place and Massachusetts was also one of the first British colonies systematically to depopulate itself of Indians and to abuse and deprive of liberty such few as remained, even those who converted to Christianity. In fact the very name 'Massachusetts' is an Algonquian word and is what the people living on the bay near Boston by the same name called themselves. Today there are no members of the tribe once known as the Massachusett. They were systematically rooted out of their homes, sold into slavery or killed and are now extinct. Only their name remains. Their crime was that they believed the land they had inhabited for uncounted generations belonged to them.

These simple illustrations sum up fairly well the history of the American relationship to the native peoples who inhabited what is now the United States before the European conquests and, for that matter, also characterize the relations of the United States with the non-European peoples in those nations upon which it has waged war most recently. American troops in Vietnam regularly called the areas outside defensive perimeters 'Indian country'. A phrase more laden with meaning could not be imagined. The originating

17

assumption was that the aboriginal tribes and clans needed civilizing and this could only be done by Englishmen. Should native peoples (or today those under American occupation) reject the American enlightening mission, the ultimate sanction was and always has been deadly violence. The substantial bloodshed accompanying the educative enterprise carried out by Americans is, and has always been, claimed to be in the service of the higher and nobler purposes of liberty, democracy, or national security.

Of course the so-called civilizing mission was always ultimately a lie. The real venture was to take land and resources from others and transfer these to the conquerors, or to open or maintain sources of gain that would deprive the other of self-determination.

Another curiosity involves the fact that in Washington, D.C. there is a museum devoted to the Holocaust perpetrated in Europe during World War II by the Nazis. The historical record clearly shows that while the United States obviously waged war upon Nazi Germany it did next to nothing to mitigate the Final Solution, the systematic extermination of Jews, so the museum presumably reflects some sense of national guilt. More curious is the absence of such a museum and the collective shame that would memorialize the holocaust that transpired in the United States, and the rest of the Americas, and the horrors and mass deaths engendered by the African slave trade. That vile traffic, in turn, was fostered when deliberate slaughter and European diseases so ravaged native populations that too few Indians remained to be enslaved. All this so that Europeans could reap the riches of the conquered peoples and lands of the Americas. When Saddam Hussein invaded Kuwait in 1990 he wasn't doing anything the Americans hadn't done too.

MICROBES: THE ALLY OF RAPE, TORTURE AND CONQUEST?

Apologists for the European conquest as a boon both for Europeans and natives insist that the destruction of native peoples and their cultures was inadvertent, owing largely to the unforeseen ravages of diseases to which the natives had no resistance. Yet, the record is clear that Spaniards, French, Dutch, Portuguese and British all took advantage of the opportunities that smallpox, measles, diptheria and many other pathogens provided to pursue dominance throughout the western hemisphere. In British North America smallpox was sometimes transmitted deliberately in the knowledge that the natives were particularly vulnerable. When illness did not carry off populations entirely, the effects of forced labor and outright slaughter did. The fact remains that, as a major historian of the American holocaust avers, 'the destruction of the Indians of the Americas was, far and away, the most massive act of genocide in the history of the world'.[1] Not even the Black Death of the European Middle Ages had approached the scale of such mass extinction, nor had there ever before been such a mass migration of people, much of it forced, from one continent to another in such brief duration.

The myth that microbes were the culprit in Europe's takeover of the western hemisphere is widespread, as is the parallel fable that the Americas were largely un-peopled. Both fantasies have been cultivated precisely to deny the fact that 95 per cent of the hemisphere's native population, numbering in the tens of millions, were killed or died as a result of the conquest within only a few generations of European arrival.[2] George Bancroft, among the first eminent historians in the United States, declared as early as 1834 that before Europeans arrived America was 'an unproductive waste...its only inhabitants were a few scattered tribes of feeble barbarians'.[3] In the late 1880s the Harvard-trained historian, Theodore Roosevelt, soon to be president and later extolled as a pioneer of environmentalism, celebrated the winning of the west and the closing of the American frontier. Said Teddy:

> All men of sane and wholesome thought must dismiss with contempt the plea that these continents should be reserved for the use of scattered savage tribes, whose life was but a few degrees less meaningless, squalid, and ferocious than that of the wild beasts with whom they held joint ownership.[4]

One hundred years after Roosevelt's screed, a standard American high school text still asserted essentially the same falsehood that 'the continents we know as the Americas stood empty of mankind and its works'. The chronicle of Europeans in the 'New World', the text assures its readers 'is the story of a creation of a civilization where none existed'.[5]

In fact the western hemisphere was inhabited by approximately 100 million individuals when Spanish conquistadors arrived. Highly sophisticated indigenous civilizations had existed since at least the classical period of ancient Greece and humans had entered both continents about 32,000 years before.[6] From the frozen tundra of the North American arctic to the southernmost territory of Tierra del Fuego, and the forests, coasts, savannahs, deserts and mountains in between, innumerable tribes of peoples had developed cultures adapted to their local conditions and had thrived for millennia.

The murderous rivalry that developed between the European Atlantic nations of Spain, Portugal, the Netherlands, Britain and France was well underway before 1492, leading inexorably to the global wars of the twentieth century, as well as much violence since. That fateful date marks the point at which the conquest of the planet by Europeans began in earnest with calamitous consequences for the indigenous peoples of Asia, Africa and the Americas.

Columbus was hardly crossing the Atlantic to prove the world was round, as children are still taught. The shape of the globe was known 25 centuries ago, probably much earlier. He wanted a shorter route to the east, to the source of luxuries that were imported into Europe via the fabled Silk Road that transversed all of Eurasia. Determined to outcompete rival Portugal in the Indies, Columbus made his first landfall on the island later named Hispaniola, today comprising Haiti and the Dominican Republic. Because he believed that he had indeed reached the eastern shores of Asia the islands retain the name, now the West Indies, hence the term 'Indian'. There he found a peaceful people similar in language and culture to those on the other Caribbean islands, who lived amidst such plenty that they had no need of a complex social system, nor did they have or desire the kind of riches after which the Spaniards lusted. But they did posses some golden trinkets, obtained in trade, which suggested more opulent societies on the mainland.

In their fever to obtain riches the Spanish observed no scruple in their efforts to discover their source. The Arawak (called so by contemporary anthropologists and also sometimes called 'Tainos' or Caribs) saw such jewelry as they had as mere trinkets but Columbus and his soldiers accused the natives of hiding their wealth. What followed has been and still is a largely suppressed aspect of American history, almost never discussed, except by indigenous peoples, during the annual official celebrations of the national holiday, Columbus Day. The barbarities perpetrated by the Spaniards upon the Caribbean peoples, and subsequently by all Spanish conquistadors and their rivals throughout the Americas, were so atrocious that their practices are quite literally comparable to those of the Nazis.

Columbus and all subsequent Spanish conquerors brought the cross of Christianity with them and priests to bring the natives to the 'true faith'. It is all but impossible to reconcile the religion they claimed, in which compassion and charity are said to be among the highest virtues, to their abysmally cruel and merciless crimes. Usually the Catholic clerics were the only literate members of the expeditions and in some cases left an honest and horrifying picture of what transpired. One such chronicler was the monk Bartolomeo de las Casas, whose diary is extensive and gruesomely detailed. He also seems to have had something like the conscience that Christians assert is a hallmark of their faith and he became an outspoken advocate for the natives in Spain. To their victims, certainly, the conquistadores must have seemed like demons from the hellish regions.

From Hispaniola Columbus dispatched forays to the islands of Jamaica, Cuba, Puerto Rico and others where, as his son Fernando airily put it, the Spanish spent their time 'looting and destroying all they found'.[7] Las Casas described his fellow Christians as behaving 'like ravening beasts'. He recounted wagers among the Spanish soldiers as to how many strokes of a sword it would take to cut a Carib in two. He related many episodes of Columbus's men throwing infants in the air to catch them at swordpoint, of training dogs to feed on human flesh, then setting them against natives for sport and watching the great wolfhounds and mastiffs devour their victims. Occasionally the Spaniards also crucified Indians (later as Indians fought back they would return the favor). Rape was universal and intended, among other things, to degrade its victims and humiliate the men who could not save women from their violators. Infants were torn from their mothers and hurled against rocks, or thrown into the jungle to die and be consumed by animals. Las Casas described one incident:

> They built a long gibbet, low enough for the toes to reach the ground and prevent strangling, and hanged thirteen at a time in honor of Christ Our Savior and twelve Apostles. When the Indians were thus still alive and hanging, the Spaniards tested their strength and their blades against them, ripping them open with one blow and exposing entrails, and there were those who did worse. Then straw was wrapped around their torn bodies and they were burned alive. One man caught two children about two years old, and pierced their throats with a dagger, then hurled them down a precipice.[8]

In response to Las Casas' plea for mercy for the Arawaks, another priest, a major theologian of the time in Spain, Juan Gines de Sepulveda, countered 'How can we doubt that these people so uncivilized, so barbaric, so contaminated with so many sins and obscenities, have been justly conquered.'[9]

Columbus himself wrote in his journal that the Arawaks were 'the best people in the world and above all the gentlest – without knowledge of what is evil – nor do they murder or steal...they love their neighbors as themselves...' Yet he also wrote that 'They would make fine servants. With fifty men we could subjugate them all and make them do whatever we want.'[10]

The Arawak were not just subjugated, they were eliminated. The real history of Columbus's arrival in the 'New World' is a woeful account of enslavement, murder, torture and genocide that, in terms of proportion and absolute numbers, was far more successful than the race murder that Hitler attempted. Within 50 years of Columbus's arrival the indigenous population of the island of Hispaniola dropped from 8 million to a mere five hundred.[11] That was only the beginning.

SPANIARDS DISCOVER CIVILIZATIONS FAR MORE ADVANCED THAN THEIR OWN – EXCEPT FOR 'GUNS, GERMS, AND STEEL'

It was in present-day Central America and the Andean region of South America that the Spanish conquistadors found civilizations to plunder beyond their fevered imaginations. Far from being the 'primitives' who were said to occupy North America (a falsehood in any case), the Aztec civilization of Meso-America, and the Maya, Toltec and Olmec ones before that, were superior by almost any measure, with the exception of steel weapons and gunpowder, to any civilization in Europe. The Aztec capital of Tenochtitlan and the Inca city of Quosco (Cuzco) were far larger, and more populated, than any city in Europe, and were cleaner too. Madrid, London and Paris were pestilential stinking sewers by comparison. It is estimated that 25 million people lived in the great valley of Mexico at the time Hernando Cortez began his conquest in 1519.[12] That was seven times the population of England. The region did not recover such a population until the 1960s.[13]

Built upon a great lake where Spaniards estimated 200,000 canoes coursed daily, Tenochtitlan employed the movement of water to cleanse the city of its wastes. The Spanish were also impressed, and made uneasy, by the personal hygiene of the Aztecs, who bathed every day, unlike Europeans, many of whom never bathed so much as once in their lives. Urban planning was singularly advanced in Central America and the Andes unlike in Europe. Architecture, engineering, art, agriculture and astronomy were far more advanced among the Aztec, and earlier cultures, and the Inca and their predecessors, than anything seen in Europe since the classical age of Greece and Rome.

In Mexico hydroponic agriculture was practiced; in Peru great terraces were carved to capture the melting waters of the Andes and thus both cultures provided food on a scale that dwarfed anything in Europe, where famine was endemic. Speaking of the great civilization he encountered, Cortez himself admitted that 'In Spain there is nothing to compare with it.' Writing to his king he declared:

> I cannot describe one-hundredth part of all the things which could be mentioned...which, although badly described, will I well know, be so remarkable as not to be believed, for we who saw them with our own eyes could not grasp them with our understanding.[14]

Primitive themselves in almost every respect, the only real advantages possessed by the Spanish were 'guns, germs, and steel'.[15]

To this very short list of advantages one would have to add rapacious cunning. In the cases of both Mexico and Peru native religions prophesied a return from the sea of white men who were held to have been the ancient progenitors of these civilizations. Both Cortez and Francisco Pizarro, the conqueror of Peru, took advantage of these beliefs, initially to ingratiate themselves, and then to betray the hospitality of their hosts. In both cases too, the conquistadors discovered that there were other indigenous peoples who wished to throw off Aztec and Inca rule.

Cortez initially encountered members of a tribe that was in conflict with the Aztec who were attempting to subordinate them. The Tlaxcaltecs inflicted heavy casualties on the Spaniards and could easily have destroyed Cortez's cohort. Seeing new and surprising weapons they instead hoped the Spanish would be their allies and help them wrest independence from the Aztec. When the conquistadors approached the capital of the Aztec at Tenochtitlan with perhaps 150,000 Indian allies, the Aztec emperor, Montezuma, sent envoys bearing gifts and then welcomed the Spanish into the city. When the Spanish saw that the gifts were made of precious metals, said one Aztec, they 'picked up the gold and fingered it like monkeys...their bodies swelled with greed, and their hunger was ravenous; they hungered like pigs for gold.' Cortez himself admitted that 'We Spaniards suffer from a disease of the heart, the specific remedy for which is gold.'[16]

Though Cortez assured the Aztec that he was an ambassador of peace he soon kidnapped and killed the Aztec ruler. When a smallpox epidemic broke out almost simultaneously, frightening and disorienting Aztecs and other tribes, Cortez seized the moment and with his native allies rampaged throughout the city, conducting a horrific slaughter in which approximately 100,000 Aztec were killed such that, as Cortes admitted 'the people had to walk upon their dead'.[17] He estimated himself that at least 50,000 people died when they were pushed into the waters of the great lake. These events were so destructive of their worldview that the Aztecs came to believe that their gods had abandoned them, thus sending them into despair. The conquest opened opportunities for the Spanish monks to convert them to Christianity, which many natives in their despondency embraced. Meanwhile the Tlaxcaltecs too were betrayed and reduced with all local tribes virtually to chattel as the Spanish quickly took over area industries, especially the mines. Within a century the population of central Mexico declined by 95 per cent, from 25 million to less than 1 million.[18]

Those who rationalize the Spanish conquest of Mexico often note that Aztecs and Maya practiced ritual human sacrifice in their religion and that Spain actually delivered a 'barbaric' society from its ills. The recent Hollywood film *Apocalypto* presents a spectacle of almost infinite slaughter of hapless captives by the bloodthirsty Maya, who are shown reveling in the streets, screaming for more gore, as countless victims have their hearts torn out and their bodies thrown tumbling down the steps of their pyramid temples.[19] But this depiction is false. The Maya did not practice slavery and while ritual human sacrifice was known it was never widespread. It is true that human sacrifices were made by Aztec priests, apparently to mollify the sun god, but hardly on the scale depicted in this film or by many exaggerated accounts today. Spanish priests at the time wrote of their revulsion against the Aztec 'atrocities', yet simultaneously in Spain, Jews and Muslims were being tortured and executed in far larger numbers, and many more 'heretics' to the Catholic faith were systematically burned at the stake by the infamous Inquisition, all of this performed amidst careful Catholic ritual. Cortez estimated that 3,000–4,000 people, almost all captives of war, were sacrificed each year in Mexico. During the period of the Spanish conquest the British were executing 75,000 people per year for petty crimes like stealing food.[20] With the exception of ritualized human sacrifice, Mexican society was quite organized and relatively peaceful compared to the wars and persecutions perpetrated by Europeans.

Thirteen years after Cortez assaulted Mexico, in 1532 Francisco Pizarro, seeking similar fame and riches, executed out the conquest of Peru. Like Cortez he was a master of treachery and deceit. By that time the Spanish had also overrun Central America and what is now Venezuela and Colombia, and smallpox had made its way to the Andes, where the Inca ruled an empire larger than China's, indeed the largest the world had seen at the time. The disease had killed the ruling emperor and thousands of local peoples and set in motion a struggle for power, eventually won by his son, Atahualpa. Incan society was thus already severely depopulated and weakened internally. When Pizarro and his 168 men approached the throne of the new emperor, who was surrounded by 80,000 of his own troops, the conquistador suddenly attacked and captured him. The Inca were astounded and frightened by the gunfire and by horses that they had never seen before. The Spaniard's armor also protected them from the stone weapons of the Inca with the result that many thousands of Inca died that day without one Spanish casualty. Subsequently, because they had invested the emperor with supreme authority, Atahualpa continued to rule in captivity at the direction of Pizarro, who demanded ransom in gold and silver. Believing that Spanish greed could be used to his advantage the Incan emperor ordered all the gold and silver in the palaces to be stripped.[21]

As they had been in Tenochtitlan, the Spanish were awed by the wealth and opulence of the Incan empire, which encompassed almost the entire coast of South America, a distance equal to that from New York to Los Angeles. Vast temples and other monumental structures abounded. Many had been built by those who came before the Inca, in some cases thousands of years before them. The skill of Andean architects was masterful beyond anything seen in Europe. Some of these great edifices still stand, immune to the shocks of Andean earthquakes which have long since destroyed many structures built by the Spanish. To this day modern scholars cannot understand how blocks of stone weighing tons were quarried and then moved miles up the slopes of towering mountains to fabled places like Machu Pichu, which, like many monuments in the capital at Quosco, the Inca maintained had been built by earlier peoples.

To pay the ransom for Atahualpa's release the Inca melted down an almost inconceivable quantity of gold and silver objects. Even so the Spanish demanded more, eventually melting the most sacred objects of the Incan religion. Conquistadors also burned the sacred and historical books in Peru and Mexico, thus depriving the world of the storehouse of knowledge that both civilizations possessed. In any case, Pizarro betrayed his promise to release the emperor and murdered him, an act which effectively decapitated the social structure of Incan society. Like Cortez, Pizarro encouraged subject tribes to revolt, and almost overnight Incan rule over their empire collapsed. Meanwhile smallpox continued its desolation of the Indian population and the Spanish ruthlessly plundered local peoples, those who had assisted them and the Inca alike. Taking over the silver mines and the coca plantations, the Spanish mercilessly worked the natives to death. Life expectancy of an Indian in forced labor during this early period in Peru was about three to four months, about the same as an inmate-laborer at Auschwitz in the 1940s.[21]

The strategy of dividing natives against each other would be the principal means by which all European conquerors would initiate their pillage and depredations, in the Americas and the rest of the world.

The story of Spanish conquest, and of the Portuguese in Brazil, the Dutch in Guyana and what is now New York, the French in the Caribbean and Canada and the British throughout North America, follows essentially the same plot. As the peoples of the Americas were subjugated, their lands taken and their riches carried off, the Europeans intensified their own murderous rivalries with each other, all aimed at further conquests throughout the planet. While the Spanish would be the first Europeans to establish colonies in North America – in Florida and the southwest – it was of course, the British who put their cultural, linguistic and imperial stamp upon what would become the United States.

Scandinavians had beaten Columbus to the 'New World' arriving in what is now Greenland and Canada centuries before he did, but those colonies disappeared for reasons that remain open to speculation – perhaps warfare with the natives, or inability to adapt to climate change, or both. After 1492 numerous mariners stopped at various points along the North American coast, trading with natives, kidnapping many as slaves and depositing their germs.

FACED WITH ECONOMIC AND SOCIAL DISRUPTION AT HOME, THE BRITISH JOIN THE GAME OF EMPIRE

At first natives of North America were not concerned about the newcomers, seeing them as weak and incapable of surviving in their attempted settlements, but also as treacherous. In fact, the Spanish attempted to establish a colony very near to what would later become the first British colony of Jamestown, but were driven off. Like the Tlaxcaltecs of Mexico, the peoples encountered by the British in their first colonies of Virginia and Massachusetts – the Powhatan and Wampanoag – attempted to use the colonists to advantage in their own relations with rival tribes. As was the case in Mexico and Peru, the British were quite successful in their strategy of 'divide and rule'. Though the assistance of natives was at first crucial to British colonists' very survival, the newcomers, who eventually came in overwhelming numbers, ended up defeating and exploiting friend and foe alike. Despite their initial assurances to the natives that they wished to live side by side in peace with them, dispossessing 'savages' from their ancestral lands was the colonial intent from the beginning.

In his narrative of the Jamestown settlement, Captain John Smith said that he told Wahunsonacock, whom the British called Powhatan, as they also called the people he led, that the colonists had come only temporarily to repair ships. But the Virginia Company was a joint-stock, profiteering enterprise, a forebear of the modern corporation, and the colonists carried with them specific instructions that they were to establish a permanent settlement in order to challenge Spain's Catholic empire.[23] The British were latecomers to Atlantic empire. Indeed, Columbus had approached the British crown for funds to make his transatlantic crossing but had been turned away. A century after Columbus, Cortez and Pizarro, Britain was contesting Spain and France for mastery of the Caribbean, establishing plantations and naval bases in Jamaica, the Bahamas and other islands, and employing piracy against Spanish galleons carrying the loot plundered from Mexico and Peru. The Spanish had already established a permanent colony at San Augustin (St. Augustine) Florida, and the French were in control of the St. Lawrence River and south-eastern Canada, and one goal of the British was to pre-empt these two enemies.

Religion was a factor since England had rejected the papacy and Catholicism and had turned toward many different strands of Protestantism, and much rhetoric was expended in the claim that Protestant Britain had a mission to bring the true faith to the heathen and impede the reach of Catholicism. Puritanism would become especially important in the British colonies of New England and would put an indelible stamp upon the American national psyche. But military advantage, and the access to wealth that made it possible, was the overriding motive of the powerful, and ordinary English colonists were impelled by forces that had been drastically altering the European world and England especially for centuries.

The Protestant Reformation had developed out of the breakdown of what historians term feudalism (though no template applied everywhere) throughout northern Europe which, in turn, had been caused by advances in food production, technology, growing populations, warfare and the fact that laws and traditions no longer accommodated the realities of everyday life. Catholic Europe was a place of tradition with an emphasis on community in a context of rigid hierarchy. Society and the production of necessities was organized around use and immediate consumption. Society was seen as static and unchanging. If there was a 'Catholic ethic' it was that the individual owed his first allegiance to the greater community.

As populations swelled, cities grew, and trade and commerce became more complex, the laws and customs of traditional society were no longer suitable for the actual conditions of life. Ever growing numbers of people dwelled in cities outside of rural tradition, many engaged in new occupations and, menacingly, in increasing unemployment. As markets grew larger so the profit motive swelled too. Soon land was seen as an opportunity to produce for the larger market and for profit and not for immediate consumption. In England peasants were evicted from the lands they had tilled for centuries and the fields were fenced in and enclosed to raise sheep for the growing wool market, not for food crops. As Thomas More, the great British theologian, remarked at the time, the agricultural process had been stood on its head; now, he said, 'Sheep eat men.' Formerly guaranteed a living as farmers, English citizens were now cast into joblessness and flooded to the cities (a process underway today throughout what has long been termed the Third World, with similar catastrophic consequences).

This displacement of countless people created a restive population with few resources and condemned to pauperization. One of the principal motives of the British colonial endeavor was to move the more dangerous elements of society from the British Isles and transfer them to America (and elsewhere). Many of them had found a kind of employment as soldiers in the various wars between the English, Scots and Irish, and then the English Civil War. Rough and violent men, they would practice their warcraft anew in the colonies.

Rather than working for immediate use and consumption this new English working class worked, when it could obtain work, for wages set by new masters. At the same time another new social class arose, known as the 'bourgeoisie', or middle class between the hereditary landed nobility and the emerging wage-earning classes. As this new social grouping grew in wealth obtained from trade and commerce, and by paying wage earners less than the value of the goods they produced, it was slowly displacing the old nobility as the new ruling class.

Newly emerging social classes were torn loose from formal convention and, loyal primarily to themselves, challenged traditional authority and fostered profoundly new institutions and laws, including new religious sects and what would become the modern corporation. All of these changes discomfited peoples anchored to tradition. Living in uncertainty and insecurity they sought solace in new ideas that would explain and rationalize the great social upheavals. These ideas took the form largely of religion. In England the Reformation challenged Catholicism and bitter internecine strife followed, with the execution of the Catholic monarch King James I. Yet the new Church of England, the establishment of which had initiated the Reformation in Britain, became a target of rebellion too, and Protestantism would soon devolve into numerous competing, and ultimately warring, sects.

The English Civil War of 1640–1660 occurred between King Charles I and his loyalists, mainly the hereditary nobility, and those members of Parliament whose social origins lay mainly in the emerging middle classes. This civil strife has often been called the Puritan Revolution because the religious persuasion of the king's opponents was prevailingly Puritan. These terms, however, disguise the real underlying issues, which were overwhelmingly social and economic. Most simply, the constitutional issue was, on the one side, between the king who claimed to rule by traditional feudal 'divine right' with his allies, the landed nobility, against many in Parliament who claimed rights and privileges independent of the crown and believed that sovereignty should be theirs. In short, the civil war that appeared to be based upon religious beliefs was primarily a class war based upon competing economic and political interests. The Puritans largely represented the commercial middle classes whose primary goal was the pursuit of profit, but also drew in members of the new class of wage earners, who joined as soldiers in their army. Interestingly, many of these foot soldiers came to profess an egalitarian ideology and later were known as 'levelers' because they wished to see a leveling of all social groupings to the same status. This set of ideas was quite radical and far in advance of its time. The real struggle lay between two different factions: one the old ruling class, the other the would-be new rulers, each seeking the upper hand in control of state power and 'property', one vested in land, the other in 'capital', or money, credit, new forms of real estate and banking. When this period of upheaval and profound change ended, feudal relationships which had been based upon use and immediate consumption were overthrown and replaced with new contract-based relations aimed at profit and future income. Modern corporate capitalism was in its first stage of development.

The Puritans triumphed for a period and though ultimately displaced, their ideas about political power and property became fundamental in the evolving structure of English society, and importantly would migrate across the sea and evolve into the 'American creed' of individual rights. Well before the Puritans took power in England, they and other Protestants, with new ideas about how society should be organized, were shaping the structure of what would eventually become the United States. Though such ideas were fostered only to encompass Englishmen, they would eventually resonate throughout American society.

Before the English Civil War, and while Protestant ideas were percolating into British society, powerful men at court invoked the 'law of God', which they claimed allowed Christian rulers to settle the lands of the 'Infidels or Savages' in order to establish 'God's worde'. Sir Walter Raleigh, soldier and adventurer, dreamed of a 'New Britannia' that would rival New Spain in its domains and raw power. Thus the royal charter of 1606 divided the North American coast into two spheres, granted to the newly organized joint stock companies, the forerunners of the modern corporation. The Plymouth group of investors would settle New England, while the London group would establish colonies from North Carolina to the Chesapeake.[23]

THE VIRGIN QUEEN'S COLONY

The first British colony was attempted at Roanoke about 100 miles south of Jamestown. These settlers were completely unprepared for the rigors of life. They seemingly expected food to drop from the air and gold to spring from the earth. Every last one of them disappeared without a trace. The settlement at Jamestown at first appeared to be heading toward the same fate. John Smith complained that the Virginia colonists disdained physical labor and were obsessed with the lure of gold. 'There was no talke, no hope, no worke, but dig gold, wash gold, refine gold, loade gold.'[24] But there was none to be had. As one settler bemoaned:

> But we chanced in a land even as God made it, where we founde only an idle, improvident, scattered people, ignorant of the knowledge of gold and silver, or any commodities, and careless of anything but from hand to mouth, except baubles of no worth; nothing to incourage us, but what accidently we found nature afforded.[25]

The only improvident people in the Virginia of 1607 were the British colonists, ironic since they claimed that divine 'providence' had set them on their course. They had chanced to arrive during a prolonged drought that had severely depleted the availability of crops, game and fresh water. Yet the Powhatan had plenty. They were hardly idle or careless and they were willing to teach the English the necessary hunting and gathering skills and to trade with them for necessities. The colonists also improvidently settled at the edge of a swamp and soon malarial fevers, dysentery and typhoid overtook them so that within a year many had died or were starving. Wahunsonacock told the new Virginians that if they would accept his rule he would protect and provision them. According to Smith Powhatan declared:

> What will it avail you to take that you may quietly have with love, or to destroy them that provide you with food? What can you get by war when we can hide our provisions and fly to the woods, whereby you must famish, by wronging us your friends?[26]

Only the willingness of the natives to provision and teach the colonists, and the fact that a momentary truce existed between England and Spain, saved Jamestown from the fate of Roanoke.

Yet the British, with rock-ribbed faith in their own superiority, were unwilling to acknowledge their debt. Rather, they maneuvered to get Wahunsonacock to accept submission to King James I. John Smith met with Wahunsonacock and told him that the English king had sent many presents that awaited him at Jamestown. Moreover, the Indian chief was to be crowned, British style, as king of the Powhatans. Wahunsonacock was not deceived, reading the ploy to make him the equivalent of an English vassal. Said the chief: 'If your king have sent me presents, I am also a king, and this my land, 8 daies I will stay to receave them. Your father the Virginia governor, (not King James) is to come to me, not I to him.'[28]

As more and more British arrived at Jamestown the Powhatan chief saw the increasing threat. He told Smith, 'many do informe me your coming is not for trade, but to invade my people and possesse my country'.[29] Though he occupied a position in the region as a chief of chiefs, he realized that if he allowed a new, independent people to plant themselves in the midst of his lands, he would lose control of the nearby tribes that owed him allegiance, and they might join with the British against him. The British would have to depart; so Wahunsonacock cut off their food. The settlers then began to attack the natives, steal food and burn their houses, leading to swift revenge on the part of the Powhatan, who quickly sealed them up in the fort at Jamestown.

The Virginia Company stockholders in England concluded that if the Indians would not accept English rule they would have to be put down with force. They recruited hardened veterans of the Irish campaigns (where the British were subduing the inhabitants of their very first overseas colony) who arrived in 1610 and immediately conducted the same kind of scorched earth policy they had inflicted on Ireland, attacking every tribe in the region, killing women and children. In one case, having captured a woman of high status whom they termed a queen, the British commander said:

> And after we marched wth the quene and her children to our Boates again, where beinge no sooner well shipped my sowldiers did begin to murmer becawse the quene and her children were spared. So upon the same a Cowncell beinge called itt was Agreed upon to putt the Children to deathe the wch was effected by throwinge them overboard and shotinge owtt their Brayns in the water yet for all this Crewellty the sowldiers weare not well pleased And I had mutche to doe to save the quenes lyfe for that Time.[30]

Despite the seeming respite the 'quene' was taken ashore and 'putt to the Sworde'. Though the English decried the cruelty of the Spaniards, and claimed that their own rule would be a model of Christian righteousness, their actual practice was, in fact, identical to the scenes described by Las Casas in the Caribbean.

In 1622 the Powhatan and other tribes rose in rebellion against the British, who called it the 'Great Massacre' after about one-quarter of the colonists were killed. Now, said the British propagandists, they could be cleared from the land. '[H]aving little of Humanitie', they claimed, they no longer had any right to be treated as humans:

> ...our hands which were tied with gentlenesse and fair useage, are now set at liberty by the treacherous violence of the Savages... so that we...may now by right of Warre, and law of nations, invade and destroy the country, and destroy them who sought to destroy us.[31]

When the uprising was crushed, the Virginia governor, Sir Francis Wyatt, declared:

> Our first worke is expulsion of the salvages to gaine the free range of the countrey for encrease of Cattle, swine &c which will more then restore us, for it is infinitely better to have no heathen among us, who at best were but thornes in our sides, then to be at peace and league with them.[32]

Once again the local tribes attempted a rebellion in 1644, this time led by Wahunsonacock's successor, Opechancanough. This uprising 'released all restraint that the company had hitherto imposed on those who thirsted for the destruction and enslavement of the Indians'.[33] Now the majority of colonists called for extermination, for the Indians 'to be rooted out from being a people upon the face of the earth'.[34] Governor William Berkeley drafted a plan to kill all the males but to spare the women and children so that they could be sold into slavery, and thus the genocide could pay for itself.[35]

The Powhatan alliance had been broken, tribes set against each other, all of them subsequently falling to British subjection. Opechancanough himself was captured, jailed and exhibited like a wild beast. Then he was murdered with a bullet to his back.[36]

Before European contact the natives of the Chesapeake were estimated to number about 100,000. By the end of the seventeenth century, as the number of British colonists rose to 60,000, Wahunsonacock's people alone were reduced by 95 per cent, to a total of 600. For the entire region the population of Indians fell by 80 per cent.[37] In the words of one colonial observer, 'those people are vanquished to their unspeakable profite and gaine'.[38]

It was, of course, exactly the opposite. Now the new Virginians could turn their attention to building up the wealth they so coveted, though not with gold and the plunder of rich civilizations, but by the cultivation of perhaps the most profitable drug in history. For that they would also pillage another continent to obtain the slave labor necessary to produce it.

A BLOOD-SOAKED CITY ON A HILL

Meanwhile the joint-stock company that was chartered in Plymouth, England, recruited members of an ultra-religious sect of Puritans who would enter history as the Pilgrims of the *Mayflower*.

While it is true that this particular group did wish freedom to practice their religious faith, as all schoolchildren are taught, they were by no means keen to extend such a privilege to others, especially to the natives they encountered throughout New England, and as events later showed, the Puritans even persecuted Quakers in much the same way that they had been. The issue of religious freedom is an ideological cloak for the real 'mission' which as the charter of the Plymouth colony attested, was primarily a profit-seeking operation. Given the riches to be harvested from New England's rich fisheries, and from the fur and lumber of its forests, this enterprise quickly became ruthlessly warlike as well.

Like the hapless colonists to the south in Virginia, the Plymouth pilgrims were hopelessly unprepared for life in Massachusetts. Most were middle class artisans, merchants or clergy, and were unskilled in growing food in England, let alone in the very different conditions of New England. They survived their first months by raiding the graves and abandoned villages of natives who had already been decimated by European diseases. They would have perished utterly, like the colonists at Roanoke, had they not been fed and taught by the local Sachem of the Wampanoag, Massasoit.

While various tribes distinguished themselves from each other, most spoke a variant of the Algonquian language known as Massachusett, though a separate tribe by that name also existed (but not for long!). In this tongue the peoples of the New England coast called their home 'dawnland' and themselves the 'people of the first light'.[39] As was the case in the Chesapeake among the Powhatan, the Wampanoag were a strong tribe often in conflict with other neighboring clans. But virtually all of the tribes had been weakened and depopulated by European diseases. When the scraggly band of Pilgrims arrived, first at what they named Provincetown, and then at Plymouth, the Wampanoag were not particularly worried about them. Even as more Puritans arrived Massasoit saw the English largely as useful tools to help him deal with rival tribes, like the Narragansett to the south in present day Rhode Island, who had been spared the plague that had ravaged the Wampanoag. Just as Wahunsonacock fed and provisioned the English at Jamestown, so Massasoit enabled the Pilgrims to survive their first winter, which, without his aid, would undoubtedly have been their last. The great feast he provided serves in legend as the first Thanksgiving, today a national holiday.

In one of history's numerous tragic ironies, the alliance Massasoit forged with the English actually enabled their colony to survive, thereby drawing ever more English settlers and ensuring the very destruction of his tribe that the great Sachem hoped to protect. Indeed, it proved utterly disastrous for all of New England's aboriginal peoples.[40]

A related irony involves the actions of another Indian named Tisquantum (called 'Squanto' in most narratives), a captive from a northern tribe held by Massasoit, who had earlier been captured and enslaved by Spanish seamen and later brought to England. He ultimately escaped and somehow made his way back to coastal New England. His great usefulness, or so it seemed to Massasoit, was that he spoke English and could thus serve as the go-between for both Indians and English. It was Tisquantum, who is still celebrated in legend, like Massasoit, as a 'good Indian' because (it is claimed without evidence) he taught the English, in their own language, the skills they needed to grow corn in the very different conditions of New England.[41] In American national mythology today there were 'good' Indians, who had the good character to cooperate with colonists in their own conquest, but who were somehow overtaken by the 'bad' Indians who fought back.

In the decade after 1620 thousands of English settlers arrived in the dawn land. Though the pact of friendship that Massasoit signed with the Plymouth colonists was to last for 50 years, the pressures brought to bear upon Indian lands by land hungry colonists proved to be its undoing. In yet another irony it would be Massasoit's son, Metacomet, who would wage full-scale war, unsuccessfully, against the people his father had saved.

As British colonists flooded into Massachusetts they quickly moved to areas north and south, coming into conflict with other peoples, but also employing divisive tactics against traditionally competing tribes. Some whites sought to understand the Indians in their own terms, and more than a few lived with natives. Thomas Morton, who would later be shipped back to England in chains as punishment for living among the Massachusett, said 'I have found the Massachusetts Indians more full of humanity than the

Christians.' But the most common response to white–Indian conflicts was increasing violence on the part of colonists.

PROPERTY AND PROFIT AS THE SIGN OF GOD'S FAVOR

Though Britons born only a century earlier would have understood the concept of land and resources held in common, the new ethic of individualism that was evolving among the British and new ideas of property made clashes all but inevitable. In New England, Puritanism gave special force to these new notions. One of the distinguishing characteristics of Puritanism was its doctrine of pre-destination. As is the case for most new cults, Puritans believed themselves to be 'a new chosen people' singled out by God with a divine mission to create a 'new Canaan', or 'new Jerusalem'. Perceiving only a 'howling wilderness', the 'Saints' (as they called themselves) believed their mission was to make the land into one 'flowing with milk and honey', not seeing that this was already the case. As Cotton Mather, the foremost New England Puritan minister from the late seventeenth to the early eighteenth century, declared: 'Here hath arisen light in darkness.' Taking their inspiration from the Old Testament Book of Joshua the Puritans also called the natives 'Amalekites', 'Amorites', or Philistines after the peoples of ancient Israel whom the Hebrews conquered and displaced. When the expedition against the Massachusett that resulted in Thomas Morton's imprisonment attacked their encampment at present day Quincy, a Puritan elder admonished John Endicott:

> There are three thousand miles of wilderness behind these Indians, enough solid land to drown the sea from here to England. We must free *our land* of *strangers*, even if each mile is a marsh of blood. [emphasis added]

It had taken only a few years for the Puritans to believe as an article of faith that the people whom they were dispossessing were the 'strangers'. For these self-styled Saints their doctrine of predes-tination informed them that individuals had been singled out for salvation even before they were born. This raised a difficult problem. How did members know they were among the saved? They resorted to circular reasoning. Their answer was that salvation was proved by the very fact that they belonged to the new community of the saved. Thus Puritanism as it flourished in the first decades of British colonization was highly self-righteous and intolerant, not only of the Indians, who were deemed pagans and devil worshippers, but also of other Protestant sects, like the Quakers.

A doctrine-like predestination was a very thin reed upon which to build a faith, so Puritans also imagined more concrete manifestations of their divinely inspired destiny. As individuals garnered more land, and raised more livestock, or caught more fish, or stockpiled more lumber, then sold these commodities for profit and in general became ever more prosperous, their very success became the needed evidence for the faith that they had been singled out for salvation. Achievement in material terms became the fundamental hallmark of God's blessing. Thus the drive to obtain land, show definitive evidence of prosperity and the accumulation of wealth became paramount. Just as enclosure became the norm in England so did the Puritans of New England begin to claim ever more and larger tracts of land, fencing them in and banning Indians from hunting or fishing or otherwise using lands that had been traditionally open to all. Such radically different ideas about land, and the relationship of people to it, was enough to bring about violent conflict. On one side land was the birthright of all, on the other land was to be held in private by individuals for their own use.

Of course this new belief system was at bottom a rationale and justification for selfishness, though its adherents believed intensely in their own rectitude. The Puritans who settled New England imposed an indelible stamp upon the later American self-conception. Their ideology took the form of religious doctrines (as did most ideas at the time) that claimed that God had singled them out as a 'New Chosen people' who were to establish a 'New Jerusalem' or 'New Zion' in the wilderness of America. They believed themselves to be among the elect, that is, those who were destined beyond question for an afterlife in heaven. What is most important is how they convinced themselves they were predestined to paradise.

Having sprung into existence as the result of the breakdown of traditional religious (Catholic) authority, and making their living in the new market economy which was very different from feudal agriculture, Puritans were highly influential in the development of the capitalist system, and the ideas which sustain it to this day. How did they know God favored them? Because they prospered; because they increased their wealth by trade, by investment and profit. It followed from such logic that those who did not profit were not among the elect and were estranged from God. In the old conception of religious community God wished people to aid each other. Now God helped those who helped themselves. Individualism would replace the collectivity and the clearest expression of God's favor was whether the individual prospered or sunk into poverty.

THE 'SPAWN OF SATAN'

So ideas of private land ownership became wedded to religious doctrine, and dogma soon coupled with racism. Whatever attitudes about the Indians Puritans brought with them, the rapidly growing conflict fed the inclination to envisage the natives as most definitely the 'unchosen people'. Indeed, they were scarcely seen as human. William Bradford, the second governor of the Massachusetts Bay Colony, wrote of his first glimpse of the new world and could see only a 'hideous and desolate wilderness, full of wild beasts and wild men'. The writings of the earliest Puritans are replete with images of the Indian as the 'spawn of Satan' or the 'devil's instruments'.

In 1636 a group of Niantic Indians killed a Briton off Block Island whom they accused of mistreating them. From Boston, Puritan leaders immediately conspired to revenge and sent an armed force to Rhode Island and Connecticut to engage in what they termed their first 'war'. Because the Pequots were the most numerous tribe in the region, and had also recently killed British subjects trespassing on their territory, they became the main focus of attack. The band of Saints set out, in their own words 'to cut off remembrance of them from the earth'. Governor John Winthrop, who is still celebrated for his injunction to the Puritans of Boston 'to be as a city upon a hill', instructed his captains 'to put to death the men of Block island, but to spare the women and the children, and to bring them away, and to take possession of the island...' What actually transpired was Puritan New England's first massacre of natives.

In reality the act of vengeance was merely a pretext to establish new colonies throughout Connecticut. As was the case throughout the Americas the Puritans had made promises to the tribal enemies of the Pequot, promising the Narragansett that for their assistance in removing their rivals the Puritans would take only Pequot land. Yet the removal of the Pequot did for the Connecticut Valley what the plague had done earlier in Massachusetts Bay. By removing one major tribal obstacle to their further colonization, the Puritans established a foothold that enabled them subsequently to suppress all the natives of the region, including, of course, the Narragansett.

The inexorable encroachment of the English upon traditional hunting grounds, and by cattle on native cornfields, finally led rival New England tribes to realize that their entire way of life was at stake. As one Narragansett sachem, Miantonomo, realizing too late that the English intended to take all native lands, put matters to his tribe:

> So we are all Indians as the English are all English, and say brother to one another; so must we be one as they are, otherwise we shall be all gone shortly, for you know our fathers had plenty of deer and skins, our plains were full of deer, also our woods, and of turkies, and our coves full of fish and fowl. But these English have gotten our land, they with scythes cut down the grass, and with axes fell the trees; their cows and horses eat the grass, and their hogs spoil our clam banks, and we shall all be starved.[42]

Subsequently, the commissioners of the United Colonies of New England authorized Miantonomo's murder because he was leading 'a general conspiracy among the Indians to cut off all the English'. Lion Gardiner, one of the principal officers engaged in the Pequot massacre, later wrote that 'although there has been much blood shed here in these parts among us, God and we know it was not by us'.[43]

Led by Captain John Mason the armed Saints fell upon the main Pequot stockade, encompassing about 400 natives. 'We must burn them,' Mason ordered. One of his officers later wrote that many Pequot 'were burned in the fort, both men, women, and children. Others [who were] forced out...our soldiers received and entertained with the point of the sword. Down fell men, women, and children.' Later about 20 captives were 'fed to the fishes'. The remaining Pequot were run to ground and as far as the Puritans could establish, literally exterminated. 'Thus did the Lord judge among the Heathen,' said Mason, 'filling the place with dead bodies...We had sufficient light from the word of God for our proceedings.'[44]

THE FIRST ALL-OUT WAR

As tensions grew all over New England only a spark was needed to initiate a conflagration. Thus the first true, all-encompassing war in British North America ensued, only a few generations after Massasoit had saved the first Pilgrims from starvation, with devastating results for the colonists and virtual eradication for the Wampanoag, the Narragansett, the Mohegan and their other Amerindian allies. This war was far more destructive on a per capita basis than any other in American history. If the New England tribes had been able to persuade their western neighbors, the Mohawks, not to believe English promises that their lands would remain untouched, that English settlement would inevitably threaten them as well and to join their fellow natives, they might well have stopped English colonization entirely at that point. However, many tribes in the north and west were swayed to ally with the British, against their traditional rivals, eventually to succumb in exactly the same way. While truly horrific in intensity for the colonists, this first colonial war resulted in total defeat for the New England natives and the extinction of their way of life.

The conflict has come to be known as King Philip's War because colonists refused to call Massasoit's son, Metacomet, by his Algonquian name. The war began when Metacomet's brother, Wamsutta, died in mysterious fashion while being held captive by the English. When a Christianized and English-speaking Indian, who had probably served the British as a spy, was murdered subsequently, colonial leaders suspected Metacomet's hand. The English were blind to the true reasons for native resentment. As the Puritan divine, Increase Mather, was to write later, the Wampanoag killed the Indian 'out of hatred for him for his Religion, for he was Christianized, and baptiz'd, and was a Preacher amongst the Indians...and was wont to curb those Indians that knew not God on the account of their debauchereyes'. Aggression against Puritanism was not the cause of the war except in the sense that it provided the rationale for the English to assume racial and cultural superiority over the natives, and to justify taking their land. The colonial and imperial project was the true cause of native resentment and war.

As more Puritan settlers arrived the economic basis of the colony changed from dependence upon trading British steel and iron tools and other goods for fur, to a more intensive and environmentally destructive economy based on agriculture, fishing and timber harvesting. Newcomers insisted upon enforcing their own Puritan code of behavior and morality, criticizing the Indians for their lack of 'modest' dress and attempting to convert the natives as well. Massasoit had barred Puritans from attempting to convert natives but a fair number who became known as 'praying Indians' did adopt the immigrant religion and soon moved out of traditional villages and adopted the English way of life. Meanwhile Indians who strayed into what had formerly been their own fields and forests were arrested and jailed for trespassing. In only the span of two generations the Indians were becoming outsiders, strangers in their own land.

When three Wampanoag accused of murder were hanged at Plymouth the tribe rose up against the English. The war quickly spread into the far west of Massachusetts and down the Connecticut Valley. Half of the 90 English settlements were attacked and many wiped out. At the height of the war villages only ten miles from Boston were assaulted. Colonists were frustrated at not being able to draw Indians into a set-piece battle. Many English men were veterans of the Thirty Years War and were accustomed to battle in open territory. Indians, however, could not stand up to muskets and cannon and so resorted to ambush and other forms of guerrilla warfare, including raids on homesteads. As the ferocity of fighting increased so did atrocities on both sides leading to the murder of women and children and to the mutilation of bodies. The ritualistic stripping of British bodies by Indians, leaving them to lie naked, particularly offended Puritan sensibilities.[45] In revenge the English made every effort to wipe out entire Indian villages. By the war's end about one in ten combatants on either side had been killed or wounded. For the colonists this was a death rate twice that of the Civil War and seven times that of World War II.[46]

Eventually the natives succumbed to a war of attrition. Metacomet was captured and murdered by an Indian loyal to the British. This son of the Puritan savior was decapitated, his body cut into pieces, and his head mounted upon a pole where it remained in the Plymouth town square for a generation. As numerous Wampanoag realized their cause was hopeless they began to surrender on the promise that their lives would be spared. They were betrayed. One after another they were hanged or beheaded. The Massachusetts Bay elders declared what amounted to 'wholesale perpetual enslavement of the Indians' who remained.[47] Those few captured Indian males who were not executed were sold into slavery abroad, while their wives and children became servants locally. Metacomet's wife and nine year old son were imprisoned and the boy was later sold into slavery.

The very basis of their livelihood now appropriated by the colonists, the Wampanoag and Narragansett and other tribes had to adjust to English ways in order to survive at all, and rapidly seemed to disappear altogether. One measure of their precipitous decline was their loss of language. Cotton Mather, one of the most powerful religious leaders of the New England colonies after the war wrote that:

It is very sure the best thing we can do for our Indians is to Anglicize them...they can scarce retain their language, without a tincture of other savage inclinations, which do but ill suit, either with honor, or with the design of Christianity.[48]

Within a generation only about 20 natives could still speak the regional language known as Massachusett.

It took the English years to recover and rebuild, but they did so, and from their new-found position of strength continued their subjugation of eastern North America. In the process of waging virtually incessant warfare with every native group, and testing their own identities against the 'devil's instruments', these English colonists were transforming themselves into a new breed: Americans.

King Philip's War is little remembered in any detail today. Yet, the cultural effect in the memory of the Puritans and other English colonists was to imprint the natives' 'savagery' forever on future generations, omitting entirely the equal atrocities initiated by the English, and, indeed, what amounted to genocide. In American national mythology it was the 'good' Indians who made the first Thanksgiving possible. In this sanctioned narrative it was the 'spawn of Satan' who trespassed upon Eden and despoiled the Puritan paradise, not the true strangers from across the sea. The 'elect of god' now enjoined themselves to establish their new promised land. The incontrovertible British design to take the North American continent from the people who already inhabited it was, and is, conveniently expunged from popular consciousness.

3
French, Indians, Rebellion and Repression

Though there is a general dread of giving too much power to our governors, I think we are in more danger from too little obedience by the governed.

Benjamin Franklin (Weeks, 1996)

THE FIRST GLOBAL WAR PREFIGURES MORE GLOBAL WAR

By the close of the seventeenth century British, French, and Spanish colonies had been firmly implanted in North America. The French dominated eastern Canada, the Spanish ruled Florida and the mouth of the Mississippi River as well as most of the south-west and California, and numerous British colonies ranged the Atlantic Piedmont from Maine to Georgia. The French claimed the vast Ohio River valley to the west of the Appalachian Mountains but the British were equally determined to claim it for themselves, especially as an outlet for a growing colonial population. Given that French policies aimed at dominating the European core, and Britain was equally adamant to prevent this, the two nations were already constantly at war. Once both had entered the race for overseas empire it was inevitable that their mutual warfare would extend across the globe. What Americans call the 'French and Indian War' is called by the British and French the 'Seven Years War'. It was the first global war, 1756–1763, fought with other European allies, all competing for advantage in the global contest and ranging across North America, Europe, the Caribbean, the Mediterranean, North Africa and Asia.

While the war did not settle matters between the French and British on a worldwide scale, the British were victorious in North America, acquiring Canada and making claim to the territories between the Mississippi River and the Appalachians, a claim obviously not recognized by the numerous indigenous tribes of the region. The effort to wrest control of Canada, and to protect the British colonies to the south, virtually bankrupted the British treasury. It was in the aftermath of victory and insolvency that the

British crown and Parliament decided to levy increased taxes upon their colonial subjects in America in order to pay for the costs of triumph. At this point the mutually opposite interests of British government officials and stockholders against those of colonial elites clashed. As British subjects who had benefited greatly from the expensive deployment of British troops, it seemed to the British that the colonials should have been willing to bear their fair share of the monetary costs, but this they were loathe to do, claiming that their losses in lives were payment enough. When the crown therefore imposed ever more financial burdens by force the stage was set for armed conflict between the colonials and their mother country. Out of this conflict grew the demand for American independence.

While Puritans and their New England successors rationalized their conquests with religious ideology and claims of divine mission, most settlers in the other British colonies justified their expansion with reference to the superiority of British civilization and practiced naked aggression. Britons had already routed the Scots, Welsh and Irish, whom they saw as inferior, and the new Anglo-Americans[1] simply took their right of conquest in North America for granted. If bellicose intent existed it was claimed to come from the other. Aggression was the charge leveled against the American natives trying desperately to hang on to their land and way of life. British colonial 'civilizationism'[2] also obsessed over 'security', ignoring the fact that British incursions into, and disruption of, ancient cultures fostered the very attacks they came so anxiously to fear. But the settlers justified this state of affairs by claiming that if Anglo-Saxons did not seize the territory then the competition would. As noted, the British were latecomers to the game of empire and thus their relentless and rapid expansion in North America quickly brought them up against the French and Spanish who had got there first, and, of course, the many indigenous tribes that had been there for millennia.

By the late seventeenth century a 'Glorious Revolution' had occurred in England that brought a good measure of power to the commercial middle classes, giving the House of Commons in Parliament considerably more authority, while weakening that of the king and landed nobility. In the process a great deal of intellectual energy was released. Treatises on politics and society abounded, such as those of John Locke, arguing a new philosophy of 'natural rights', and these ideas percolated throughout the British social structure, with the result that ordinary British citizens, including those at the bottom of the hierarchy, began to develop a new sense of their own individuality and right to liberty. Liberty meant not having to live at the sufferance of others and that meant having property. The primary measure of property was still land, and most of that was already claimed in England. But the vast bulk of North America was still up for grabs. While most of the early colonists would indenture themselves as servants to the wealthy in order to gain passage to America, their terms of servitude would be limited, if harsh, and they had every hope of achieving personal independence by settling the rapidly expanding frontiers of the British Empire. Once this autonomy had been achieved, most quickly adopted the characteristics and outlook of 'free born' Britons. They asserted a self-evident right to foster the extension of that empire and they pushed westward implacably.

After the initial setbacks were overcome, when the natives of New England and the Chesapeake and deeper south were defeated, an immense surge of immigration took place from the late seventeenth to the mid eighteenth century. While there were some aristocrats who immigrated, and others who aped their manners, most British subjects interacted with each other without the deference expected in England. In the American colonies Britons could escape subordination and pauperism. As Adam Smith put it, there 'was more equality among the English colonists than among the inhabitants of the mother country'.[3] Thus, at a very early stage the principal ingredients of American ideology – divine mission, 'exceptionalism', or qualitative difference in social relations from Europe, fierce individualism, and racism – were already being fashioned.

Just as the original colonies of Virginia and Plymouth were fostered by joint-stock companies, so prominent landowners and merchants in both these colonies, and the others that had been established, created such companies themselves to exploit the lands west to the Appalachian Mountains. Many states like Massachusetts and Virginia claimed everything west to the Pacific Ocean![4] In mid eighteenth-century British America, the 'far west' referred to the Ohio and Mississippi valleys. Men sufficiently well-connected to have a stake in one of the many land grant companies stood to make fortunes by speculation if their claims to the trans-Appalachian west could be enforced. If ordinary settlers wished to move into those lands they would have to pay those who had gotten it virtually for nothing, but only if the British crown could occupy and hold the land. The French already claimed the territory and then there was the problem once again of the natives who occupied it. By the time of the American Revolution many of these speculators were none other than the 'Founders' and, as we shall see, they had a profoundly vested interest in securing these lands away from England, and toward themselves.

It is often forgotten that most American colonists just prior to the revolution considered themselves British citizens, even more British than the British. Empire was rapidly becoming a way of life for England and the vanguard of this imperialism were those busy colonizing America and defending British frontiers. While the Puritan Revolution had been defeated and its rigidity had diminished, the English still took the religious superiority of their various Protestant faiths seriously, and gloried in British citizenship. For them there was no difference between Old England and New.

England's perennial clash with France intensified after the Glorious Revolution when power at the London court passed to men committed to crafting a vast maritime empire that historians call mercantilism: the transfer of wealth to the mother country in the early stage of modern capitalism. Colonies existed to enrich the metropolis, not primarily to benefit the colonists themselves. Thus, a collision developed between the American colonials' idea of empire, acquiring territory, and London's goal of maritime supremacy. At all times, however, British authorities calculated the advantage over France (and Spain as well, though the Spanish empire in the Americas was already on the wane). London wished to clear both rivals from the Caribbean islands and thereby assert primacy over the entire Atlantic.

New France's empire in North America was larger in area, but considerably smaller in power than her enemy's, and centered largely on trade with natives, not colonization. While England controlled the eastern coastal region, France claimed the area surrounding English colonies to the north and west, and the vast area from the great lakes down the Mississippi Valley to New Orleans. Given the scale of British immigration, however, Britons soon vastly outnumbered the French in North America.[5] Anglo-Saxon settlers, most of whom were escaped indentured servants or those whose terms were about to expire, were now experiencing overcrowding and wanted the territory the French claimed.

The natives in the region bestriding or west of the Appalachian chain, like the Iroquois, Seneca, Delaware, Cherokee, Creek and others, retained their unity and strength. Those who lived between both the English and the French, like the Huron, tended to favor the French simply because they did not alter the environment and destroy the Indian way of life. One Indian leader put it this way:

Brethren, are you ignorant of the difference between our Father (the French) and the English? Go and see the forts our Father has created, and you will see that the land beneath their walls is still hunting ground…whilst the English, on the contrary, no sooner get possession of a country than the game is forced to leave, the trees fall down before them, the earth becomes bare.[6]

Between 1689 and 1748, after King Philip's War had been resolved, the British and French fought three wars in North America. Though the British certainly wanted the French expelled from the continent, London was far more concerned about France in Europe and the Caribbean, so the government temporarily called a halt to the out-migration of British colonists to the west. At least temporarily London wished to preserve a balance of power in North America, and vetoed attempts to enlarge it. In 1745, for example, a force of 4,000 New England colonists attacked and took the French fortress at Louisbourg on Cape Breton. But Parliament soon returned it to France, much to the consternation of the colonials. Now the growing contradiction between London's aims and those of colonists was coming more sharply into focus. Anglo-Americans were more than willing to wage war against France (and Spain). Refusal by Parliament to allow settlement beyond the Appalachians that would lead inevitably to war with France led to overcrowding in cities like Boston, New York, Philadelphia, Baltimore and Charleston and spurred more resentment on the part of lower-class Britons anxious to obtain land and the independence land was seen to ensure. Thus, for Anglo-Americans the issues that led to war with France were largely domestic but they dovetailed with England's greater goal of global empire. The new Americans needed 'living space'.

One of the chief colonial proponents of imperial expansion at the expense of France and the natives was Benjamin Franklin:

I have long been of the opinion that the foundations of the future grandeur and stability of the British Empire lies in America… Britain itself will become vastly more populous…the Atlantic sea will be covered with your trading ships, and your naval power will…awe the world.

He asserted further, 'Already in the old colonies many thousands of families are ready to swarm, wanting more land.'[7] Many other Americans agreed with Franklin, who would soon play a momentous role in separating from Britain and ultimately taking its place on the North American continent. The French and Indian War was ignited by none other than George Washington in 1754 (although he was under orders from Virginia's governor). Aiming to establish an outpost in French territory, Washington's Indian allies attacked a French force, resulting in a terrible massacre. The French responded just as brutally and London decided to break the truce, dispatched thousands of British regulars to the colonies and immediately set out to conquer Canada and drive the French from the continent entirely. In this endeavor London had the wholehearted support of American colonists.

The war in North America quickly led to naval engagements in the Caribbean, the Mediterranean and Asia. Thus the Seven Years War was the first truly global war which foreshadowed ever more destructive wars and signaled the degree to which imperial rivalries would shape the future of the planet. In this early stage of worldwide struggle for supremacy, unconventional methods of warfare would first make their appearance. Warfare in the forests of America did not suit the tactics practiced by professional soldiers on either side, who simply formed ranks en masse in open areas and fired at each other almost at point-blank range. Though they had roundly condemned such practices when they had been employed against them, American colonists quickly adopted the guerrilla tactics of the Indians whom they recruited as allies against the French and the tribes that lined up with them. They would do so again when the time came to face their British cousins.

The earliest contact between Europeans and natives involved the fur trade. Indians were happy to provide pelts in return for more durable European tools and weapons, which clearly improved native material prosperity. But this new commercial relationship also altered Indian ways of life and undermined traditional culture and spiritual values. Competition between English and French traders also caused competition to develop between tribes and gradually forced them to choose sides, drawing natives 'into a market economy where their trading partners gradually became trading masters'.[8] Natives gradually adopted European habits, including the consumption of alcohol which their new patrons exploited, much to the growing erosion of tribal cohesion. As furs became depleted due to overhunting in certain areas, tribes began to trespass on the territories of neighbors. As the strength of the Europeans grew it became increasingly apparent to Indians that they would have to make serious calculations as to which group would become dominant, which could aid against rival tribes and which offered the lesser of evils. Aboriginal Americans were being forced to choose sides in the hope that by doing so they could best preserve their own positions.

The presence of the French and their native allies in Canada and the Mississippi Valley were the obstacle to British colonial advancement into the west, and thus, while colonial spokesmen like Franklin insisted their support of the war was simply patriotism, it was in fact naked self-interest. London deployed 40,000 troops to North America and with the added support of colonial militias waged war on a scale never before seen on the continent. France was forced to cede Canada and the Mississippi Valley and most possessions in the Caribbean. While Spain was given New Orleans, it gave up much of Florida to English control. Thus the colonists believed that land was opened up to settlement. Speculators rushed to make their claims. Throughout the war merchants luxuriated in military contracts for food, uniforms and ships. British colonists who did not volunteer for military service, or who were not dragooned, enjoyed record employment opportunities and high wages. The French and Indian War appeared to have resulted in all that the colonists desired.

AMERICANS WHO WANTED WAR NOW REFUSE TO PAY FOR IT

There was bound to be a down side and there was. Human losses were astounding for the era. Muster lists for Boston, for example, indicate that virtually all working-class families contributed soldiers. In a town that then counted only 2,000 families, 700 men perished.[9] Such extensive widowhood 'feminized poverty' and required expanded poor relief. The situation was similar across the colonies. The cost to the British government for the war was enormous and the subsequent tax burden increased exponentially and would eventually become crushing to many, leading to foreclosures, homelessness and pauperization in American cities not unlike that of metropolitan London. Colonists had migrated to American colonies precisely to escape such conditions drawn by higher wages and the lure of cheap or free land.

In return for the aid of their Indian allies British authorities had promised them a 'racial boundary' that would preserve western lands for various tribes. The Proclamation of 1763 ordered all colonial subjects then living in the west to withdraw east of the Appalachians and forbade further British emigration beyond the line. Needless to say the colonial subjects ignored the edict and tensions began to simmer between the crown, Anglo-Americans and natives, both those who had aided the British and those who sided with the French.

The British crown also wanted colonists to pay their fair share of the costs of war. Despite all the advantages that accrued to Anglo-Americans they quickly renounced any responsibility for it. In a speech to the House of Commons in 1766 Franklin essentially falsified recent history, repudiated his own previous grandiose pronouncements and claimed the war had not been fought for colonial interests at all but was a 'British war', in which the colonists had 'no particular concern or interest'. Since Parliament could not allow Americans 'to benefit from Britain's protection without contributing anything in return'[10] it shortly began to levy deeply unpopular taxes and imposed 'intolerable' acts upon the colonists leading many to assert that their rights as free-born Englishmen were being violated. The British government was impairing their liberties and reducing them to 'slaves'.[11]

Franklin, previously the champion of British citizenship and empire, now asserted that America would 'in less time than generally conceived, be able to shake off any shackles that may be imposed upon her, and perhaps place them on the imposers'. Alexander Hamilton mused that some day the British crown would serve the interests of her 'prodigal offspring'.[12] In short order most of the most influential men in the colonies, those now celebrated as the Founding Fathers, were saying much the same thing.

In the United States the American Revolution is celebrated as a near impossible victory over a mighty and tyrannical empire made possible by the heroism of those who introduced the concept of equality and self-government into a benighted world. The revolutionary generation took terrible risks. Only a few short years before they were shining exemplars of British citizenship but after 1776 they were committing treason. Had the crown not been so preoccupied with continental threats from France the real strength of imperial Britain would had been deployed, instead of inept commanders and foreign mercenaries. The colonial rebels would have been trounced and Washington, Jefferson, Franklin, Hamilton et al. would have swung from the gallows, their names mere footnotes to history today. But luck and circumstances were with the new republic.

'All men are created equal' are, as everyone knows, Thomas Jefferson's words. Even though the Founders exiled all Africans from the very ranks of human beings, Jefferson's words did not even apply to the majority of white men in the colonies at the time. The signers of the Declaration of Independence and the US constitution selected themselves as representatives of 'We the People' but acted primarily in their own interests. Virtually all of them were plantation owners and slaveholders, or had extensive commercial and banking interests, and all feared genuine popular democracy. When Jefferson also wrote in the Declaration that all men are entitled to the 'pursuit of happiness' he was paraphrasing the British philosopher John Locke, whose ideas were widespread among all colonial classes. In late eighteenth-century America, happiness was identical to the possession of property because property enabled the individual to be free of subjection. Independence meant self-sustenance, not servitude. Those who failed to prosper were judged to be indolent, or incompetent, and certainly not fit to govern. The most widespread form of property was land and there was land aplenty in North America. If Jefferson's 'empire of liberty' was to exist it could only do so if the troublesome natives were removed and, by 1776, if the British could be prevented from interfering with the pursuit of land and profit.

Most emigrants from the British Isles left because they had no land or any other property and desired above all to acquire some. Most had to indenture themselves, to commit to servitude under others for a time in order to buy their passage to the colonies, but the promise of land and profit thereafter became the animating motive of colonists. Many of the founders had invested in companies that bought cheap land west of the Appalachian Mountains before the British had attempted to put a stop to western settlement in deference to their Indian allies against the French. Their speculative plans to sell this land at a significant profit to the restive mass of immigrants in the eastern cities was at risk, even as their own fortunes dwindled from the imposition of the hated taxes.

Colonies had also established their own money to facilitate trade. When the British demanded payment of taxes or duties in pounds sterling or gold sovereigns the local currencies were devalued and the overall colonial economy was impoverished. Middling businessmen could no longer obtain credit to build their enterprises. Those colonists whose futures were limited as wage earners in the east also realized that continued taxation would limit job growth and keep wages lower. So a community of interest had built among all classes against the British. But the American elite had the most to gain.

Many American colonists, probably a third, rejected rebellion and remained loyal to Britain. In what was really a civil war they were persecuted and killed and their properties confiscated. Many fled to Canada or the Caribbean. Franklin's own son remained a loyalist and the father never spoke to his son again.

THOSE WHO MADE THE GREATEST SACRIFICES ARE BETRAYED

In the first blush of rebellion many rushed to volunteer. But leaving farms and shipyards entailed great sacrifice so recruitment and retention soon proved problematic. Unable to pay troops in hard currency the Continental congress issued 'scrip' or promissory notes, or entitlements to western land should victory be theirs. But promises did not send money home to wives and children, so the majority of revolutionary soldiers sold their scrip to bankers and speculators at usurious discounts for currencies that could purchase necessities. They also sold their notes to western land. Thus they were never paid the full value of their service, and as the war went on their families, farms and small businesses fell further into debt. One revolutionary soldier's narrative spoke for most:

> When those who engaged to serve in the war enlisted, they were promised a hundred acres of land, each, which was to be in their own or adjoining states. When the country had drained the last drop of service it could screw out of the poor soldiers, they were turned adrift like worn-out horses, and nothing said about land to pasture them upon.[13]

Meanwhile vast sums of scrip and entitlements to land fell into the hands of speculators that they expected Congress to redeem at full face value when victory came. Thus men who sacrificed little profited from the risks and hardships of those who sacrificed much. Many of the 55 men who wrote the US constitution were among these speculators and represented their interests at Philadelphia.

The British declared that all slaves fighting on their side would be freed. Since colonial opposition to the crown was not universal and recruitment and retention in the continental army proved problematic when the rigors of extended war became apparent, slaves were dragooned. Some Americans recognized the irony of fighting for liberty with slaves and suggested that those on the American side should be freed as well. But southern leaders objected strenuously, fearing slave rebellions more than defeat.[14]

The most democratic of the founders was one reviled by most of the others, though his popularity was certainly used to the fullest extent. Tom Paine's pamphlet *Common Sense* did far more to win mass support for rebellion than anything Jefferson or Washington had to say. But his opposition to monarchy, insistence on popular democracy, universal suffrage, the abolition of slavery, free public education and even a minimum wage, led most of the other Founders to regard him as a dangerous radical, a demagogue and promoter of genuine democracy.

For the fact is that most of the Founders feared democracy as surely as any monarchist. To them the great mass of common people were the 'mob', stupid and drunken, incapable of self-governance owing to their ignorance.

Thus a 'republic' in which the choice of governing officials would be limited strictly to the prosperous and propertied was the only option for them. Though they rejected monarchy, they embraced the principle of representative and divided government and strictly limited suffrage. The US Senate and House of Representatives were clearly modeled on Britain's Houses of Lords and Commons. The upper chamber had the power of veto over the lower and would thus serve as a brake on any perceived radicalism. So the American revolution was not really a revolution. It was a rebellion that was fortunate to win and while it instituted key reforms and unique adaptations, such as a written constitution and a Bill of Rights, it was really a transfer of power from the British government to an American self-selected elite who ensured that governance would be held by them. When they spoke of equality, by no means did they mean 'all'. Yet by articulating this ideal they had let the proverbial genie loose and the democratic ideal would soon gather a life of its own, thence to bedevil future generations of the ruling elites.

The US constitution was established to foster centralized government with the power to tax and raise an army. Many American historians assert that the American revolution fostered 'universalist' values and principles that were intended to enlighten a benighted and backward world. The founders intended this only in the most limited sense. Just as the British nobility had opposed the rise of the commercial middle classes to power, so did the new ruling class oppose the political participation of the commoners, and this was just as true in America as in Britain. The proof was not long coming.

THE NEW AMERICAN ELITE TAXES AND FORECLOSES ON THOSE WITHOUT REPRESENTATION

In 1786 a rebellion broke out in western Massachusetts that, more than any other event, spurred the American elite to write the US constitution and centralize power in their hands. Veterans of the revolution had returned to their farms only to find them in disarray and burdened with debt and taxation that they viewed as unjust, since many did not meet the property qualifications to vote. In Massachusetts property qualifications had increased and hence many were being taxed without representation![15]

Boston merchants and bankers had borrowed heavily during the revolution and were now squeezing their debtors. Because former soldiers had not been paid fairly for their military service they were in debt and behind with their taxes, so the business elites who controlled the courts soon began to confiscate farms and homes as payment, and to put veterans in debtor's prison. Many organized themselves to prevent sheriffs from evicting them from their properties. When the state militias were called out to suppress the growing rebellion it soon became apparent that many were fellow veterans and they refused to oust their former comrades-in-arms. This led Boston elites to establish their own private militia, which the governor then placed under state command, and this force was deployed to put down what was now known as Shays' Rebellion. (Daniel Shays had served as a captain in the Continental Army and, like many veterans, had returned to a neglected ruined farm.)

The hypocrisy of so many of those who initiated the revolution is clearly illustrated by their response to this upsurge of popular democracy against similar injustices perpetrated by the new domestic ruling class and the governments they controlled. Samuel Adams, an icon of the revolution, now condemned men he had inspired to rebellion who were resisting the very sort of 'taxation without representation' and tyranny that he had denounced. Adams claimed that British agents were fomenting treason and as a member of the new ruling class drew up legislation that suspended the age-old Anglo-American rule of *habeas corpus* and, making a distinction between rebellion in a republic and a monarchy, called for the execution of the Shaysites.[16]

The upheaval in Massachusetts was the worst. Similar events were taking place in every state. Alexander Hamilton fulminated against the impudence of the mob:

All communities divide themselves into the few and the many. The first are the rich and well-born, the other the mass of the people. The voice of the people has been said to be the voice of God; and however generally this maxim has been quoted and believed, it is not true in fact. The people are turbulent and changing; they seldom judge or determine right. Give therefore to the first class a distinct permanent share in the government.[17]

James Madison, the 'father of the Constitution' wrote that class conflict arose from 'the various and unequal distribution of property. Those who hold and those who are without property have ever formed distinct interests in society.'[18] It was obvious to him and most other of the Framers of the Constitution that the haves should rule over the have-nots. Benjamin Franklin concurred: 'though there is a general dread of giving too much power to our governors, I think we are in more danger from too little obedience by the governed'.[19]

Washington himself was so alarmed by the universal spirit of rebellion, which in truth was sparked by the revolution itself, that he was induced to come out of his comfortable retirement at Mount Vernon to preside over the convention at Philadelphia in 1787.

Most of the 55 self-selected men who drew up the constitution were lawyers; most of their wealth was in the form of land, slaves, manufacturing or shipping; half of them had money loaned out at interest and 40 owned government bonds. All represented their fellow citizens of wealth and were intent on protecting property and wealth and 'to repress domestic faction and insurrection'.[20] Most also had speculated in the continental scrip and land certificates issued to soldiers who had been forced by privation to sell them at a loss for hard currency. Holders of these bonds, scrip and certificates wanted the central government to redeem them in full and that would only be possible with a new form of government with the power to tax. Manufacturers desired protective tariffs; moneylenders wanted the federal government to put a stop to the issuance by states of their own paper money; land speculators wanted military protection for invading Indian lands; slave owners wanted federal protection against slave revolts and to capture escaped slaves; bondholders needed a federal government able to tax and so pay off bondholders with interest.[21] A single representative of the interests of small farmers and wage earners, those who had made up the very backbone of the revolution, was nowhere to be found. In the end the material interests of the propertied elite were met virtually in full while the lower orders fended as best they could.

All American schoolchildren learn early of the sanctity of the Bill of Rights. Few learn that these first ten amendments to the original constitution were opposed by most of the original framers. The document issued in 1789 had omitted to ascribe rights of free speech, assembly, trial by jury of peers, freedom from arbitrary search and seizure and many others precisely because they did not want the common people to exercise them. But opposition to the ratification was so deep that promises of the later amendments had to be made or the constitution might have been rejected. Thus did the genie of democracy work its spell. While the universal right to vote was not among the new rights extolled, the ones that were enumerated were sufficient to lead many to believe that they were genuine citizens and not mere subjects. This would have far reaching consequences.

The Founders had made one thing very clear. The threat to liberty came primarily from vested government, though once that power was in their hands they deemed it sacrosanct. But the lesson was absorbed by those who had borne the brunt of distress and sacrifice in the revolution. The Second Amendment to the Constitution of the United States providing for the right to bear arms was instituted as a defense against the new government's potential to replicate the tyranny of the crown. Armed militias would provide a counterweight to the standing army should that be employed against the people, as the British army had been. Since that time numerous legal cases have ruled that this right is embodied in the National Guard and since that agency can be federalized the original intent has been nullified. It was one thing for popular eruption to create the US; it was another if similar upheavals were to contest the decisions of the new American governing class.

No sooner had the Bill of Rights been adopted than the Whiskey Rebellion broke out in western Pennsylvania and spread to Virginia. The new Secretary of the Treasury, Alexander Hamilton, and Congress lost no time in exercising the newly established power to tax. The justification was to draw down the national debt but Hamilton also wished to impose taxes 'more as a measure of social discipline than as a source of revenue'.[22] But most importantly Hamilton 'wanted the tax imposed to advance and secure the power of the new federal government'.[23] Suppression of the tax rebellion would constitute the first exercise of armed force by the new government against its own citizens.

Hard currency was scarce in this rural region and farmers could not easily get their corn to eastern markets, so they usually converted corn they could not sell or barter to whisky. Often the whisky itself served as a medium of exchange. Congress levied taxes on all distillers but the larger industrial producers (George Washington was the largest) were charged rates significantly lower than small farmers. Since voting rights were limited by property qualifications many small farmers could not vote and saw imposition of the tax in much the same terms as did colonists at the time of the Stamp Act. As in Shays' Rebellion many of the whisky rebels were veterans of the revolution and their issue was taxation without representation and the clear bias in favor of the wealthy.

By the summer of 1795, civil protests became armed rebellion. As word of the upheaval spread across state lines tax collectors were assaulted and resistance took other forms such as robbing the mail and stopping court proceedings. With Shays' Rebellion still fresh in their minds Washington and Hamilton declared martial law and themselves led the new army of the United States into the west to crush the rebels. The firm precedent was established. Though the United States itself had come into existence by armed rebellion, the new national government would not tolerate the same from Americans. The unintended result channeled popular frustration at the biased power exercised in the capital toward universal suffrage, a fundamental right not fully recognized in law until 1964.

With the spirit of rebellion temporarily squashed the elites turned their attention toward the shape of the economy. American settlement by Britons had from the start been a profit-making enterprise and citizens of the new nation were as committed to pecuniary self-advancement as ever. Though the Founders feared 'faction', political differences were inevitable. Thus two main camps and two different visions emerged. Jefferson imagined the vast continent filling up with independent 'yeoman' farmers, while Hamilton envisioned a strong centralized industrial and commercial economy, a central bank and an army of wage earners to serve it. To the Jeffersonians, Hamilton's system seemed too closely akin to Britain's but the Federalists understood that continued upper-class control would require greater centralization. Only that would enable the US eventually to out-compete Britain. Since the age of the self-dependent yeoman was over, and an increasingly global market was the focus of all production – agricultural as well as industrial – the result of the split between the Hamiltonian

Federalists and Democratic-Republican Jeffersonians was a system that combined both conceptions. The vast American hinterland would be opened up to agricultural enterprise producing for eastern and European markets, while the American cities would evolve around banking, trade and manufacture. But first the west would have to be won.

4
An Empire for Liberty?

Wage war and call it self-defense.   Fisher Ames, 1798 (Ames et al., 1854)

What good man would prefer a country covered with forests and ranged by a few thousand savages to our extensive Republic studded with cities, towns and prosperous farms...?

Andrew Jackson, Second Inaugural Address, 1830 (US Government, 2001)

Now that the restive lower orders were contained, the political elites of the new nation set about fostering a sense of nationalism that they saw as necessary to channel popular frustration that would otherwise be directed at them. Jefferson's espousal of a republic, based on widespread ownership of land by a self-sustaining independent class of small farmers constituting the great majority, is still seen as the first great advocacy of popular democracy, yet the vast majority of people could not vote, including most white males. Hamilton and his fellow Federalists feared the growth of Jefferson's 'yeomanry' and knew the day was not far off when its white, male members would demand suffrage, and with it perhaps overturn the aristocrat's grasp on power and destroy the Hamiltonian goal of an industrial society with centralized banking and control of money. So, expansion was necessary to Democrats and Federalists alike in order to provide the growing white population with at least a small stake of property in the new system. The new nationalism would be based on whipped up fears of foreign plots both to contain Americans and deprive them of their vaunted birthright. The result would be aggression turned outward toward the native peoples and the imported slaves.

CREATING AN ENEMY TO THWART THE BILL OF RIGHTS

Though American independence could not have been won without the alliance with France, the new Federalist government soon waged undeclared war against its former benefactor. The French monarchy was overthrown in 1789 and many Americans initially viewed this event as a replication of the American revolution. However, Federalists viewed revolutionary France, and its radical call for democracy, as a threat to established order. They feared the infection would penetrate the United States.

Because conditions there were vastly different than those that obtained in the US, the French revolution became self-destructive, eventually leading to military dictatorship under Napoleon Bonaparte, who proceeded to conquer much of Europe and renew war with Britain.

Despite the recent animosities between the two nations, most Federalists remained Anglophiles and understood that their own wealth and power depended mainly on trade with their former rulers. As Hamilton put it: 'I have always preferred a connexion with [Great Britain] to any other country, we think in English, and have a similarity of prejudices and predilections.' Meanwhile the French sought to cut off trade between Britain and the former colonies, while the British seized American vessels bound for France. The continued Franco-American alliance would deprive the US of the one market that sustained it. Although President Washington had declared American neutrality, many members of his administration, especially Hamilton, plotted to ally with England and to seek its favor mainly to expand into the west. The treaty signed by Chief Justice John Jay won agreement from Britain to withdraw from forts in the Northwest Territory, thereby opening up that land for settlement. In response to what they saw as a repudiation of their alliance the French now seized American vessels. The erstwhile enemy was now ally, the former confederate a bitter adversary.[1]

Jeffersonian democrats had viewed the French more positively and desired to keep the alliance. Their opposition to the real but undeclared war with France led to an even deeper split between the two opposing camps that would soon evolve into the two-party system. Hamilton's followers hoped that the Anglo-American alliance would enable the US to seize Florida and Louisiana and, to gain popular support, spread propaganda that Napoleon's *Grande Armée* would soon invade the US. 'Our game will be to attack where we can,' said Hamilton, 'France is not to be considered as separated from her ally [Spain]. Tempting objects will be in our grasp.'[2]

For the first time, but not the last, the extreme war party in the US had created an enemy in order to focus domestic fear and attention on a false threat from abroad, then employed war as the means for expansion and engrossment of their own fortunes.

Deliberately instilling xenophobia and drawing attention to the large number of immigrants not of English ancestry, the Federalists under the second president, John Adams, passed a new Naturalization Act increasing the time required for citizenship from five to 14 years. The Alien Act enabled the president to arrest and jail or deport the 25,000 French who resided in the US, or any other of the foreign born who dissented. Most chilling of all was the Sedition Act that effectively nullified the First Amendment to the constitution and led to the arrest of numerous journalists and editors who voiced opposition to the war with France. They were condemned as traitors. These measures, coming so soon after passage of the Bill of Rights, were an overt attempt to invalidate it and revealed how deeply many of the Framers opposed popular dissent and democracy itself, especially when the issue was war or peace. Their counterparts in every subsequent era of American history would enact similar measures intended to cow the voice of popular opposition, right up to the present.

In 1800 the French, faced with enormous casualties and attempting to suppress slave rebellion in Haiti, agreed to remunerate the US for its shipping losses, thereby undercutting the war hawks, who had grown so unpopular that Jefferson ascended to the presidency that year. Termination of the war turned out to be a stroke of good luck for Jefferson's vision because he would not have been able to 'purchase' the vast Louisiana Territory only three years later otherwise. The French had forced the Spanish to 'retrocede' Louisiana (France had turned it over to Spain in 1763 to avoid losing it to Britain after the Seven Years War) and Napoleon, in need of funds, 'sold' the region for $15 million.[3] An area larger than the nascent US itself, Jefferson envisioned its settlement from the first. He had his 'empire for liberty', but its 200,000 native inhabitants had not been informed of the real estate transaction.

War between France and England spread to other European states and proved a boon to the infant US in other respects. At the beginning of the nineteenth century the US became 'a world class commercial power'.[4] European economies suffered tremendously and so demand for American goods and foodstuffs exploded exponentially in the belligerent states. While trade expanded there new markets in China, Latin America and the Mediterranean were also opened up. Yankee merchants from New England were the first Americans to ply the seas of Asia. From that moment on the vast 'great China market' would loom in the imagination of American entrepreneurs, eventually to result in five bloody wars (against Japan,

Korea, China and Vietnam and the war of Philippine independence) in the attempt to bend it to the American agenda.

Also, at that moment, the new American nation intervened for the first time directly into the affairs of another. Pointedly, this involved what would later come to be known as the Middle East.

The quasi-war with France had spurred the creation of the American navy and a new threat led to its buildup. 'Barbary pirates' were seizing and enslaving merchants and sailors in the Mediterranean and then holding them for ransom. With insurance rates increasing and profits diminishing Jefferson soon deployed warships to counter these predations. By 1804 almost the entire navy was in the Mediterranean. In 1805 the American consul in Tunis asked for permission from Jefferson to overthrow its ruler and replace him with another more inclined to US interests. Secretary of State James Madison deplored meddling in 'the domestic contests of other countries' but decided the cause was just and approved the exploit. 'Jefferson took a Hamiltonian pleasure in the way his military venture had earned the respect of European great powers.'[5] The paradigm for more such meddling in the not too distant future was set. Now it was time to build a continental empire.

MANY TRAILS OF TEARS

We shall be obliged to drive them [natives] with the beasts of the forest into the Stony Mountains.

Thomas Jefferson, 1808

I see not how the Indians could have been treated with more equity or humanity than they have been in general in North America.

John Adams, 1818

Whether the whites won the land by treaty, by armed conquest, or both...mattered little so long as the land was won...all men of sane and wholesome thought must dismiss with contempt the plea that these continents should be reserved for the use of a few scattered savages whose life was a few degrees less meaningless, squalid, and ferocious than that of the wild beasts.

Theodore Roosevelt, *The Winning of the West, Vol. IV*

In his private correspondence Jefferson often indicated a paternalistic concern for the fate of the American natives, usually claiming that their best interests would be served by abandoning their traditional ways and assimilating into what he clearly believed was a superior civilization. In letters to native leaders he would call them 'my sons' and their peoples his 'children'; to whites he would claim that 'in body and mind' the native was 'equal to the white man'. But as was the case with his anti-slavery pronouncements, hypocrisy lurked just below the surface.

All Americans know that the native peoples of the Americas were largely displaced but little attention is paid to the methods. Just as Indian lands in the seventeenth century were 'expropriated through trickery, legal manipulation, intimidation, deportation, concentration camps, and murder', so the model continued, becoming, in short, the prototype of what is now condemned by the US as 'ethnic cleansing'.[6] All of these measures have been employed against every non-white enemy the US has created for itself: from Virginia to Vietnam, from the Pequot massacre to Sand Creek, to Wounded Knee, to My Lai to Haditha and Faluja.

When the Louisiana Territory was obtained Jefferson wanted to see the Chickasaws of the south-eastern states removed to the farthest west, though they had been among the few tribes to take the American side in the revolution. Jefferson claimed that there were no other tribes in the west, ignoring both differences in climate and geography that would utterly disrupt Chickasaw way of life and the fact that they would then come into conflict with the Plains tribes. Alarmed that white settlers were pouring into both the Northwest territories and Louisiana Territory, a number of Indian leaders like Tecumseh attempted to bring about a confederacy of the many tribes in resistance. To this Jefferson responded:

> We too are preparing for war against those, and only those who shall seek it, and if we are ever constrained to lift the hatchet against any tribe, we shall never lay it down until that tribe is exterminated, or driven beyond the Mississippi. In war, they will kill some of us; we shall destroy all of them.[7]

It was Jefferson who provided the impetus for Andrew Jackson's later ethnic cleansing of the entire south, ultimately the annexation of Florida, Texas and the conquest of the far western lands and tribes. At the time of the Louisiana Purchase these were territories claimed by Britain and Spain, but Jefferson alleged that his acquisition included not only these lands, but also Oregon.[8] Mexico's independence brought Texas under that new nation's rule, but by 1844 James Polk would claim that at least part of Texas had also been included in Louisiana. As we shall see this was simply a ruse to take all of Texas and more.

With Florida completely surrounded by the United States, the Spanish had every reason to think that their claim would be the next to be absorbed. While many high school texts refer to the acquisition of Florida as a 'purchase', it was brought about by a man who would become the most bellicose president in US history, Andrew Jackson. Born of Scots-Irish ancestry in the Appalachian region of North Carolina that was fiercely contested between whites and natives, Jackson was orphaned by the age of 13 and suffered brutal wounds at the hands of the British during the revolution. These traumatic experiences left him with an implacable hatred of the Indians and the British, and a desire for vengeance that he exercised without mercy. Climbing in southern society to become a land speculator and slave trader at the very moment the invention of the cotton gin caused the explosion of cotton as the prime plantation crop, Jackson yearned above all to cleanse the region of those he considered savages, though his own rages led him to knife fights and to engage in a number of pistol duels, killing one man. (The 'gin' derives from 'engine'. This was a revolutionary invention by Eli Whitney in 1794 that enabled slaves to remove the seeds from cotton much faster and in more bulk than they could previously do by hand.) When escaped slaves and members of various tribes sought refuge in Spanish-held Florida among the Seminoles, Jackson took it upon himself to invade the area. Though his actions were condemned by President Monroe and his Secretary of State, John Quincy Adams, their rhetoric was largely diplomatic camouflage. They wished to annex Florida too and were perfectly happy for a rogue to accomplish it. Realizing they would lose the land anyway the Spanish then sold it to the US. Jackson became the territory's first governor.

LAND HUNGER PROVOKES AN UNNECESSARY WAR

Jackson had become the nation's first military hero since Washington because of his decisive defeat of the British during the war of 1812. Jackson's victory at the Battle of New Orleans actually came after the peace treaty between Britain and the US had been signed, but communications by sea delayed the message. As during the revolution, Britain's best troops were pre-occupied with France. Had the full might of England been brought to bear the outcome would have been very different. Every American war aim failed. Most land battles were lost, though some naval engagements passed into legend, and the hysterical clamor for war reinforced what was already a growing sectionalism between North and South. Indeed, New Englanders even contemplated secession, long before the Confederacy of 1861. Boston merchants continued to trade with their prime partners, the British, even as war commenced. While a pugnacious nationalism emerged, it was also balanced by an equally assertive sectionalism. The very solidarity of the Union was weakened.[9]

The bitter conflict between Napoleon and England escalated in 1803 and at first benefited the US tremendously. Attempting to remain neutral, American merchant vessels traded with both nations but because each belligerent sought to strangle the other's economy by depriving it of necessary supplies both France and Britain soon began seizing American vessels. Despite the losses American shippers found ways to smuggle goods to either side and thus kept American ports busy and profitable. Then when the British fired upon a US frigate, the *Chesapeake*, Jefferson's party, the Democratic-Republicans, passed the infamous Embargo Act prohibiting all commerce with both sides. The result was an instant economic depression. Federalists in the North, especially New England, seeing their profits crash, were outraged and threatened to withdraw from the Union, but many farmers in the border states who were hungry for more land envisioned a conquest of Canada and the total removal of the British from North America.

Many Americans accused the British of arming Indians in the West to block their westward migration. As tensions mounted the British continued to seize vessels and impress American sailors into their own navy. Certain Federalists were suspected of secret dealings in order to rejoin with Britain. The war hawks who carried the day desired material benefits but their words showed little hint of anything more than 'national honor'. President Madison declared that 'To have shrunk under such circumstances from manly resistance would have been a degradation...' In the manner typical of the war hawk who himself will bear no cost of war but only its benefits, Senator Henry Clay asserted that the greatest boon would be 'the reproduction and cherishing of a martial spirit among us', and added:

> But I prefer the troubled ocean of war, demanded by the honor and independence of the country, with all its calamities and desolations, to the tranquil, putrescent pool of ignominious peace.

Despite the language of honor the underlying motive was land hunger. By a slim margin Congress voted for war.

Americans celebrate this war in the words of their national anthem, the 'Star-spangled banner'. But the British burned to the ground the new capital at Washington and forced President Madison to flee for his life. The attempted annexation of both Canada and East Florida were disasters. For the British the affair was a sideshow to their war with France and would not have come about (and it scarcely figures in their history).

But for Americans who now poured into the West, the second war against the most powerful empire, by *not* ending in re-subjugation, was perceived as a glorious victory and vindication of a new order. The new 'American system' was acclaimed as the vanguard of human progress, thus lending license to an exultant and belligerent nationalism that propelled settlement of the Louisiana Territory and would lead to uncompromising demands for more land and influence beyond its boundaries. As Clay put matters, the US now had the 'power to create a system of which we shall be the centre' and added that America would become 'the place of deposit of the commerce of the world'.[10] The requirements of war had now led all parties to accept increased federal authority, especially in levying tariffs to enlarge the army and navy, and on capital improvements like canals and roads to foster the development of a national market. No longer willing to be at the mercy of trade with England, all the new nationalists desired to engross American territory and open new foreign markets. With the Spanish empire tottering and losing its colonies to independent states the only real rival in the western hemisphere was England and, though Americans believed they had defeated her, Britannia still ruled the waves and would for some time to come. At best the new republic would make a temporary accommodation.

LAYING CLAIM TO THE HEMISPHERE

Though the first of the American pronouncements known as 'doctrines' bears the name of James Monroe, it was formulated by John Quincy Adams. Unlike his fellow New Englanders, many of whom regretted the break with England, Adams was a committed nationalist with a grand vision of America's future, one that had no room for Britain. Like his Puritan forebears he believed that God had appointed the US to civilize the New World. Anticipating the doctrine of 'Manifest Destiny' he said as early as 1811, 'The whole continent of North America appears to be destined by Divine Providence to be peopled by one nation, speaking one language, professing one general system of religious and political principles.'[11]

As Spanish power collapsed dramatically in the western hemisphere, Adams led those who worried about British advantages in the competition to establish trade, mining concessions and loans in the emerging Latin republics.[12] But he still had to acknowledge British strength. London's rulers were well aware that the only resistance they faced in the Americas now was their former colony. So the British foreign minister, George Canning, proposed that both Britain and the US combine their power to prevent any future colonization of the western hemisphere. In addition to blocking France, Spain and any others from the hemisphere, both Britain and the US would also agree not to annex any more territory themselves. Both nations would concentrate on commerce. American officials certainly desired an end to European colonies but they absolutely rejected such a constraint upon the United States. Canning's stipulations would have hemmed in the US and barred it from future annexation of Texas, California, Oregon, or Cuba and Puerto Rico, already being envisioned. As for commerce, the US wanted to supplant Britain in the markets of the world.

So, instead of a joint declaration the US government issued the Monroe Doctrine unilaterally and proclaimed audaciously that the western hemisphere was no longer open for European colonization. American effrontery was remarkable in the face of British power. The United States could by no means militarily enforce its claim and it had no standing in domestic or international law. The British shortly repudiated the doctrine by establishing a new colony in the Falkland Islands. But the upstart nation had asserted that it would do what it insisted Europeans could not. It would continue territorial acquisition and it seemed to avow that it would one day dominate the hemisphere.

As Spain's western hemispheric colonies struggled for independence the US extended rhetorical support. But most Americans viewed Catholics in Latin America as backward 'papists' who were incapable of the virtues of liberty and self-government characteristic of Anglo-Americans. All Spanish territories, moreover, possessed large numbers of natives who were deemed utterly inferior. When Mexico achieved independence the US formally congratulated its neighbor but the new nation also claimed lands that many in the US insisted were part of the Louisiana Purchase. In any case, the legalistic argument over Mexico's border hid deeper desires among Americans to seize a great deal more than the region known as Texas.

The agricultural and industrial prosperity of the United States were two sides of the same coin. As a result of mechanical improvements, and above all, slave labor, cotton had become the most important export crop throughout the South. It was also a vital commodity necessary to textile manufacturers and the workers they employed in New England and other areas of the North. While the movement to abolish slavery was strongest in the North, even there most Americans believed that the 'peculiar institution' was vital to continued profits and employment. The American farmer, north or south, whether producing cotton or corn for export, did so as part of a growing market system and therefore required more and more land to profit in that system. Enormous pressures were in place to settle the western continent beyond the boundaries of the Louisiana Territories. Profits engendered by slave-based cotton production were so great that representatives of the slavocracy demanded that south-western lands be acquired to spread that source of wealth.

But much land in the Deep South was still held by natives. Jefferson had been the first president to call for the removal of Indians but it was not carried out until the 1830s. Historians refer to the 'Age of Jackson' as the period when demands by lower class white men for the right to vote were led and met by a president who stood for full democracy against the privilege of entrenched aristocratic power. While it is true that universal white male suffrage was obtained during this era, most of those who obtained it were no more democratic than their opponents. White men still barred women and every non-white from exercising the same right. Now that their votes were needed by both parties they could exact pressure on federal and state governments to confer advantage on them. The benefit most sought was the land of those Indians who held title to it by treaty. Jackson was the most prominent voice calling to shred these treaties.

The governor of Georgia stated flatly that treaties 'were expedients by which ignorant, intractable, savage peoples were induced without bloodshed to yield up what civilized people had a right to possess'.[13] And when the land promised in treaties was desired then such expedients could be ignored.

'ANGLO-SAXONISM' AND THE MARCH TO THE PACIFIC

Anglo-Saxonism was coming into full bloom. A senator from Virginia put matters in unmistakable terms:

> It is peculiar to the character of this Anglo-Saxon race of men to which we belong, that it has never been contented to live in the same country with any other distinct race, upon terms of equality; it has, invariably, when placed in that situation, proceeded to exterminate or enslave the other race in some form or other, or, failing that to abandon the country.[14]

Few suggested the land be abandoned.

In yet another of history's ironies it was Jackson who introduced the phrase 'As long as grass grows or water runs' to ensure the peoples who had been removed that the new lands they would be given would forever be theirs. Between 1831 and 1838 approximately 125,000 Cherokee, Chickasaw, Choctaw, Creek and Seminole Indians were forcibly removed from millions of acres in the South.[15] Most of these tribes had sided with the Americans against the British, and some had also given up their traditional ways to adopt American-style market agriculture. They had done what Jefferson had advocated they do. But the whites wanted their land. Though the words of the Lakota Sioux elder, Black Elk, were spoken many years later, they apply to all relations between whites and natives in the Americas: 'The white man made us many promises but he only kept but one. He promised to take our land and he took it.'[16]

The Choctaw were first and it is from their tragedy that the term 'Trail of Tears' entered history, but all tribes had their own journey of sorrows as they were driven from their ancestral lands across the Mississippi to occupy what would be called the Oklahoma territory. Subjected to forced marches in bitter cold, deprived of food, suffering from disease, all tribes had similar tales of savage abuse that compare easily with the infamous Bataan Death March inflicted on American soldiers during World War II. The pattern of ethnic cleansing set in the seventeenth century still worked efficiently. A Confederate soldier wrote many years after these events: 'I fought through the War Between the States and have seen many men shot, but the Cherokee Removal was the cruelest work I ever knew.'[17]

In 1844 James Polk, a wealthy slave owner and cotton planter, was elected president and quickly became the agent of war and more expansion. Pretext would again be the method as it would for virtually every war thereafter. The first stage of the war against Mexico, the real aim of which was to annex all of what is now the American south-west, California and Oregon, began by bringing what was then called the independent republic of Texas into the Union. Mexico had allowed Americans to establish farming communities in its territory, believing they would live under Mexican law. Mexico had abolished slavery but some Americans flooding into Mexican territory established cotton plantations based on slave labor. Mexico attempted to rein in this problem but there were too many Americans. Though most American settlers in Texas did not have slaves themselves, they resented the idea that they had to live under the rule of 'inferior' Mexicans. So, claiming that they were following in the tradition of the American revolution, the Texans were able to win independence in 1836 but many held out hope of becoming a state in the American Union.

Polk claimed to be 're-annexing' Texas, asserting falsely that it had been included in the Louisiana Purchase. At the same time he called for the 're-occupation' of Oregon though the US had never occupied it in the first place. By this time many prominent northern intellectuals and religious figures were openly supporting abolition but that did not mean they opposed expansion. Polk and his followers believed that by including Oregon they would mollify northerners concerned about slavery's expansion in the south-west. Northerners and southerners alike desired the ports of San Francisco, San Diego and Seattle. Abolitionism, noble as it was, was far outpaced by a virulent racial nationalism claiming scientific evidence that melded into the doctrine of 'Manifest Destiny'. While the phrase itself is attributed to an obscure newspaper editor, the ideology was already in wide circulation.

Well before the nation of Germany came into existence the roots of Nazi race theories were being set in the United States, and for the same reasons. New pseudo-sciences of phrenology and 'craniology', in response to abolitionism, focused on claims of African inferiority, but were also put to use rationalizing the conquest of Mexico and native peoples. These ideas were paralleled by the ever more popular doctrine of 'Anglo-Saxonism'.[18]

Daniel Webster, Senator from Massachusetts, asserted that 'on this continent *all* is to be Anglo-American from Plymouth Rock to the Pacific seas, from the North Pole to California'.[19] Secretary of State James Buchanan said that 'Anglo-Saxon blood could never be subdued by anything that claimed Mexican origin'. Sam Houston, the president of Texas when it had been independent, stated that 'The Mexicans are no better than the Indians and I see no reason why we should not go in the same course now, and take their land.'[20] One journalist's estimation of Mexicans reflected broad opinion: 'There are no people on the continent of America, whether civilized or uncivilized, with one or two exceptions, more miserable in condition or despicable in morals than the mongrel race inhabiting New Mexico.'[21]

Abolitionists in Britain, where slavery had been banned in 1834, made weak attempts to bring independent Texas into the British orbit, but there was really no chance of that. American slaveholders desiring annexation then used the well tested tactic of 'danger from abroad' to whip up popular support for Texas' entry in the Union, as well as to lay groundwork for subsequent acquisitions. In 1845 Texas became the twenty-eighth state.

TO THE HALLS OF MONTEZUMA

Both Mexico and the United States had recognized the Nueces River as their common border but now Polk insisted that the boundary was the Rio Grande, about 150 miles to the south. He sent a large American force under General Zachary Taylor to that river while also sending an emissary to Mexico City to 'resolve' the issue diplomatically, fully realizing that Mexico would not simply sign away its territory. All that remained was to wait for an incident that could then be used to justify war. It was not long in coming. On April 25, 1846 an American patrol was ambushed by Mexican forces and 16 soldiers were killed, the rest wounded and captured. Polk had his pretext. He declared that 'Mexico has passed the boundary of the United States, has invaded our territory and shed American blood on American soil.' War, 'notwithstanding all our efforts to avoid it, exists by the acts of Mexico herself'.[22]

One of the ranking officers in Taylor's army, Colonel Ethan Allen Hitchcock, wrote in his diary:

> I have said from the first that the United States are the aggressors... we have not one particle of right to be here...It looks as if the government has sent a small force on purpose to bring on a war so as to have a pretext for taking California and as much of the country as it chooses...My heart is not in this business...but, as a military man, I am bound to execute orders.[23]

In Congress, recently elected Abraham Lincoln rose to demand that he be shown on the map the very 'spot' that American blood was shed 'on American soil', adding that Polk's charges were the 'half insane mumbling of a fever dream'.[24] John Quincy Adams spoke vehemently against war but later voted appropriations, as did Lincoln.

Only two members of Congress voted against war. One of them, Joshua Giddings of Ohio, labeled it 'an aggressive, unholy, and unjust war'. Later, after war had been declared, he also refused to vote funds for the war, saying that 'In the murder of Mexicans upon their own soil, or in robbing them of their country, I can take no part either now or hereafter. The guilt of these crimes must rest on others – I will not participate in them.'[25]

Only rarely in two centuries of American history has a voice as honest and courageous been raised in the halls of Congress against the pretexts and machinations of those who would wage war in open contravention of the principles upon which the nation claims to stand. But they were lonely voices against a rising tide of war frenzy.

Ralph Waldo Emerson, one of the leading intellectual proponents of the supposedly humane philosophy of Transcendentalism, passively opposed the war but said little and clearly counted himself among the manifest destinarians:

> It is very certain that the strong British race, which has now overrun so much of this continent, must also overrun that tract [Texas], and Mexico and Oregon also, and it will in the course of the ages be of small import by what particular occasions and methods it was done.[26]

Theodore Parker, Boston minister and abolitionist, sighed: 'God often makes the folly and the sin of men contribute to the progress of mankind.'[27] Walt Whitman, whose compassion for the wounded in the Civil War is celebrated, showed that it did not extend to Mexicans: 'Yes! Mexico must be chastised...America knows how to crush as well as expand!'[28]

American forces marched all the way south to Mexico City, where US Marines stormed 'the halls of Montezuma'. The port city of Vera Cruz was bombarded with 1,300 shells, leading a reporter to write that few soldiers were killed while 'the destruction among women and children is great'.[29] Many American units behaved brutally towards occupied civilians. One commander, George G. Meade, later the hero of the battle of Gettysburg, wrote that some of his men 'killed five or six innocent people...for no other object than their own amusement...they rob and steal the cattle of poor farmers, and in fact, act more like a body of hostile Indians than civilized Whites.' Even General Taylor acknowledged that 'There is scarcely a form of crime that has not been reported to me as committed by them.'[30] Rape was widespread. One officer wrote in his diary that his men 'were emulating each other in making beasts of themselves'. Another wrote to his parents that 'Old women and girls were stripped of their clothing – and many suffered still greater outrages...it gave me a lamentable view of human nature...and made me for the first time ashamed of my country.'[31] After Mexican surrender, when he became military governor of the 8 million people of Mexico City, General John A. Quitman revealed what he thought of his new charges. They are 'beasts of burden', he said, 'with as little intellect as the asses whose burdens they share'.[32]

With victory, the desire on the part of many Americans to annex all of Mexico came to the fore. The *Boston Times* envisioned the conquest of Mexico as 'necessarily a great blessing to the conquered. It is a task worthy of a great people who are about to regenerate the world by asserting the supremacy of humanity over the accidents of birth and fortune.' In Philadelphia Commodore Robert Stockton exulted in what he saw as a mandate from heaven: 'It is because the spirit of our pilgrim fathers is with us; it is because the God of armies and the Lord of hosts is with us.' He called upon his government to 'redeem' the Mexicans.[33]

But opposition to 'All Mexico' came from those who feared trying to rule over an immense non-white population. Senator Edward Hannegan of Indiana spoke in Congress: 'Mexico and the United States are peopled by two distinct and unhomogeneous races. In no reasonable period could we amalgamate.' Andrew Donelson, Polk's ambassador to Mexico, declared that 'We can no more amalgamate with her than with negroes.' The *Cincinnati Herald* railed against taking southern Mexico. How could the United States incorporate 8 million Mexicans it asked 'with their idol worship, heathen superstition, and degraded mongrel races?' Senator John C. Calhoun advised that the US should keep only the sparsely populated areas: 'What we want is space for our growing population.'[34]

Despite the enormous military losses it suffered, the government of Mexico would not surrender. Polk had sent an envoy to Mexico telling him to demand Baja California as well as the original demand for Upper California and the vast New Mexico territory. Nicholas

Trist nevertheless formulated the Treaty of Guadalupe Hidalgo, settling for the original war aims. Polk was enraged but had to submit the treaty to the Senate. He consoled himself by predicting that the California ports would provide an excellent jumping off point for further expansion, both commercially and territorially, into the Pacific and on to Asia. He was correct.

The cost to Mexico was enormous. At least 50,000 died as opposed to about 11,000 Americans (the vast majority to yellow fever and other diseases, not combat) and it lost half of its territory. Many of Mexico's art treasures from its long history were looted as well. Years later Ulysses S. Grant regretted the role he had played as a young officer. 'I had the horror of the Mexican War...only I had not moral courage enough to resign.'[35]

Victory over Mexico provided the environment for yet more war. As they reached the Pacific Ocean, Americans immediately set their sights on Asia and the island stepping stones to the riches they believed had loomed with promise since the earliest days of the republic. Within a decade American warships would enter Japanese waters and forcibly 'open' Japan to the larger world, thereby fostering a crisis in the island nation that would lead it to militarize against the westerners and join the game of empire itself. Back on the mainland, acquisition of new territories in the southwest opened up growing antagonisms between North and South over the extension of slavery and ultimately led to the Civil War.

5
From Ashes to Empire

I can hire one half of the working class to kill the other half.

Jay Cooke, Wall Street baron, 1877 (LaFeber, 1980)

This is a government of the people, by the people, and for the people no longer. It is a government of corporations, by corporations...

John Hay, 1886 (LaFeber, 1980)

God has not been preparing the English-speaking and Teutonic peoples for a thousand years for nothing but vain and idle self admiration. No, he has made us the master organizers of the world...

Senator Albert Beveridge, 1899 (LaFeber, 1980)

NOT FIGHTING TO FREE SLAVES

The Civil War is taught in American primary and secondary schools in such a way as to leave children with the impression that it was fought primarily to free the slaves. Nothing is further from the truth. While the issue of slavery was the underlying cause of the war, the principal issue before the nation when Lincoln was elected in 1860 was whether slavery should be limited to the regions where it already existed, not its abolition. Most shipwrights from Massachusetts, farmers in Pennsylvania or blacksmiths from Indiana did not enlist in the Union Army to free slaves but rather to preserve the Union above all. Until that problem of disunion was resolved, the Civil War would bring a halt to expansion while the nation rent itself asunder.

Abraham Lincoln chose to wage war against the secessionist Confederacy to emphasize his commitment to the Union and so did hundreds of thousands of northerners who volunteered rather than see the nation split in two. From the beginning of the American experiment the founders had desired to see the nascent republic dominate the entire hemisphere and most political and economic elites thereafter also earnestly pursued this goal. The rapid expansion of the US across 3,000 miles of territory, from 'sea to shining sea', in a mere 67 years (1781–1848) testifies to that, and on the eve of the Civil War the US had already initiated inroads into the Pacific, Asia and Central America. Northern industrial and financial interests were also dependent upon southern cotton and the vast profits the crop engendered, and the black slave labor upon which it all relied. The loss of these to a new independent nation would have weakened the position of the US against its principal commercial rival, Britain, which was more than happy to have its challenger torn apart. The breakup of the United States, had secession been allowed by Lincoln's administration, would have strengthened the already formidable hand of Britain in the Caribbean and South America, and destroyed any hope of achieving the American goal of hemispheric dominance. Union was an absolute necessity to carry out the primary goals for which the United States had been established.

The Civil War was the bloodiest and most costly of all American wars because Americans were killing Americans. Approximately 620,000 died on both sides, and the toll of other casualties was catastrophic, especially in the South, where entire cities like Atlanta and Richmond lay in ashes and the countryside was stripped of crops and livestock. While most northern states were spared the agonies of battles and physical destruction, the human toll was nevertheless staggering. The phenomenon of 'soldier's heart', or what today is called Post Traumatic Stress Disorder (PTSD) was widespread. Across the nation, north and south, tens of thousands of soldiers were homeless and psychologically or physically incapacitated, reduced in many cases to begging. This was in an era when there was no Veteran's Administration to provide care or benefits. Some states, like Massachusetts, established homes for the stricken, but many, and especially in the devastated south, could not afford these measures. The carnage of the war was so horrific that it altered the American concept of death itself, as civilians at home tried to come to terms with overwhelming loss. Both sides, for different reasons, adhered to a faith that the fallen had died for transcendent and noble purposes, rather than in ignominy.[1]

For about a generation Americans were sickened by the very thought of war, at least between white Americans. Though the conquest of natives throughout the west continued apace this was largely out of sight and mind for most, since Indians scarcely counted as human. While the central government in Washington laid claim to the vast territories of the west, the aboriginal peoples of the region had never been a party to the transfers of 'ownership' that occurred either by treaty, as in the case of Oregon, or by war with Mexico. Consequently native peoples did not accept white settlement peacefully. Meanwhile, in the decade following the Civil War, federal forces continued to occupy areas of the South until the infamous 'Compromise of 1877' (see below) when the ostensible beneficiaries of the war were dishonorably betrayed, an event so fraudulent that it alone demolishes the national fantasy that the Civil War was joined in order to free the slaves.

Lincoln did not issue the famous Emancipation Proclamation until 1863, two years after the war began, and to a great extent did so out of expediency. While Lincoln himself opposed slavery on moral grounds, he emphasized in his campaign speeches that he had no intention of abolishing slavery, but merely wanted to limit it to the areas where it already existed. In 1863, despite every advantage, the North was losing the war. Conscription had been implemented and it was violently opposed, leading to destructive draft riots in northern cities. One reason the Emancipation Proclamation was issued was to provide incentives to northern blacks to enlist in the Union Army. Until that moment black people saw the conflict as a white man's war. If the goal of abolishing slavery could be added to the preservation of the Union, blacks would overwhelmingly support Lincoln. Once the proclamation was issued over 200,000 free blacks and escaped slaves did enlist and they played a major role in winning their own freedom.

The Emancipation Proclamation freed all slaves in areas not occupied by the Union Army (which meant in 1863 that it freed not a single slave! Delaware, Kentucky, Maryland and Tennessee remained slave states and in the Union) but their legal status at the end of the war after the Confederacy surrendered remained unclear. So 'radicals' in Congress, all northerners or representatives of border states, fostered the addition of the Thirteenth Amendment to the US Constitution in 1865, declaring all slaves henceforth free. At first this was deemed adequate to ensure that freedmen were now American 'citizens'. But few whites treated them as such, and not only in the defeated South. So in 1868, and again in 1870, the Fourteenth and Fifteenth Amendments were added, granting citizenship and the right to vote to all freed *men*. The eleven states that had seceded were not to be re-admitted to the Union, or allowed to vote in any elections, until they had ratified these three amendments. They did so but only under duress and throughout the South freed blacks could exercise civil rights only where federal troops were stationed to protect them. But in the north the public tired of the seemingly endless occupation, weary of those waving the 'bloody shirt' of the rebellion and calling for further punishment of the South, and demanded that the troops be brought home once and for all.

THE COMPROMISE OF 1877: SELLING THE FREEDMEN OUT

In 1876 the former states in rebellion were finally allowed to vote in presidential elections. The election of that year was by far the most corrupt and contentious in American history. Lincoln was the first Republican president and the Republican Party ruled in Washington. No white southerner would vote for a party so identified with defeat and occupation. Although many northern whites, known as carpetbaggers, moved into the South their numbers were not enough to overcome the opposition of white southerners to Republican rule. While freed blacks certainly identified with the Republicans, most were effectively disenfranchised by the Ku Klux Klan and other terrorist organizations. The Klan had been founded by bitter confederate veterans at the close of the war who were committed to white supremacy despite defeat. Thus, in the key election of 1876 white terrorists prevented many blacks and northern whites from ever reaching the polls. By these corrupt measures Democrats claimed victory.

Republicans objected and the result was that in three key states (Florida was one) dangerous disputes arose over which party had actually won electoral votes. The argument grew so violent that civil war was brewing again in some areas. Northerners were in no mood to resume hostilities and so pressure mounted to resolve the issues. At first it was proposed that Congress rule on the matter, but since it was dominated by Republicans that was not acceptable. Then the problem was tossed to the Supreme Court but the same dilemma obtained there. A special commission was appointed but its membership contained eight Republicans and seven Democrats. The political stalemate threatened to break out into renewed warfare in the South and so a great 'compromise' was reached behind closed doors in smoke and whisky filled rooms. If Democrats would give up their claims and allow Rutherford B. Hayes (known thereafter as 'his fraudulency') to assume the presidency, he would subsequently remove all federal troops from the South. The return to self-rule and white supremacy, rather than who occupied the White House, was of far greater importance to southerners and so the compromise was accepted.

Virtually on the day that Union forces left the South, the Ku Klux Klan took over and the former slaves were stripped of civil and political rights and most were reduced virtually to the same status as under slavery. Though technically 'free' they had no land and no means to self-sufficiency and were at the mercy largely of their former masters. Most became tenant farmers or remained as domestic servants. Unable to vote and alter their circumstances the majority of blacks remained trapped in debt servitude. Tenants were bound to the land by debt incurred when tools, seeds and livestock were loaned by landowners at usurious rates. Very few were able to get out of debt and profit to the point where they could buy land outright for themselves. When courageous freedmen and women attempted to exercise their newly promised rights they were faced with the Nazi-like evil of the Klan. One prominent politician and abolitionist, Carl Schurz, wrote to President Andrew Johnson that:

Dead bodies of murdered Negroes were found on or near highways and byways. Gruesome reports came from the hospitals – reports of colored men and women whose ears had been cut off, whose skulls had been broken by blows, whose bodies had been slashed by knives or lacerated by scourges.[2]

Despite horrific obstacles to full citizenship and humanity, the abolition of legal slavery did enable some to escape debt bondage, to prosper and educate themselves and eventually to lead the struggle for equality and full civil rights, though the attainment and enforcement of voting and civil rights nationally would take a full century after the end of Civil War, because of the power wielded by the various white supremacist organizations that continued to terrorize the African-American population with the connivance of state and federal officials.

MASSACRES IN THE WEST

Meanwhile the territories ceded by Mexico and Britain in the far west would have to be settled, and this meant the conquest and displacement of yet more native tribes. The pattern of Indian removal and genocide followed the template set in the earliest years of colonization. In the Dakotas, Wyoming, Montana, New Mexico, Arizona and California, the US government and state officials signed formal treaties with the Sioux, Cheyenne, Arapaho, Nez Perce,

Apache, Comanche, Hopi, Navaho and many other tribes, granting them ownership of territories in 'perpetuity'. But whites poured into these lands in violation of the treaties and demanded that the federal government not only protect them, but enable them to settle. It was not long before official American government actions effectively betrayed commitment to the treaties. As natives fought back, more and more troops were rushed into the west and the natives were gradually defeated and forced to live on reservations, usually on the worst land with fewest resources. A number of signal events occurred that were celebrated as great victories over tribes in the west but were really gruesome slaughters.

The infamous Sand Creek Massacre occurred on November 29, 1864. By a treaty of 1851 with the US government, the Cheyenne and Arapaho had been granted a vast territory encompassing parts of Colorado, Kansas, Nebraska and Wyoming. When gold was discovered in Colorado in 1858 whites demanded a revision of the treaty. The native chieftains knew they could not defeat the US Army so they signed an agreement accepting a reservation about one-thirteenth the size of the original area. This caused many younger tribesmen who called themselves Dog Soldiers to revolt which brought renewed warfare between them and American soldiers.

Nevertheless the chiefs who had signed the acceptance attempted to keep it. They were told to camp their people numbering about 400 old men, women and children, near Fort Lyon at Sand Creek, where they would be regarded as friendly. Despite this, Colonel John Chivington of the Colorado Militia led a force of 800 drunken men to attack the camp. Even though the Cheyenne chief, Black Kettle, waved an American flag given him by Abraham Lincoln, a terrible massacre ensued. Small children were used as target practice. Men and women alike were scalped and their private parts cut out to be worn and later displayed as trophies in Denver. Virtually all the people in the encampment were killed. About 50 soldiers also died from their own 'friendly fire' induced by their drunkenness.

As a direct result of this wanton slaughter the Dog Soldiers took their revenge on thousands of American civilians. A committee to investigate the massacre held an open meeting in Denver only to be greeted by a huge crowd shouting 'Exterminate them, Exterminate them all!' Many soldiers claimed the natives had fired first, though this was impossible since no native warriors had been present. One of Chivington's officers, Captain Silas Soule, who had refused to attack, bore witness to what had really happened. He was murdered a few weeks later.

The Cheyenne and Arapaho clan structure and way of life was effectively destroyed. Chivington was criticized by the committee but no punishment was levied. He would later justify his savage acts with the words 'Nits make lice.'[3]

The fate imposed upon the native peoples of the Americas has justifiably been called the 'American Holocaust'. As Stannard rightly says in *American Holocaust*, 'massacres of this sort were so numerous and routine that recounting them becomes numbing'. Another almost identical massacre occurred at Wounded Knee in South Dakota against the Lakota Sioux 36 years later. The genocidal impulse of many Americans is captured by an editorial written for a Dakota newspaper at the time:

> The nobility of the Redskin is extinguished, and what few are left are a pack of whining curs who lick the hand that smites them. The Whites, by law of conquest, by justice of civilization, are masters of the American continent, and the best safety of the frontier settlements will be secured by the total annihilation of the few remaining Indians.

These words were written by L. Frank Baum, later to become the beloved author of *The Wizard of Oz*.[4]

INDUSTRIALISM RENEWED AND THE ASCENSION OF FINANCE

From 1865, at the close of the Civil War, to 1898, the United States underwent change so transformative that it emerged suddenly as a nation primed to leap upon the stage of global power to compete for empire with Europe and Japan. No comprehension of this process can be complete without understanding the enormous social and economic upheavals and dislodgments that resulted throughout this period from a renewal of the industrialization that had been on hold since the outbreak of civil war. One major result of the Union victory was the collapse of the political power of the old southern 'plantocracy' and its transfer to the industrialists and financiers centered on Wall Street. Soon to be known as plutocrats this new ruling class quickly legislated more centralized banking, fostered high tariffs to ward off competition from abroad and passed the Homestead Act to rapidly populate the west and develop interior markets.

Americans settled more land after 1870 than they had in the previous 300 years.[5] Meanwhile Congress simply gave away vast acreage to the railways as well as agricultural, livestock and lumber interests which, in turn, stimulated colossal iron, steel and mining industries. The transcontinental railroad was completed in 1869 and numerous other lines were built to connect to it and to the rapidly evolving industrial system of capitalist production, leading virtually overnight to immense population shifts westward. The revived machine age led to numerous innovations in machine technology and the internal combustion engine was employed to drive new devices in agriculture which increased the quantity of foodstuffs and cotton; while in or near the cities huge manufacturing plants produced massive amounts of finished goods like clothing, tools, furniture, canned goods and many other necessary commodities for everyday life that had previously been made by hand by independent craftsmen. A truly transformative national system of production and distribution evolved rapidly.

The new system, however, brought equally massive dislocations of people. The pre-existing domestic population was not large enough to meet the increasing demand for unskilled labor in the proliferating factories. Resulting pressure by industrialists on the government forced changes to immigration laws and allowed huge numbers of foreigners to enter the country. But innovative agricultural technology rendered American farmhands obsolete and reduced their numbers, so rural dwellers were forced to move in huge numbers to urban areas for work, or to uproot to settle the far west.

Industrial capitalism produced immense profits but the new wealth was not shared equitably. Great fortunes were being made for a minority (though a much larger middle class also emerged) but extensive poverty was the lot of a huge part of the population. A major consequence of these many developments was the rapid change in the character of cities. As rural peoples and immigrants moved to urban centers, most cities in the north increased exponentially in size and population. Alongside the mansions of the rich, and the stalwart abodes of the new middle classes, slum dwellings multiplied overnight. Here, infrastructure such as clean running water and sanitation services were non-existent. Public privies in congested alleys were the norm. Horses still abounded and dropped their wastes in the streets, there to remain. Overcrowding and disease followed inexorably. These conditions, coupled with work days often 14 hours long, led to life expectancy being far shorter than today.

CYCLES OF BOOM AND BUST PRODUCE POLITICAL INSTABILITY

As if these multiple evils were not enough, they were exacerbated by the sheer instability of the finance system and the production cycle of boom and bust. There were no methods to judge the ability of this growing population to consume the vast quantities of commodities flooding the domestic market. As industrialization commenced the ideology of 'laissez-faire' became fashionable among those who benefited primarily from the new wealth and it therefore became the predominant doctrine of the master classes. This new secular religion held that the government should not interfere to regulate the marketplace lest it throw its 'natural' tendency to equilibrium out of balance. In the end, its proponents argued, the market would right itself. This completely ignored the fact for millions of people at the bottom end of the employment scale, wages were too often inadequate for necessities and the situation was far worse when unemployment rose, as it did with regularity.

People who had been independent artisans making a living under their own command, or who owned and ran small farms, now found themselves out-competed by machine-driven corporations, forced out of business and into the new class of wage-laborers, or 'wage-slaves' as they called themselves. With nothing but their labor to sell in a marketplace that was becoming the overarching regulator of social and economic life, they had no choice but to take jobs as factory workers, usually for considerably less money than they had made while their previous artisanal skills were still of use and value.

The ideology of laissez-faire also ignored the basic reason for the cycle: overproduction. In the scramble to profit in the new economy manufacturers had to rely on 'economies of scale'. Huge factories would produce consumer goods willy-nilly, with no way of knowing the limits of the public's ability to buy and consume them. Sooner or later such anarchic production would flood the market with more goods than the people could consume. This, in turn, would require the shut-down of manufacturing and the subsequent lay-off of much of the work force. This then led to a drop in the ability of the unemployed to buy, leading to further damage to other sectors of the economy in a cascading ripple-effect.

Such business downturns had always characterized the American economy, but in the post-Civil War era the scope and size of the industrial economy meant greater dislocations and consequences for millions. Between 1873 and 1877, and 1893 and 1896, two catastrophic depressions occurred with dismal results for those in the bottom half of American society.

By 1886 railroad construction had virtually ended, leaving large numbers of the approximately 200,000 iron and steel workers unemployed with few other opportunities.[6] The steel plants themselves had been built with borrowed money and this had to be repaid, so new outlets for their enormous output had to be found. At the same time European imperialists were using their conquered territories in faraway Africa and Asia to increase agricultural production, thereby lowering the price of wheat and other commodities, thus forcing many American farmers into bankruptcy.

CLASS WAR INTENSIFIES

While industrialists and financiers were quick to grasp the new opportunities made available by mechanization, they were equally quick to contradict their own doctrine of laissez-faire when depression eroded profits. They formed political organizations, like the National Association of Manufacturers, the National Board of Trade, the American Banking Association and others, to lobby government for special favors in the form of tax breaks, land deals and legislation protecting them from foreign competition, and especially laws to limit the freedom of wage workers to unionize or strike. While claiming that the American creed gave them the right to pursue self-interest in the market, plutocrats were keen to deny similar guarantees to their work force. Thus the new working class came rapidly to the conclusion that it had to organize in the form of labor unions and new political parties in order to meet the power of the industrial and financial magnates and to obtain a fair share of the profits their labor produced. Small farmers also formed the National Farm Alliance in an attempt to counter the railroad owners and middlemen who profited even as the farmers went bankrupt. As the political clout of the new plutocrats increased, the movement of those whose labor was key to the entire industrial enterprise grew in intensity.

When boom turned to bust, and life became intolerable for the poor and unemployed in both the urban slums and rural areas, the only alternative was strikes, walkouts and boycotts as victims of the downturn attempted to force those profiting from the system to share the wealth they derived from the very labor of those they treated with contempt. Many new immigrants came from countries in Europe with traditions of socialist politics and they brought these ideas to the US where they were immediately branded 'un-American'. A great ferment of social discontent and rebellion among the native and foreign-born stirred the land. Violence rocked cities, factories and railways.

Long known as 'robber barons' the new industrialists, and the financiers who were their partners, used their wealth to buy political authority, becoming effectively the powerbrokers behind the 'throne' of constitutional government. Thus they could enact legislation that outlawed strikes and mass demonstrations and could jail labor leaders. Elected officials would often be openly referred to as the 'senator from the Standard Oil Company' or the 'congressman from Dupont'. Even John Hay, Abraham Lincoln's former secretary and soon to be secretary of state under McKinley, deplored the situation: 'This is a government of the people, by the people, and for the people no longer. It is a government of corporations, by corporations, and for corporations. How is this?'[7]

Walter Q. Gresham, a former secretary of state, declared that the situation 'seemed to portend revolution', adding that 'Our revolutionary fathers...went too far with their notions of popular government. Democracy is now the enemy of law and order.'[8] The *New York Tribune* editorialized that 'social restlessness was arraying class against class and filling the land with a nondescript Socialism as dangerous and revolutionary as it is imbecilic and Grotesque'.[9] Jay Gould, one of the principal lords of Wall Street, openly feared a great social revolution. Another, Jay Cooke, sneered at the prospect of a great union movement across industries, arguing that unemployment worked to employers' advantage. 'I can hire one half of the working class to kill the other half,' he blustered.[10] He was not alone and many among the barons concurred. They hired private armies of thugs to break strikes and intimidate those who would join them. In some cases state militias were ordered to fire upon striking workers, and did so, as in the case of the infamous Ludlow massacre.[11]

But the more perceptive among the oligarchs understood that open class warfare was ruinous to profit and would strangle their golden goose as surely as periodic crises of overproduction. The newly emergent working classes would have to be appeased in some fashion that would ensure that no real power was ceded to them, while simultaneously ensuring that wages could be raised, working conditions improved, the cities cleaned and the illusion cultivated that the rebellious classes had significant democratic influence in the political system. While the doctrine of laissez-faire claimed that competition among producers led to efficiency and rational distribution of resources, it was soon clear that contention between firms also lowered the rate of profit, the very essence of capitalism. The problem of falling profits owing to increasing competition was solved by the mechanism of oligopoly. Entire industries agreed to set prices and share markets rather than drive each other into bankruptcy. Thus giant cartels were created completely dominating production in steel, oil, railways, mining, lumber, livestock, meatpacking and many others. Formerly any profits to be had were shared by millions of small entrepreneurs, farmers and artisans. Now Big Business was poised to garner the greater share of the nation's wealth.[12]

Even though the western territories were vast they soon filled up with those who wished to settle there. The US Army was inexorably vanquishing Indian resistance to white settlement and the railroads had connected the west and east. The course of population movement had always been to the west. Now at the shores of the Pacific the limit of the continental *frontier*, the 'safety valve' for excess population in the east, had finally been reached and with it the limits of domestic consumption of the immense production engendered by the new industrial system.

A Gordian knot of crisis in the late nineteenth century afflicted the nation. By all measures the depression of the 1890s created 'a greater loss and more suffering than ever before in the history of the country'.[13] The falling rate of profit, the inability of the domestic population to consume the surplus, unemployment, collapsing wages, bankruptcies, demands by wage earners for a greater share and better working and living conditions, violence in the streets and workplaces, failing farmers and the continental limit to population migration – all resulted in a profound intellectual, political and economic consensus among the barons. For them the answer was expansion overseas and consolidation of power at home. The United States would henceforth go abroad in search of new markets, new sources of raw materials, cheaper labor and continued profit. If the restive population demanded a greater share of the economic pie, the conclusion reached among the rulers was to increase the size of the pie.[14]

TO CONTAIN THE REVOLT OF THE MASSES AND RESTORE PROFITABILITY, THE PLUTOCRATS OPT FOR EMPIRE

The profound crisis engendered by the Depression of 1893–1897 catalyzed the consensus among elites that has been the driving force of American foreign policy ever since. Driven by the universal conclusion that the limits of production and consumption in domestic markets had been reached, convinced that continental territories necessary for population expansion were also limited, historians, social theorists, naval strategists and religious figures developed intellectual rationales across all disciplines that ultimately met and conflated. Deeply influenced by what appeared to be a consistent and coherent theoretical solution to the growing crisis, political and governmental elites embarked upon the course of expansion and empire. To foster domestic stability, provide employment, sell commodities – in essence to maintain the integrity of capitalism itself – new foreign markets would be found, or created, and they would also be defended against rivals, or from peoples who would reject American intervention in their lands.

Simultaneously, the barons understood that their foreign industrial competitors, chiefly Britain but also the rising nations of Germany and Japan, were experiencing similar problems. Thus, the leap upon the stage of empire would also intensify existing imperial rivalry. The US had by far the greatest advantage in industrial strength; it would soon maximize that advantage by building one of the most powerful navies on earth, to project American power into the far reaches of the planet.

As early as 1853 William Seward, later Secretary of State, reflected the unapologetic expansionist sentiment of the political classes:

> Multiply your ships and send them forth to the East. The nation that draws most materials and provisions from the earth, and fabricates the most, and sells the most of productions and fabrics to foreign nations, must be, and will be, the great power of the earth.[15]

Later, he added that the:

> ...borders of the federal republic...shall be extended so that it shall greet the sun when he touches the tropics, and when he sends his gleaming rays toward the polar circle, and shall include even distant islands in either ocean.[16]

Seward also congratulated the Canadians for developing 'states to be hereafter admitted to the Union' and predicted that Russian settlements in the Pacific north-west would 'yet become outposts' of the United States, a prophecy that became fact when he acquired

Alaska. The American destiny was limited only by the boundaries of the earth itself, but the first phase required the conquest of the North American continent. 'Control of this continent,' he avowed, would ensure the US 'in a very few years the controlling influence of the world.'[17] 'The world contains no seat of empire so magnificent as this...the nation thus situated...must command the empire of the seas, which alone is real empire.'[18]

In the early years after the Civil War, President Ulysses S. Grant issued an edict that announced perhaps the first real enforcement of the Monroe Doctrine. Known as the 'non transfer principle', the statement declared that 'hereafter no territory on this continent shall be regarded as subject to transfer to a European power'.[19] Grant then sought to annex Santo Domingo (the Dominican Republic today) but was stymied by a Congress opposed to incorporating the largely non-white population. In 1872 the US Navy acquired its first Pacific beachhead, gaining rights to the harbor of Pago Pago in Samoa. When newly unified Germany later attempted its own acquisition of Samoan islands and found itself blocked by the US, the German Foreign Office complained that the United States was effectively extending the Monroe Doctrine to the Pacific, treating it as an American lake.[20] He was correct.

In 1889 the Cleveland Administration convened a pan-American conference aimed at creating a permanent customs union and a tribunal to arbitrate conflict between western hemispheric nations. Secretary of State James G. Blaine declared the conference had created a new 'Magna Carta' but the Argentine statesman Roque Saenz-Pena said that Blaine had desired 'to make of America a market, and of the sovereign states, tributaries'. The Latin American nations could not overcome their understandable distrust of the colossus to the north, given the history of American intervention in the region. They had seen nothing as yet.

Attention then turned to Hawaii where commercial growers of sugar and pineapples had long been investing in the islands, leading Secretary of State Blaine to assert in 1881 that since sugar producers in Hawaii had become utterly dependent on the US continental market, the islands had become 'part of the commercial system of the American states'. In 1888 another secretary of state, James Bayard, said the US had only 'to wait quietly and patiently and let the islands fill up with American planters and industries until they should be wholly identified with the United States. It was simply a matter of waiting until the apple should fall.'[21] By the mid-1890s Senator Henry Teller of Colorado, who would later disavow the outright annexation of Cuba, had no such compunction about Hawaii. 'We want those islands,' he avowed. 'We want them because they are the stepping way across the sea…necessary to our safety, they are necessary to our commerce.'[22] Theodore Roosevelt declared that it was 'a crime against white civilization not to annex' the islands.[23] Senator Henry Cabot Lodge of Massachusetts was even more aggressive and swaggered that: 'We have a record of conquest, colonization and expansion unequalled by any people in the 19th century…we are not to be curbed now. For the sake of our commercial prosperity we ought to seize the Hawaiian Islands now.'[24]

The descendants of American whalers and missionaries to the islands, though a minority, had become the predominant economic force and by the 1880s coveted outright political control. In 1887 they forced King Kalakaua to establish a representative government that guaranteed power to the planters and other Americans. The Hawaiian monarchy, they claimed, was not consistent with 'a modern system of property and economics'.[25] In 1893 his heir, Queen Liliuokalani, challenged that constitution on behalf of the majority population and was overthrown by the landowners. Acquisition of Hawaii followed much the same pattern that had brought Texas into the American Union. An 'American' population declared 'independence' then sought annexation to the United States.

Lodge's challenge was quickly taken up; Hawaii was annexed in 1898. While the preponderant aim was economic, there were many among the elite who had ulterior motives. The new proponents of naval power, especially Theodore Roosevelt, had long cast covetous eyes upon one of the Pacific's most desirable anchorages at Pearl Harbor. Establishment of the American naval base there, followed almost simultaneously by acquisition of a similar base in the Philippines, greatly worried Japan and set the two nations on a collision course.

THE MONROE DOCTRINE ENFORCED

In 1895 a dramatic dispute between Britain and Venezuela nearly brought the US and London to the brink of war but resulted finally in Britain's acquiescence to the Monroe Doctrine. Venezuela had long chafed at Britain's claim that its colony of Guiana extended across the Orinoco River. When gold was discovered in the disputed region Britain threatened to send troops to enforce its claim. Britain had also recently landed forces in Nicaragua, and British investments throughout Latin America threatened American determination to solve domestic economic problems by increasing exports to the region. Thus, if this claim stood it would guarantee continued British naval power in the Caribbean and thwart American objectives. The Cleveland Administration therefore insisted that Britain submit its claim to international arbitration. US officials cared little about Venezuela's concerns; indeed, in the end Britain got to keep the territory. The issue boiled down to American desire to thwart British power in the Caribbean.

Arguing that the Monroe Doctrine's enforcement was 'important to our peace and safety as a nation and is essential to the integrity of our free institutions and the tranquil maintenance of our distinctive form of government', President Cleveland stated flatly that 'The duty of the United States is to resist by every means in its power, as a willful aggression upon its rights and interests, the appropriation by Great Britain of any lands or the exercise of governmental jurisdiction over any territory, which after investigation we have determined belongs to Venezuela.'[26] In his now famous 'extension' of the Monroe Doctrine, Secretary of State Richard Olney decreed:

> Today the United States is practically sovereign on this continent, and its fiat is law upon the subjects to which it confines its interposition. Why? It is not because of the pure friendship or the good will felt for it...it is because, in addition to all other grounds, its infinite resources combined with its isolated position render it master of the situation and practically invulnerable as against any and all other powers.[27]

Though doubting the issue would come to that, the Cleveland Administration sent a message to Congress stipulating that if Britain refused the finding of the arbitration commission then the US would be prepared for war. In the Senate Henry Cabot Lodge worried that 'if we allow England to invade Venezuela nominally for reparation...really for territory, our supremacy in the Americas is over'.[28] Though Britain was on the verge of a disastrous war in South Africa, and clearly wanted no part of conflict with the United States, the 'jingoes' led by Roosevelt exulted over prospects of war. 'Let the fight come if it must,' said Teddy, 'I don't care if our sea coast cities are bombarded or not, we would take Canada...the mere fact that Canada would inevitably be rent from England in the end would make the outcome an English disaster.' Later, Roosevelt would condemn the advocates of diplomacy as craven. 'Personally,

I rather hope the fight will come soon. The clamor of the peace faction has convinced me that this country needs a war.' He could hardly restrain his 'disgust' at the 'cowardice' of some members of his own party who ought to have supported 'Americanism'.[29]

England's acceptance of the arbitration effectively certified that nation's submission to the Monroe Doctrine and American dominance of the western hemisphere. But this was not enough for the coterie of full-blooded imperialists waiting in the wings to win power and initiate the 'American century'.

The dawning of this new American empire was buttressed by key intellectual rationales, the fundamental outlines of which are critically necessary to understanding the age and the events which followed.

THE IDEOLOGY OF EXPANSION

Fredrick Jackson Turner's famous thesis on the closing of the American West, *The Significance of the Frontier in American History*, had enormous influence. Noting the deep anxieties caused among ordinary American workers and farmers, as well as elites, about depression, agrarian unrest, labor strikes and large-scale immigration, this historian argued that the previous availability of land had conferred a significant measure of economic power and independence to many average Americans. But industrial expansion, railroads, electronic communications and population explosion had put an end to the traditional frontier as a 'safety valve'. The American west no longer offered escape. The drawbacks of industrial capitalism had now brought the United States to a 'watershed' moment. Either American institutions would have to be radically altered to suit a non-expanding society, or a new frontier would have to be found.

> For nearly three hundred years the dominant fact of American life has been expansion. With the settlement of the Pacific Coast and the occupation of the free lands, this movement has come to a check. That these energies of expansion will no longer operate would be a rash prediction; and the demands for a vigorous foreign policy, for an inter-oceanic canal, for a revival of our power upon the seas, and for the extension of American influence to outlying islands and adjoining countries, are indications that the movement will continue.[30]

Captain (later Admiral) Alfred Thayer Mahan's *The Influence of Sea Power Upon History, 1660–1783* is still studied at the US Naval Academy and was the basis for the buildup of the American navy in the 1890s and its subsequent projection into the distant oceans of the world. Agreeing with Turner, Mahan declared that having lost its landed frontier, the US would have to turn to its 'omnipresent frontier', the sea. Grounding his thesis in the shared belief that outlets for the American surplus production would have to be found, Mahan argued that 'colonies' of two types would have to be acquired. The first would be colonies as markets, the second as strategic bases to protect markets and enforce American policies. These measures, in turn, would require the swift construction of a modern battleship navy. Though he employed the term 'colony', his vision, and that of his political and economic supporters, was really akin to the modern concept of 'neo-colonialism'. Mahan's acolytes, among whom were Theodore Roosevelt, Henry Cabot Lodge and John Hay, did not wish to transfer large American populations to these places, as was the case with classical colonialism, but to exploit them in the manner he prescribed, reaping mainly an economic and strategic advantage over European, and the growing Japanese, rivals.[31]

Brooks Adams was the great grandson of John Adams, and grandson of John Quincy Adams. His studies, including *The Law of Civilization and Decay: An Essay in History* and *America's Economic Supremacy* led him to conclude that a 'law' ruled history and that societies arise on the basis of economic growth but soon fall into 'spiritual' decline as selfishness and greed become the predominant motivations. He believed that the centers of civilization had moved progressively from east to west and that the United States had become the new locus of human civilization and empire, but that it was at the verge of spiraling downward into inevitable decay. Adams argued that it was possible to 'repeal' the law that was at that moment crushing the United States by following policies that he stipulated. These included centralizing the economic and political life of the nation so that key stores of energy could be acquired and safeguarded, gaining control of Asia and the markets therein and elevating a man 'brimming with martial spirit' to lead the American people on this 'crusade'. For Adams, this 'man on horseback' was Theodore Roosevelt, who would shortly fulfill that role as one of the most bellicose of American presidents.[32]

In an age of scientific discovery that accelerated the industrial revolution, new ideas in the biological sciences were bound to influence events too. Charles Darwin's ideas about evolution, particularly those of natural selection, were rapidly adapted by those calling themselves social scientists into the doctrine of 'Social Darwinism'. This pseudo science lifted ideas from the earlier era of scientific racism, grafted them to the new theories from biology and applied them to society in order primarily to justify the already existing social and political hierarchies that obtained within individual states and in the relations between the colonizers and colonized, and to argue that such relationships reflected the natural order of evolution. Thus the primacy of white Europeans over their colonial subjects was held to be the inevitable result of the fundamental laws of biology. In white popular culture 'survival of the fittest' meant that the rule of white Europeans over others was fated by genetics. The primary champions of Social Darwinism held professorships at the elite universities of the great powers. In the United States, William Graham Sumner at Yale popularized these ideas, and though he was himself in the camp of 'anti-imperialists', the ideas were immediately used to justify the continuing conquest of the native tribes and the continued subjugation of African-Americans in the era of post-Civil War reconstruction, and were then employed as validation for the leap on to the stage of empire.[33]

A key aspect of Social Darwinism also became a permanent part of the American creed and dovetailed with earlier religious conceptions of poverty as evidence that the individual was not among the elect. The domestic social hierarchy was also taken for granted. Those who failed to prosper and rise in the social order had no one to blame but themselves. They were by definition unfit for anything other than the place they held. Thus Social Darwinism also served to rationalize and justify the exploitation of the many by the few.

Inevitably, as had been the case since the first colonization of the Americas, religion would also become an element in the rationale for the new American empire. Ironically, religious advocates were also quick to adopt Social Darwinism to their causes. Among the most influential advocates of 'Anglo-Saxon Christianity' or 'Christian imperialism' was Josiah Strong. Born on the frontier, he became secretary of the Home Missionary Society, and was among two or three of the most influential religious figures of the late nineteenth century. His book, *Our Country: Its Possible Future and Its Present Crisis*, sold over 175,000 copies, an enormous figure for that time. Though he decried the ills of industrial capitalism and the 'idolatry' of money and capital, he also claimed that 'The world is to be Christianized and civilized...commerce follows the missionary...A

Christian civilization performs the miracle of the loaves and fishes and feeds its thousands in a desert.' For Strong the salvation of America lay in the fulfillment of the Anglo-Saxon mission to reshape the world. Hearkening all the way back to the Puritans he claimed that 'we are the chosen people' who nevertheless could not remain imprisoned on the North American continent:

> The unoccupied arable lands of the earth are limited, and will soon be taken. The time is coming when the pressure of population on the means of subsistence will be felt here as it is now felt in Europe and Asia. Then will the world enter upon a new stage of its history – the *final competition of races, for which the Anglo-Saxon is being schooled*...Then this race of unequaled energy, with all the majesty of numbers and the might of wealth behind it – the representative, let us hope, of the largest liberty, the purest Christianity, the highest civilization – having developed peculiarly aggressive traits calculated to impress its institutions upon mankind, will spread itself over the earth. If I read not amiss, this powerful race will move down upon Mexico, down upon Central and South America, out upon the islands of the sea, over upon Africa and beyond. And can any one doubt that the results of this competition of races will be the 'survival of the fittest'?[34]

Among the nation's decision-makers these ideas flowed into one another and became virtually a seamless explanation of social reality while also pointing toward action. For Theodore Roosevelt these views were luring the nation toward a glorious future.

Of all the European powers that the US had wished expelled from the western hemisphere, Spain with its continued control of Cuba and Puerto Rico rankled most. A great measure of prejudice derived from Spain's Catholicism which fed longstanding attitudes about that nation's 'backwardness'. Spanish rule in Cuba was especially cruel because of constant uprisings by Cuban *independentistas*, and the misery of the Cuban population was a constant theme in the American press. But these issues were useful camouflage and propaganda for the deeper desire on the part of elites to seize the islands, establish control over their economies, build naval installations and consolidate control of the Caribbean; thence to take up the issue of a canal through the isthmus of Central America.

President McKinley was very much an economic nationalist. As he put it himself his 'greatest ambition was to round out his career by gaining American superiority in world markets'.[35] McKinley is often characterized as a man consumed with anguish over the 'necessity' of war with Spain. One story handed down is that, lost in prayer, McKinley came to believe that God desired the United States to seize the islands controlled by Spain, in order to liberate them into a new dawn of freedom and democracy. Others in the McKinley Administration, however, had ulterior motives. As Roosevelt, then undersecretary of the navy, put matters:

> I should say that I would welcome a foreign war. It is very difficult for me not to wish war with Spain for that would result at once in getting a proper navy...In strict confidence I should welcome almost any war...[36]

Roosevelt's desires were by no means purely strategic. Like most members of the era's political/economic elites he accepted the general consensus that the creation and protection of export markets was central to American policy. The war with Spain would give the US bases in the Caribbean and in the Philippines, the doorstep to the east. Even Roosevelt's political opponents agreed. As Mark Hanna put it:

> We can and will take a large slice of the commerce of Asia. That is what we want. We are bound to share in the commerce of the Far East, and it is better to strike for it while the iron is hot.[37]

More than any other individual Roosevelt ensured that war with Spain would ensue despite efforts to the contrary.

It is often forgotten that Roosevelt was a Harvard-trained historian whose written works were fundamentalist panegyrics to American supremacy and expansionism. Thus he was central to that growing coterie of intellectuals within the circles of power who saw him as their 'man brimming with martial spirit'.[38] Roosevelt, Lodge, Mahan and Adams spent much of their time in each other's company. Together they joined the strategic, economic and ideological justifications for renewed American expansion in the late nineteenth century. Perhaps the clearest expression of this group's objectives, one conflating all of them, was made by their political ally, Senator Albert Beveridge. Speaking of the brutal Philippine

War of 1900–1902 and the desire to annex the islands, he uttered the following on the Senate floor:

> God has not been preparing the English-speaking and Teutonic peoples for a thousand years for nothing but vain and idle self admiration. No, he has made us the master organizers of the world…that we may administer government among savages and senile peoples…The Philippines are ours forever…and just beyond the Philippines lie China's illimitable markets…We will not renounce our part in the mission of our race, trustee under God, of the civilization of the world…China is our natural customer. The Philippines give us a base at the door of the East…It has been charged that our conduct of the war has been cruel. Senators, it has been the reverse. Senators, remember that we are not dealing with Americans or Europeans. We are dealing with Orientals.[39]

This remarkable statement encapsulates the prevailing doctrines then entering American public ideology and which would characterize the American mind-set thereafter to one degree or other, despite its overlay with traditional rhetoric about democracy and liberty. First, there is the renascent idea of 'Manifest Destiny' in which God is presumed to have ordained a special mission for America as the inheritor of Anglo-Saxon civilization to set the agenda for the world. Second, an emphasis on American commercial interests in 'China' (greater East Asia) that would require military and naval bases to protect those interests. Finally, there is Social Darwinism and its embedded racism, insisting on Anglo-American racial superiority and justifying the mass killing of Filipino civilians as racial inferiors standing in the way of 'progress'.

The year 1898 would become one of the most momentous in US history. That year the US would actively seek war with Spain, claiming officially that the goals were to banish the corrupt and brutal Spanish finally from the western hemisphere, put an end to the constant violence that threatened American investments in tobacco and sugar and promote freedom for the colonized peoples in Cuba, Puerto Rico, Guam and the Philippines. That year the United States would also issue the first of its Open Door Notes, articulating the policy that remains the bedrock of American relations with the rest of humanity.

6
War with Spain, then Another and Another

The power that rules the Pacific...rules the world.

Senator Albert Beveridge, 1899

...this war is the first gun in the battle for ownership of the world.

Brooks Adams, 1898

AS A PRETEXT FOR WAR, SPAIN IS DECLARED A THREAT TO AMERICAN SECURITY

In San Francisco's Union Square a towering triumphal column celebrates Admiral George Dewey's victory over the obsolete and dilapidated Spanish fleet at Manila on May 1, 1898. It would not have been out of place in the Rome of the Emperor Trajan. Reading the lengthy inscription on the monument a tourist could easily believe that the courage, daring and valiant sacrifice of American forces had saved the republic from imminent invasion. In fact, it was one of the most one-sided 'victories' in the annals of American warfare, a classic case of the elephant versus the ant. The Spanish fleet was destroyed in a matter of hours and no American died from Spanish gunfire. The remainder of the war was only somewhat more consequential in terms of casualties. Indeed, more Americans died from illness, due primarily to poisoned foodstuffs provided by corrupt suppliers, than from the effects of battle. More Americans would die later, in the subsequent war waged against Filipino insurgents attempting to win the independence that had been promised them by President William McKinley, an assurance that was betrayed.

The focus of American hostility towards Spain was its presence in Cuba. The Spanish fleet in the Philippines posed no conceivable threat to American security, yet the naval squadron commanded by Dewey had been secretly ordered by Assistant Secretary of the Navy Theodore Roosevelt to position itself to attack at Manila the moment that the war he machinated to bring about began. As a major proponent of Mahan's navalism, Roosevelt believed that acquisition of the Philippines was necessary for further American expansion and power as he exclaimed on so many occasions well before war actually broke out.[1] Roosevelt, among many others, was determined to provoke war with Spain and to use the certainty of a one-sided victory to propel the United States into the club of great powers.

Though it is often claimed that President William McKinley opposed war, and was ultimately overcome by political opposition, it was McKinley who approved Roosevelt as assistant secretary (though he was a well-known jingo and expansionist), who approved Roosevelt's secret order to Dewey and who ordered the battleship *Maine* to Havana. The president was merely rhetorically for peace, while his policies carried the nation inexorably toward war. Though he declared in his inaugural address that 'we want no wars of conquest, we must avoid the temptation of territorial aggression', his inaugural parade involved crack troops and cavalry marching with precision in a display of martial discipline not seen in the capital since the Civil War.[2]

Spain's glory days had been over for more than a century and it clung with desperation to the last island remnants of its once vast empire. Spain, whether in the Caribbean or Pacific, posed no threat whatever to American national security. Its sin was that its continuing hold on Cuba and Puerto Rico stifled the US's longstanding desire to control the entire Caribbean, and was a glaring reproach to the Monroe Doctrine. On the far side of the Pacific, Spain's colony of the Philippines, with its strategic harbors, offered a 'doorstep' to the 'China market' that would enable the US to contest for economic supremacy against the established empires, as well as emerging Germany and Japan. In brief, Spain's tottering empire posed an obstacle to the rising American one.

As in many other cases of American conflicts the Spanish–American War was fomented on outright lies and trumped up accusations against the intended enemy, and was foisted by politicians, press and pulpit on a public reeling from the grim consequences of a lengthy depression.

There had always been a bloc in Congress lobbying for annexation of Cuba, Santo Domingo and Puerto Rico. The slavocracy had desired the islands in order to expand slave production in sugar, tobacco and cotton. Later, in the early years after the Civil War when the issue of equal rights for black Americans grew ever more contentious, opponents of outright seizure objected on the basis that incorporating more blacks into the union would only worsen an already undesirable problem. By the late nineteenth century, however, as the multifaceted crisis of overproduction, depression and unemployment deepened, political and economic elites committed American policies to expansion. Thus their spokesmen began to look upon Spain's possessions as vital requirements to the new American empire. Senator Lodge declared:

> ...We should build the Nicaragua canal...and when the Nicaraguan canal is built the island of Cuba... will become a necessity...the great nations are rapidly absorbing for their future expansion and their present defense all the waste places of the earth...as one of the great nations of the world the United States must not fall out of the line of march.

While such men employed the language of armed might with frankness and candor to each other, they understood that war with Spain could only be sold to a public as all American wars are packaged. They claimed that 'security' of the hemisphere was endangered by the brutal Spanish requiring an unpleasant but necessary mission to liberate oppressed Cubans and provide them the gift of democracy. The political elites pitched arguments, duly carried in the press and clearly intended to overcome profound anxieties caused by the depression, that the expulsion of the Spanish from the islands would open them up to American economic development and the construction of the new navy would thus benefit the US economy as a whole. Despite these rationales war fever in the general population never reached a critical temperature until the accidental sinking of the USS *Maine* was deliberately, and falsely, attributed to Spanish villainy.

Cuban exiles living in New York constantly agitated in the press for American intervention to save the populace from the cruelties practiced by the Spanish army. Cuban rebels on the island operated then, as all guerrillas do, against armies of overwhelming superiority, and as American Minutemen (a volunteer militia said to be ready in a minute's notice) did against the British in 1775. They conducted hit and run tactics and then vanished into the vast sea of the population. The Spanish responded, again as all imperial powers do, by attempting to dry up the sea. They drove masses of people off their land and into what amounted to concentration camps. They also practiced summary execution of rebels, and purely innocent civilians alike. These *reconcentrados* quickly became breeding grounds for disease and starvation, so huge numbers died. This situation was appalling enough but the so-called 'yellow journals', newspapers that traded in sensationalism, embellished, exaggerated and invented ever more lurid and graphic accounts of Spanish atrocities as they sought to inflame public opinion on the side of intervention. In an example intended deliberately to whet the prurience of a Victorian-era public, the Spanish were accused of strip-searching a Cuban woman aboard an American vessel. The reality was that the woman was searched by other women, and not stripped. The vessel had been boarded by Spanish forces because it was secretly smuggling arms to Cuban rebels and the woman was carrying documents involving her in the Cuban struggle. Another prevarication issued from Congress, when Senator John Morgan claimed that American citizens in Cuba were 'now literally starving to death for want of provisions and supplies'.[3] War hawks were now declaring that Spain's re-concentration policy was aimed at Americans too.

THE PRESS REVEALS ITS RACISM AND LUST FOR EMPIRE

Then, as now, with rare exceptions, the press largely sided with the opinions and goals of the corporate and political elites determined to find some pretence for war with Spain. Usually the issue was framed in terms of humanitarianism and the idea that Cubans were engaged in a struggle all but identical with that which the Americans had waged against Britain in 1776. Yet, the *Washington Post* put matters in the rawest and most primitive terms: 'We are face to face with a strange destiny,' the paper editorialized. 'The taste of empire is in the mouth of the people even as the taste of blood.'[4]

Had solicitude for the welfare of Cubans, a majority of whom were of African descent, been genuine, then editorial concern for Americans of African descent would also have been in evidence. At that moment, however, the political liberties and civil rights ostensibly guaranteed by the 13th, 14th and 15th amendments to the US Constitution at the close of the Civil War were systemati- cally being stripped, and terrorist organizations like the Ku Klux Klan were visiting virtually indistinguishable atrocities upon black Americans, and the press was silent. When elites communicated with each other they were far more honest than they let on to the public. One predominant reason that President Grover Cleveland had refused to intervene in Cuba in 1895 despite the efforts of men like Roosevelt was his fear that a Cuban victory might result in 'the establishment of a white and a black republic'.[5] In an article in *The Saturday Review* the young Winston Churchill, whose mother was an American, wrote that:

> A grave danger represents itself. Two-fifths of the insurgents in the field are negroes. These men would...in the event of success, demand a predominant share in the government of the country... the result being, after years of fighting, another black republic.

The Spanish themselves, in an effort to ward off American intervention appealed to traditional European racism saying that 'In this revolution, the negro element has the most important part...and the result of the war, if the Island can be declared independent, will be a secession of the black element and a black republic.'[6]

On the other hand many of the emergent socialist organizations and traditional trade unions made their sympathies for Cuban rebels explicit, advocating for American aid to them, but at the same time they decried the run-up to outright American intervention and the hypocrisy of the plutocrats' concern for the welfare of ordinary Cubans. The socialist *Appeal to Reason* editorialized that elites often cooked up pretenses for war 'to distract the attention of workers from their real interests'. The American Longshoremen's Union told its members: 'If there is a war you will provide the corpses and the taxes.' The International Association of Machinists remembered a massacre that occurred during a coal strike in Pennsylvania when the local sheriff and his deputies shot strikers at point blank range killing 19, all shot in the back. Its journal decried '...the carnival of carnage that takes place every day, month and year in the realm of industry...the blood tribute paid by labor to capitalism...Death comes in thousands of instances in mill and mine, claims its victims, and no popular uproar is heard.' Though the president of the American Federation of Labor, Samuel Gompers, served as a cheerleader for war, he acknowledged that even when there was no income tax levied on most wage earners, taxes were increased on daily necessities, so the war led to a reduction by 20 per cent, of the purchasing power of workers' wages.[7]

CUBANS ON VERGE OF WINNING INDEPENDENCE ON THEIR OWN ALARM WASHINGTON

In their efforts to banish Spain from the hemisphere US policy-makers faced a glaring problem. The Cuban liberation movement was winning and it seemed quite likely that Spain would grant independence to the Cubans. Since the real goal of US policy was to take over from the Spanish and then label American rule a victory for 'democracy', this turn of events simply would not do. American war hawks now moved with alacrity.

In January 1898 McKinley warned Spain against outbursts of anti-Americanism and ordered the USS *Maine* to Havana harbor, ostensibly to protect American citizens. In a cryptic message to a diplomat Senator Lodge wrote that 'There may be an explosion any day in Cuba which would settle a great many things. We have got a battleship in the harbor of Havana, and our fleet, which overmatches anything the Spanish have, is masked at the Dry Tortugas.' Then on February 15 the prescribed explosion occurred, killing over 250 sailors and marines, resulting in the worst (at the time) naval disaster in US history. While it is generally agreed today that the USS *Maine* was sunk by the internal buildup of coal dust, war hawks at the time rapidly blamed the sinking on Spanish treachery. Though McKinley appointed a naval board of inquiry few believed it would be impartial, much less blame the navy for the catastrophe no matter where the evidence lay. Indeed, the board ultimately ruled that a 'submarine mine' of unknown provenance had destroyed the *Maine*, implying that the Spanish had some covert role. McKinley immediately demanded that Spain lay down its arms, allow the US to mediate between the Spanish government and rebels and revoke the re-concentration measures. Secretly, however, he ordered the US ambassador to inform the Spanish government that the US would devote its 'friendly offices' to Cuban independence. This was the one stipulation, McKinley knew well, that the Spanish must reject, though Spain met his first demands. Ignoring these concessions McKinley ordered Dewey to commence battle even before he addressed Congress to demand 'the forcible intervention of the United States as a neutral to stop the war, according to the large dictates of humanity...'[8] Unwilling to declare war Congress passed a resolution authorizing armed intervention. The American fleet would unmask itself, crush the hapless Spanish, and Cuba, Puerto Rico, the Philippines and Guam would be freed from Spain's sovereignty only to be ruled from Washington and New York.

In short order, with a crushing victory over Spain, the Caribbean Sea became, as the Romans used to say, *mare nostrum*, 'our sea'. All four island-nations became *de facto* American colonies, exploited as bases for the American navy and for their resources, their people now serving American masters. Cuba's constitution was written in Washington and came with the proviso known as the Platt Amendment that the US could intervene militarily on the island any time American interests were said to be at risk. The Philippines had been promised outright independence but Manila Bay put the US at 'the doorstep to Asia' and no imperial advantage such as this could be surrendered no matter what had been guaranteed. When Filipinos rose in rebellion against the army that had claimed to free them, the US had its first counter-insurgency jungle war which it waged with utmost brutality, killing upwards of 200,000 civilians, the greatest number of civilian deaths up to that time.

With the riches of Asia looming, which of the new empires would dominate?

At this critical stage the US enunciated its plans for the future and on first sight these seemed benign, and equitable as well. The Open Door policy asserted the right of all nations to access the wealth of China on equal terms. But since the US economy could already out-compete its capitalist rivals, and would begin with a clear-cut advantage, American rivals understood that the US could potentially close the doors to them. Japan especially took notice. Washington was asserting the fundamental rules of a new game, applicable to the entire world, even if the US was not yet powerful enough to enforce them. But the message was clear. Henceforth, the markets and resources of the world would remain open to American penetration. From that moment on the US would rely increasingly on its arms to enforce what would come to be its overarching policy.

Meanwhile, the shores of the new American lake had to be pacified. American marines were landed in Mexico, Nicaragua, Honduras, Haiti and the Dominican Republic, and those nations brought to heel. Colombia was refusing to allow a new inter-oceanic canal through its province of Panama to enable the American navy and merchant fleet to pass easily between the Atlantic and Pacific. Roosevelt's solution was simple. He told Washington's handpicked Panamanian rebels to declare independence and then dispatched the navy and marines to prevent Colombia from doing anything about it. Some in Congress objected to this naked land grab but, said Teddy, 'I took the Panama Canal, let Congress debate!' Only a few years later Woodrow Wilson would justify the new war against Mexico with the words 'I will teach them to elect good men.'

The United States had joined the club of empire.

7
World War I: Making the World Safe for American Capital Investment

In American national mythology World War I is represented, in the words of President Woodrow Wilson, as the war waged 'to make the world safe for democracy'. It was also claimed to be the 'war to end all wars'. In the standard version of American entry into World War I Wilson strove heroically to keep the US neutral and out of the war but German violations of American neutrality and international law had shattered the global system. Thus, he claimed, events out of his control finally forced him to intervene because only American power and righteousness could restore international order. The reality was that Britain was the first to breach maritime law. Wilson merely pretended neutrality while his policies were carrying the country inexorably into the war.

American public opinion was overwhelmingly opposed to intervention of any kind, so war hawks in both parties, and especially Wilson, had to walk a political tightrope to avoid endangering their real agenda and careers. The Republican opposition, which had launched the nation on to the stage of global competition and aggression only a generation previously, and was still anxious to extend American power, cast Wilson as weak and unable to promote American 'preparedness' and national security in the face of Germany's alleged threat to the Americas. Yet Wilson was serving their ends, if not as expeditiously as they wished. Meanwhile, Democratic Party bosses anguished at the ferment of real democracy represented by the demands of progressive reformers and used the war to call their 'patriotism' into question. The country's major financiers and industrialists grew fearful that defeat for Britain and France would bankrupt both nations, cause profits to plummet and wreck the corporate economy already in depression. For Wilson the war presented the precious opportunity to advance himself as the savior of international order, and at the same time to hasten the ascendancy of the United States to global preeminence. But to realize his grandiose vision Wilson needed to ensure that he would have to enter the war and he required a place at the table when the peace was crafted.[1] After almost three years of pretended neutrality, and policies calculated to spoil that neutrality, the United States did enter the war, at precisely the moment when the addition of American military power to that of England and France broke Germany's military position. Wilson now had his international stage, though his political opponents would soon demolish his 'internationalism' and therefore his glory.

While the United States would be catapulted nearly to the pinnacle of global power, the war solved little between its European rivals. The so-called 'peace' that followed the war was merely a temporary truce. The world was made safe for more war. Round Two would ensue soon enough. The failure of the peace after World War I would intensify totalitarianism in the shape of Nazism, Stalinism and Japanese militarism, as the traditional and victorious European powers maneuvered desperately to maintain the illusion of their own sovereignty and cling to their empires. Subsequently, as renewed crises unfolded in the 1930s, and as more sophisticated internationalists ascended to power under President Franklin Roosevelt, the moment approached when the US could achieve global dominance and restructure the global system to serve American ends, or lose that opportunity and watch as the planet divided into autonomous and mutually exclusive blocs.

The war erupted in 1914 but its real origins lay deeply buried in Europe's history, as a result of alliances and secret deals between the European powers, each seeking its own advantage and aggrandizement. Britain, France and Russia had entered into an alliance known as the Triple Entente, while Germany, Austria and Turkey had fostered the Triple Alliance, promoting a dangerous arms race that promoted paranoia and mistrust all around. In both cases secret agreements were made such that, in the case of war, territories, resources and markets under the control of the enemy would pass to the opposite side. When immense reserves of oil in Persia (present day Iran) were discovered, with similar fields certain in Mesopotamia (Iraq and Kuwait), where Britain, France, and Germany vied for influence, the great prize of the Middle East was also at stake. All that was needed in such tinder was a mere spark. That flashpoint arrived with the assassination of the Austrian heir to the throne in the Austro-Hungarian province of Bosnia by a Serbian. When Austria declared war on Serbia, Russia then came to the aid of its Slavic cousin. This set in motion Germany's treaty obligation to Austria, then Britain and France entered as allies of Russia. While Germany is usually blamed for the war by its enemies, culpability lay with all of the competing European powers. Their self-aggrandizing, imperial antagonisms all but ensured war.

GERMANY'S POTENTIAL DOMINANCE IN EUROPE A THREAT TO THE OPEN DOOR

While German submarine warfare against American shipping in the Atlantic was the stated cause for American entry into the war, the most important issue for American elites was the growing preeminence of Germany in the European heartland, its challenge to the stability of the global system as it then existed and to their hope to take charge and rationalize that system themselves. Germany and the United States (and Japan) had arrived upon the stage of great power simultaneously in the late nineteenth century, each in their own way testing the strength of the empires already established. German military men, economists and politicians spoke openly of Germany's right to a 'place in the sun' and for a self-contained central European empire that they termed 'Mitteleuropa'.[2] In this scheme Germany would dominate Europe's industrial heartland, as well as the Balkans and near Eastern periphery. Germany would thus become an economic powerhouse on the scale of the United States and be able to compete throughout the world for markets and resources (and deny them to the United States).

This brought the issue of the Open Door in Europe into question for the US. The European core was the largest consumer of American industrial and agricultural commodities. American banks drew great profits from financing this trade, while the US government allowed corporate giants to flout the new anti-trust laws in their overseas operations.[3] Britain too had an enormous but largely protected empire from which American producers had been all but banished. Now Germany might foster a self-contained economic empire over much of the continent and exile or limit American exports. From the perspective of the most far-seeing internationalists in government (most of whom came from elite business and financial backgrounds) the war seemed a ripe and necessary opportunity to alter the balance of power in America's favor.

At the war's outset President Wilson issued an executive decree calling for American neutrality, but this did not have the power of law and could not be enforced. Nor was it intended to be. In truth, neither Wilson nor any of his major advisers (with the exception of William Jennings Bryan, who would soon resign) were remotely neutral. Some members of Congress earnestly wished to avoid

American entanglement and passed laws that certain commodities were contraband, like weapons and ammunition, and could not be sold to either warring side. American bankers and industrialists preferred to deal with both sides, wherever there were profits to be made, and traded contraband items surreptitiously.

THE STANDARD INTERPRETATION OF AMERICAN ENTRY IS SUPERFICIAL

The standard interpretation of America's entry into the war focuses on two precipitating events: the decision by Germany in early 1917 to resume attacking merchant vessels, including the 'neutral' vessels of the US, with the new sea weapon the submarine, and the widespread anger toward Germany when the Zimmerman Note was revealed, a so-called plan to reward Mexico with territories lost in 1848 in exchange for declaring war on the US. The reality lay behind-the-scenes.

Wilson believed that the US had arrived at a moment ripe for the US to assume international supremacy and for him to promote himself as rescuer of global order. Unlike his predecessor Theodore Roosevelt, who openly demanded war with Germany, Wilson proclaimed his desire to keep the US neutral, while actually seeking a way to enter the war under conditions that would enable the US to broker the final outcome. This meant a careful, calculated approach to intervention, and dishonesty with the American electorate.

The age of corporate domination of the American economy had begun in the previous century but the reform movements of Populism and Progressivism had placed unwelcome obstacles before the new oligarchy. Even Republicans like Theodore Roosevelt had to pay lip service to surging anti-monopoly opinion, though the famous Sherman Anti-Trust law ultimately proved all but impotent. While Wilson had won the presidency in 1912 as a self-proclaimed champion of the progressives, his real fiscal and economic policies had benefited corporate oligarchs, though not to the satisfaction of most Republicans or Wall Street. The movement of farmers, labor and small businessmen had pushed the Democratic Party to profess many of their goals and created the illusion that a political realignment had occurred. But bosses in both parties feared this outbreak of popular democracy and the real threat that it could lead to popular sovereignty. The outbreak of war in Europe signaled the prospect of stopping these movements dead in the political waters.

'Free Trade' was the watchword of the British in their heyday of supremacy in the nineteenth century. It had the ring of magnanimity and egalitarianism but the British showed flagrant hypocrisy as their warships and armies battered down all resistance to their imperial scheme throughout Africa and Asia, and their tariff barriers ensured that preference in trade would only apply within the British dominions. In other words free trade meant freedom primarily for Britons, based upon British power.

The Open Door policy was America's answer to British free trade. Liberal internationalism, as Wilsonian policies have been termed,[4] was defined in much the same way. The principle of 'fair' competition was paid lip service when the Open Door notes were first issued a generation earlier. Ostensibly, the US insisted that all western trading nations, and Japan, could partake of the 'great China market'. It soon became apparent that the Open Door policy was intended for the entire world. The advantages the US enjoyed were overwhelming to any competition. Though the Open Door notes had been issued by Republicans, the Democrat Wilson had endorsed them well before becoming president when he declared in a speech that 'the doors of nations which are closed must be battered down'.[5] By 1916, as Europe's war undermined the belligerents' economies, the US had become the creditor nation to the world. As Wilson emphasized, the US was clearly 'the mediating nation of the world in respect of its finances'. For example, the aggregate resources of the national banks of the United States exceeded by $3 billion the aggregate resources of all the other powers and Japan combined. Wilson continued, 'We can determine to a great extent who is to be financed and who is not to be financed...we are in the great drift of humanity which is to determine the politics of every country in the world.'[6] The reality of international competition spoke not to a harmonious concert of the industrialized western nations in which all shared equally in trade and commerce, but to a struggle for advantage between them for access to resources and markets. One nation's gain was usually another's loss.

This was precisely why Germany had taken an aggressive stance in international relations. By the time many German-speaking states had unified as the nation of Germany in 1871, many of the fruits of the world had been taken and locked up by the other powers. Wilson himself said that it was a matter of 'England's having the earth and Germany's wanting it'.[7] He carefully omitted the fact that the corporate and political elites of the United States wanted it too. The already existing members of the imperial club resented Germany as an interloper (which is how they also saw the US and Japan). To gain their own advantages these powers had employed military force, often quite brutally, and to ensure continued benefits they had deployed their armies and navies around the globe, facts not lost on Germany. There was no such thing as friendly competition. The more competitors who entered the contest the more insecure did the others become. Thus a costly arms race and covert alliances with secret agreements promising divisions of spoils was all but inevitable.

Wilson's faith emphasized the moral superiority of capitalism, especially the emerging American corporate variety, and what he claimed was its potential to order the world in a peaceful, cooperative and just manner. He was utterly indifferent to the stark realities that economic competition, the no-holds-barred contest to acquire control over access to vital resources, markets and the key factor of labor (all of which constituted the very essence of capitalism), had led and would inevitably lead to other forms of international strife, especially war. The evidence was right there before him when the European war broke out, but Wilson claimed that European nations, especially Germany, were still practicing 'atavistic and irrational' patterns of behavior. All that was necessary, he asserted, was that Europeans accept American leadership of a global condominium of the industrialized nations. In this way the system that had previously been led by Britain, but which had gone astray as a result of outmoded imperial practices, could be set aright on a rational and orderly basis.

Wilson was also a religious idealist, a 'Christian Capitalist',[8] who firmly believed that the US had been singled out by his deity to 'lead the way along the path to light'.[9] In that sense Wilson, and many of his closest advisers like William Jennings Bryan and Robert Lansing, both of whom served his administration as secretary of state, were missionary ideologues who took seriously Turner's Frontier thesis, which really hearkened back to the doctrine of Manifest Destiny and even to Puritanism's concept of a 'new chosen people'. They, like so many before them, asserted that America had a unique mission. It had been led 'to be the champions of humanity and the rights of men. Without that ideal there would be nothing to distinguish America from her predecessors in the history of nations.'[10] But just as these doctrines had always also rested on a base of racism so did Wilson, a southerner raised during the era of Reconstruction and its betrayal of black Americans, believe that the preservation of 'white civilization, *and its domination over the world*, rested largely on our ability to keep this country intact...'[11] (author's emphasis).

Throughout the first two years of war the Wilson Administration assured the public that the US had no reason to enter the war. Indeed, Wilson's campaign slogan for the election of 1916 was 'He Kept Us Out of War'. Yet, within months of his re-election the president stood before Congress to ask for just such a declaration.

BRITAIN VIOLATES AMERICAN NEUTRALITY BUT WILSON DOES NOTHING

While Britain was certainly aware of its increasing dependence on American finance, London had hardly reached the point where it was ready to accept its loss of leadership, much less to surrender it to the upstart former colony. Yet such a sea change was well under way, brought about in part because of Britain's own imperial over-stretch, and what was proving to be the unparalleled disaster of the war.

The Royal Navy still dominated the seas. The British government had won international acceptance of the Declaration of London in 1909, a codification of the rules of sea warfare asserting legal rights for neutral nations in time of war. Americans were entitled under this international agreement to deliver exports to nations at war and to other neutrals equally without interference from belligerents.[12] As soon as war broke out, however, the British declared they would not abide by the very rules they had crafted, arrogating to themselves the decision as to what was contraband and quickly prevented neutrals from docking at both German and nearby neutral ports. British marines also boarded American ships to search for what they termed forbidden goods, even foodstuffs, effectively halting American trade with the coalition of Germany, Austria and Turkey. Britain now controlled neutral commerce between neutral nations. Indeed, this violation of international maritime law could well have been a cause for war with Britain under other circumstances. Certainly, Britain's violation of American neutrality enraged many Americans who wanted some kind of retribution. Robert Lansing of the State Department wrote to Wilson that the US 'cannot consent' to Britain's unilateral revision of the London Declaration and that its measures were 'wholly unacceptable'. The president refused to send such a message to London, in effect collaborating with Britain's violation of American neutral rights.[13]

Unable to reciprocate in kind against its enemy, the Germans began to employ the new sea weapon, the submarine, sinking British merchant ships carrying American goods in a counter effort to cripple the British economy, as the British blockade was slowly crippling

Germany's. Valuable American cargoes sinking to the bottom of the sea did not sit well with American insurance underwriters and, as British losses mounted, questions arose in both private and public financial circles as to how they would be able to pay for all they were buying on credit, and losing. Meanwhile, American banks were extending significant credit and loans to the British and French to cover the cost of their American imports. American shippers were also violating the president's proclaimed neutrality policy by secretly loading contraband aboard ships bound for Britain. German spies abounded in American ports so they knew of such contraband and violations of American neutrality. If the Germans knew then so did official Washington but virtually nothing was done to stop the trade in contraband.

THOUGH ITS BLOCKADE DAMAGES THE AMERICAN ECONOMY THE HOUSE OF MORGAN INVESTS IN BRITAIN

With German markets all but vanished those at the commanding heights of the American economy saw that they were building up a vested interest in the outcome of the war. The British blockade had diverted American export trade to Britain and France thereby making general American prosperity, and corporate profits, dependent on transactions with the Allies alone.

The United States' economy had been in deep recession just prior to the outbreak of war. The New York Stock Exchange had even shut down for a time. Before the war, steel production fell to 50 per cent of capacity and cotton, chemicals, copper and agriculture suffered similarly. As the New York *Financial Chronicle* put matters, 'deadening paralysis has settled over the country's industries'.[14] When war broke out American financiers and manufacturers would have preferred to trade with both sides. Nevertheless, the business with the Allied side produced the greatest expansion of its trade in American history up to that time. The US became the allied source for food, raw materials and foodstuffs and the allies became the indispensable stimulus to the entire American economy.

The investment banking firm of J.P. Morgan had become the official agent for Britain and France in American capital markets, loaning both governments over $2.3 billion itself and arranging for $3 billion in contracts with American exporters. Most of the most powerful political figures in both parties were also dependent on Morgan money, so Morgan interests were thus a pivotal force behind the scenes pushing the American government towards war.

Some of the greatest industrial giants, US Steel, Bethlehem Steel and Du Pont were *de facto* satellites of Morgan. Should Britain and France lose, the peace terms imposed on them by Germany would undoubtedly render them unable to repay loans and credits, and German victory might mean the closure of many European markets too, or at least restrict them on German terms at odds with the Open Door policy.[15] As Thomas W. Lamont, a Morgan partner bragged, '...our firm was never for a moment neutral. We didn't know how to be.'[16] Wilson's real policies clearly favored the British and his public stance of neutrality was calculated to mollify American public opinion which was overwhelmingly opposed to entering the war, or to favoring either side.

Republican Party bosses were worried because they were taken in by Wilson's pose of neutrality. Republicans were agreed on the necessity of American intervention and the overriding motive of enhancing American power on the international stage, although, like Wilson, they could not be open about this, owing to widespread popular opposition to US entry into the war. While many Republican oligarchs had invested heavily in Allied securities and certainly desired a guarantee of these investments, they also saw war as the necessary device to thwart the 'muckrakers' who had been constantly exposing their corruption and limiting the partnership between industry, finance and politics. War would of necessity marry corporate America to government and result in an immensely profitable alliance that would also silence the restive attempt by progressives to resuscitate popular democracy.[17] In order to mount the stage as the savior of global order, Wilson knew he had to involve the United States directly, yet he also had to be perceived as the valiant stalwart holding the line against being drawn into the war. His own failure to confront British violations of neutrality and his willful refusal to end the illicit traffic in contraband were steadily eroding that pretense. Meanwhile, enormous political and economic pressure was placed on him by financial interests in league with bosses in both parties to enter on the side of the Allies, the majority of Americans be damned.

WILSON'S NEUTRALITY A CHARADE

In 1915 the Germans learned that the British passenger liner, the *Lusitania,* was covertly loading banned ammunition and rifles in its hold. The German government informed Secretary of State William Jennings Bryan and also took out large advertisements in New

York daily newspapers, warning the passengers that the presence of weapons aboard the ship made it a legitimate enemy target. The Germans made their intention to sink the ship very clear, warning passengers not to embark. Bryan attempted to intervene but was rebuked. He had his finger on the source of the problem. 'Money is the worst of all contraband,' he said, 'because it commands everything else.'[18] Later he said that 'Germany has a right to prevent contraband from going to the Allies, and a ship carrying contraband should not rely on passengers to protect her from attack.'[19] He said further that 'A person would have to be very much biased in favor of the Allies to insist that ammunition intended for one of the belligerents should be safeguarded in transit by the lives of American citizens.'[20] Unable to deflect Wilson from his increasingly interventionist policies, Bryan resigned.

Many congressional leaders declared that Americans should not board British ships at all, but Wilson did not support such calls. Despite the ominous and very public warnings from Germany, passengers were told by the shipping line that the Germans would never dare to sink the ship. The *Lusitania* was sunk with the loss of 124 American lives and 1,070 British passengers. Wilson could have intervened against the departure of the *Lusitania*, after all, given well-publicized German warnings, he knew of the ongoing and extensive trade in contraband. Despite his proclaimed neutrality Wilson did nothing to stop this traffic, which intensified the drift toward war increasingly demanded by those sectors of the business classes who had suffered losses as a result of the closure of German trade, and were now also losing money to the submarines.

Wall Street and much of the press immediately raised the slogan 'freedom of the seas', while hawks in Congress stoked the furnace for war. But the American people overwhelmingly voiced the opinion that American citizens should not embark upon belligerent vessels. Germany backed off and promised to cease attacks on merchant vessels leaving the US. The drumbeat for war nevertheless intensified from many quarters. The American ambassador to Britain, Walter Page, declared that if the British navy should be defeated and the Reich gain dominance over the European continent, then Germany's increased power and influence throughout the world would force the US 'out of the sun'. Wilson's closest confidant, Colonel Edward House, claimed that if Germany were to win 'our turn would come next'. Under Roosevelt the US had begun to build the world's strongest navy and this effort continued intensely under Wilson. Though the general in charge of coastal defense stated publicly that the shoreline could easily be made impregnable, the panic-mongering continued.[21]

Senator Robert M. La Follette, a leader of the Progressives, accused Morgan, and his satellites Du Pont and Bethlehem Steel, of consolidating a 'propaganda machine' of 197 newspapers to promote lurid stories of German atrocities and imminent danger to the American continent itself. 'Preparedness' parades were organized in every major city by groups calling themselves patriotic organizations. Under the pretext of promoting stronger military defenses to safeguard the peace, their real aim was to whip up war hysteria. Roosevelt declared frankly that his motive was to 'get my fellow countrymen into the proper mental attitude'. One former assistant secretary of state said that 'there are 50,000 people who understand the necessity of the United States entering the war…but there are 100,000,000 Americans who have not even thought of it. Our task is to see that figures are reversed.'[22] Wilson himself, the self-professed champion of neutrality, was induced to march in a 'patriotic parade' and made numerous speeches justifying war preparations by quoting from the Old Testament.[23]

For a time Germany was extremely careful to mollify American concerns. Yet the British blockade continued with devastating effects on the German economy as Germany's ability to sustain both its troops and citizens at home became ever more difficult. Public opinion in the US took careful note of Wilson's hypocrisy in condemning German submarines attacking merchant ships that were armed, or carrying contraband of war, while all but endorsing Britain's mining of the North Sea, thereby making it impossible for American vessels even to approach Scandinavian ports. Indeed, the first neutral ship to be sunk was sent to the seabed by a British mine. Britain had even declared foodstuffs headed for neutral ports to be contraband.[24]

WILSON POSITIONS HIMSELF TO BE GLOBAL MESSIAH

In 1916 Wilson sent a secret note, known as the House–Grey Memorandum, to London saying that he would propose a conference led by himself to end the war. Should Germany refuse to attend, or to accept American proposals, the US would then enter the war to 'defeat militarism' once and for all. Germany was well aware that American neutrality was a sham. Later, when the conference was actually announced, one of the public proposals endorsed returning the provinces of Alsace and Lorraine to France, having been taken previously by Germany in 1870. This was a proposition that new Secretary of State Robert Lansing knew Germany must reject. Therefore, Wilson would have his pretext to enter the war. In desperate straits domestically because of the blockade and fearing American entry, Germany announced unrestricted submarine warfare against any and all vessels attempting to dock in England and almost immediately sank two American ships. Wilson called for Congress to allow 'armed neutrality' by providing guns for every merchant ship. Congressional opponents argued that if the US could accept Britain's nullification of American shipping then it could suffer Germany's too. But, of course, that would have plummeted the American economy into instant depression. The one-sidedness of American 'neutrality' had made entry on that side inevitable.

The infamous Zimmerman Note was revealed in a manner timed to inflame public opinion. British espionage had intercepted a telegram from Germany's foreign minister to his ambassador in Mexico informing him to endeavor to persuade Mexico to ally with Germany should Germany's efforts to keep the US neutral fail. In exchange for a declaration of war, Germany would aid Mexico to regain the American south-west, lost almost 70 years earlier in the Mexican War. The proposition was never actually delivered to Mexico. Wilson could have dismissed the Zimmerman Note as the desperate nonsense it was; Germany was in no position to give military aid to Mexico in North America. But Wilson was now leading those forces most concerned about the unfavorable long term effects on the American corporate economy and on their control of domestic politics. Hence, 'Teutonic treachery' suddenly became the watchword of the day.

The threat to shipping would undoubtedly diminish the overall value of trans-Atlantic trade, but of equal importance was the growing indebtedness of the Allies which had reached $2.3 billion, an enormous sum in 1917. From his post in London, US Ambassador Page wired the State Department to alert them to the 'international situation which is most alarming to the financial and industrial outlook of the United States'. He continued:

> The inevitable consequence will be that orders by all Allied governments will be reduced to the lowest possible amount and that trans-Atlantic trade will practically come to an end. The result of such a stoppage will be panic in the United States... it is not improbable that the only way of maintaining our preeminent trade position and averting war is by declaring war on Germany.[25]

The House of Morgan, and the great financial and industrial conglomerates tied to it, thus had their reasons for war but the twin outrages of renewed submarine attacks and the Zimmerman Note provided all that the right-wing popular press and hawks needed to stimulate public outrage and an appetite for American intervention. Wilson asked for and received a Congressional declaration of war. Only months previously he had been re-elected on the pretext that he would keep the US out of war and yet events throughout his presidency, many of which he orchestrated, had been impelling him towards exactly the opposite. In fact he admitted as much later in testimony to the Senate Foreign Relations Committee declaring that the US would have become embroiled even 'if Germany had committed no act of injustice against our citizens'.[26]

BOLSHEVIKS TAKE RUSSIA OUT OF THE WAR AND POSE A NEW THREAT TO THE OPEN DOOR

A factor equal in importance to the challenge posed by Germany to the continued evolution of a liberal capitalist world system was the Bolshevik Revolution. Germany was also at war with Tsarist Russia, a corrupt, tottering regime whose prosecution of the war ruined the peasant agricultural economy, viciously exploited the industrial working classes and sacrificed the lives and limbs of millions of soldiers. The result was two distinct revolutions. The first was welcomed by the Wilson Administration as a step for Russia away from feudal autocracy and towards what it claimed would become liberal democratic capitalism. Most importantly, the new Russian government under Alexander Kerensky, continued to wage war on the eastern front against Germany. When this liberal revolution took power Wilson was able to claim that the war had been redefined as one between democracy and autocracy, hence his declaration to Congress that 'the world must be made safe for democracy', re-emphasizing his hopes that the liberal democracies of Britain and France, and now Russia, would prevail and usher in a new age. Since they would be heavily indebted to the US they would have little choice but to accept American leadership.

Yet the ravages of war for Russia cut too deep. Popular discontent and agitation against the war raged, enabling the small but highly organized Bolshevik Party to seize power and to win enough public support to govern, at least in the larger cities and nearby regions. The leaders of the Bolsheviks, especially Vladimir Lenin and Leon Trotsky, thundered against the capitalist nations and blamed the war on imperialist competition, which they said was the inevitable outcome of capitalism. They vowed that their revolution would overturn capitalism throughout the west and replace it with a more humane and just system run by and for ordinary workers and peasants. When the Bolsheviks signed a separate peace treaty with Germany that took Russia out of the war, enabling millions of German troops to be transferred to the western front, thereby jeopardizing the entire Allied position, Wilson's hope for a speedy end to the war and a new global order was profoundly endangered. The US, Allies (and Japanese) were so frightened by the communist revolution that they even redeployed troops into Russia itself in an effort to strangle the Bolshevik hold immediately. This effort failed, but undoubtedly constituted the first blow in what would eventually become the Cold War.

So there was the twin specter of German submarine warfare against American shipping, and the prospects of communist revolution in Europe, both of which constituted profound threats, not only to Wilson's idealistic desires, but to what was coming to be a consensus in the ruling circles of the US for a more rationalized world system open to American economic penetration. American entry to the war would be sold as making the world 'safe for democracy'.

The American public's opposition to the war was overcome by the German attacks and the Zimmerman Note, and an intense propaganda campaign was initiated to frighten the population into believing that a new domestic menace, 'the Reds', now endangered democracy at home, though the American Justice Department had already whittled away at what remained of that. Pumped-up jingoism became the norm and all opponents of entry into the war were accused of disloyalty, cowardice and even treason. Roosevelt derided anti-war activists as 'mollycoddles' and 'weaklings'. Nativism was made to raise its bigoted head yet again. German and Irish immigrants were condemned for their 'anti-Americanism'. 'Hyphenated-Americans', said Roosevelt, could not be trusted. True, 'red-blooded' Americans would not hesitate to rise to their country's defense.

AMERICAN ENTRY TIPS THE BALANCE THOUGH GERMANY IS NOT MILITARILY DEFEATED

American entry, coupled with Germany's increasing inability to equip troops and feed its domestic population as a result of the British blockade, tipped the balance of the war. Facing eventual military defeat, Germany was forced to ask for an armistice. It is vitally important to understand that this was *not a surrender* but a cease-fire in which Germany hoped at least to gain some of its war aims. What happened subsequently would have profound consequences for the future. The terms of the Peace Treaty of Versailles were draconian for Germany. Despite Wilson's attempt to achieve 'peace without victory', the British and French took advantage of the collapse of the German economy, and the simultaneous outbreak of what amounted to civil war within Germany, to impose a crushing burden.

Germany had not been defeated but neither had it won. Many Germans hoped that in the peace negotiations that would follow the armistice they would achieve at least some of their war aims. What actually followed is critically important in understanding why the Nazis would be so successful in the early 1930s. Though at the time of the armistice German troops had been beaten back, they had not technically surrendered and they still occupied French soil. Thus German leaders, soldiers and its people believed that 'honor' could still be salvaged. Yet despite the armistice Britain continued its blockade, thus intensifying Germany's economic collapse, with grievous conditions for civilians. Simultaneously, the success of the Bolsheviks in Russia emboldened German socialists and communists and a civil war broke out between them and rightists who claimed that Germany had been 'stabbed in the back' by traitors like the leftists and Jews. In the Peace Treaty of Versailles Germany was obliged by its weakness to accept humiliating terms. It had to take full culpability for initiating the war, though there was blame aplenty to go around among all the belligerents, and to pay enormous reparations for the costs of the war to Britain and France, thereby leaving Germany unable to care even for its millions of maimed and wounded. It also had to accept the profound humiliation of French troops occupying German soil, especially mortifying because Germany had stopped fighting while it still occupied French territory.

Wilson proposed sweeping peace terms known as the Fourteen Points calling for an end to secret diplomacy, arms reductions, self-determination for ethnic minorities in the fallen empires, trade barriers and trade equality among all nations and the establishment of a League of Nations committed to preventing another general war. Germany looked favorably upon these proposals because they promised the most lenient peace terms. But Wilson failed to prevent the vengeance Britain and France wreaked upon Germany, thus also precluding the reconstruction of Germany along the lines that would have re-integrated it into that concert of western industrial nations he believed was the only hope for future stability. The seeds of the next round of war were being deeply planted. The US Senate would not be a party to the Versailles Treaty, nor would it enter the League of Nations that Wilson himself had proposed as a guarantee to prevent future wars between the industrialized nations. France and Britain insisted on the most punitive sanctions, while Wilson's opponents at home like Roosevelt and Lodge assailed his calls for internationalism as detrimental to American national security. Both ridiculed Wilson's concept of the league as effectively subordinating American national sovereignty to a foreign power. Wilson was a dreamer, they exclaimed, if he thought that the US could lead the world by moral suasion. Roosevelt and Lodge and their allies wanted the United States to lead the world but to do so from a position of strength. Roosevelt even called for continued military conscription though a draft was loathed by the population at large.

WILSON'S PEACE PLAN FAILS BUT THE US BECOMES THE GLOBAL FINANCE CAPITAL

Despite setbacks the US was catapulted by the war to the very forefront of international power. Its economy had grown exponentially as a result of war production and New York had effectively replaced London as the finance capital of the world. The US stood as virtually the only creditor nation. From 1914 to 1918 'a massive international transfer of wealth from the eastern to the western shore of the Atlantic' occurred.[27] As a result of Britain and France's withdrawal from international trade during the war, the US had entered markets previously dominated and restricted by these nations. In Latin America especially, as British weakness forced a withdrawal of London's capital from the region, the US share of markets accelerated dramatically. The US had moved from a marginal player on the international scene and now stood poised at the very threshold of potential supremacy.

A WAR AGAINST DEMOCRACY AT HOME

Yet having waged a war to make the world safe for democracy, Americans quickly saw that very little in the way of such democracy had developed overseas and this would foster within a generation the preconditions for round two of the war. Moreover, democracy was mortally wounded at home. The era of popular democracy, progressivism and reform was at an end. War production had made giants of many of the corporations that still dominate the American economy.

Many groups had been outraged over Wilson's betrayal of neutrality. His government's response was to enact legislation designed to silence the opposition, going so far as to jail many of those who took the First Amendment at face value. A highly unpopular draft law was enacted, only the second in American history. The Espionage Act of 1917 outlawed speech against the war as interference with military recruitment and carried 20-year jail sentences for those convicted. Eugene Debs, head of the Socialist Party and one of the most prominent dissident politicians in the nation who had been one of Wilson's opponents in the election of 1912, was sentenced to ten years in prison for a compelling speech he made against the war. His judge claimed that because there were draft-age youths in his audience his words 'would obstruct the recruiting or enlistment service'.[28] Effectively nullifying the First Amendment to the US Constitution, the Sedition Act of 1918 made any speech against the government's wartime policies illegal. The Supreme Court upheld these acts. In the *Schenk vs. the United States* case of 1919, the imprisonment of a member of the Socialist party who urged draftees to use their First Amendment rights to employ legal methods to overturn the conscription law was upheld. Justice Oliver Wendell Holmes delivered the majority ruling arguing that just as someone in a crowded theater has no protected right to shout 'fire', thereby causing panic, so no citizen could endanger the security of the US in a time of 'clear and present danger'. Later court decisions amended and weakened this ruling but not before severe damage had been done to the Bill of Rights, and the power of the executive had been engrossed far beyond the original Constitutional intent.

Wilson created what amounted to the nation's first ministry of propaganda in the shape of the Committee on Public Information. One of its newspaper advertisements encouraged citizens 'to report the man who spreads pessimistic stories. Report him to the Department of Justice.' One socialist, Kate Richards O'Hare, had the courage to say in a speech that 'women in the United States were no more than brood sows to raise children to get into the army and be made into fertilizer'.[29] For her temerity she was sentenced to five years in the Missouri state penitentiary. Never before had the First Amendment been so suppressed, even leading the attorney general to brag that 'never in its history has this country been so thoroughly policed'. Anti-German propaganda spewed from multiple sources resulting in the victimization of naturalized Americans of German ancestry. Vigilante groups attacked German-American social clubs and spied on citizens accused of disloyalty. The US Post Office even revoked the mailing privileges of anti-war organizations and of journals publishing articles the government deemed disloyal.

Even after the war Wilson's Department of Justice continued its war against pacifists, socialists and trade unionists during the infamous 'Red Scare', which led to the creation of the Federal Bureau of Investigation. After a series of bombings, including the home of the Attorney General, A. Mitchell Palmer, by a fringe anarchist group, a new wave of xenophobia was directed against immigrants. Thousands of immigrants who held unacceptable political views were deported. Numerous American citizens were jailed for belonging to the International Workers of the World (IWW, or wobblies as they were called because they said they would start the globe shaking on its axis). The American Legion, the nation's largest veterans' organization, was established mainly to go on the offensive against 'anti-Americanism'. Though most Americans have been conditioned recently to perceive the FBI as a primary force in the 'war on terror', its initial mandate was to intimidate political opposition to the dominant parties. It was also during this time that the Ku Klux Klan expanded its numbers exponentially, especially in the northern mid-west, virtually without opposition from law enforcement, thereby enabling this terrorist organization to increase its racist attacks upon black Americans whose contributions during the war had raised their demands to achieve the constitutional guarantees denied them since the end of the Civil War.

A WORLD MADE SAFE ONLY FOR MORE WAR

Russia, formerly an ally of Britain and France, had withdrawn from the war in a state of collapse, then to succumb to the Bolshevik Revolution. In response Washington sent troops, with others, to intervene in an ongoing civil war on the side of forces loyal to the discredited monarchy, with hopes of strangling the communist baby in its cradle. This armed intervention in Russia is all but forgotten in the United States, but what would American history books say had Russian troops ever intervened in America's own past? Many historians date the actual onset of the Cold War to this armed incursion into Russia. One thing is certain: the extremely hostile response of the western capitalist nations to the Russian revolution had the effect of tightening the grip of totalitarianism in that country.

Faced with constant aggression from outsiders, the Soviet state quickly descended into a brutal struggle for power internally, a clash won by the most ruthless of the Bolsheviks, Stalin.

The victory of communism in the Soviet Union stimulated communists in Germany to attempt a similar revolution there. Communism, as a modern political force, had originated in Germany in the mid-nineteenth century and German communists had opposed the war. As Germany's economy collapsed after the war, civil war broke out between communists, socialists, and right-wing veterans of the war. Though the leftists were routed, and many murdered, Germany's resulting weakness ensured that it would have to accept the humiliating *diktat* of the Versailles Peace Treaty. It is difficult to convey to readers today the enormity of Germany's collapse at this point. Despite the armistice, Britain maintained the blockade of Germany's ports. In some areas of Germany starvation approached. Unemployment and inflation reached epidemic proportions. War orphans dependent on a bankrupt state existed at subsistence levels. Amputee veterans begged in the streets. As the 1920s progressed vengeful war veterans and disaffected youth would form the nucleus of the Nazi Party and they would seek a terrible retribution from those they blamed for defeat – the 'disloyal' communists, the Jews and the victorious British and French. The seeds of World War II and the Holocaust were sown in the so-called 'peace' after World War I.

Though most of the carnage of World War I had devastated Europe, the war also penetrated the far side of the globe. Japan, newly emerged as a great power after its crushing defeat of Russia in 1904, had allied with Britain and as a result had occupied Germany's possessions in the Far East. Having penetrated northern China, annexed Korea and taken areas of Siberia from Russia, Japan now expanded economically in regions previously dominated by Europeans. But Japan also rankled at the treatment it received as an ally of Britain against Germany. Japan was not allowed to keep possession of some of Germany's Pacific colonies, while Britain and the US attempted to impose second-class military status on the nation in the hope of averting further Japanese expansion into mainland Asia. Both approaches eventually resulted in exactly the opposite of what was intended. As one historian noted, 'From an economic point of view, the First World War was won by the United States and Japan.'[30] Now a major world power, Japan intensified its imperial ambitions and quickly came to be perceived as a threat to the European colonies in Asia, and to the American colony in the Philippines. It would not be long before Japan would deliver the most serious challenge to the very bedrock of American foreign policy, the Open Door.

Also in Asia the hopes of tiny Vietnam for independence from France were dashed when the plank of self-determination for ethnic minorities in the old European empires in Wilson's Fourteen Points was declared to apply only to the small nations of Europe and not to Europe's colonies. Rejected by Wilson at Versailles, the Vietnamese delegation abandoned any faith in liberal internationalism and turned instead to the Soviet Union and its promise to assist Europe's colonies in their efforts to win national independence from their imperial overlords. The nucleus of Vietnam's communist party was engendered by World War I, as were many national independence movements throughout the colonized world, and the political forces of communism and nationalism would eventually confront the United States decades later at the very moment it moved to assume global hegemony.

In south-west Asia the long-tottering Turkish Empire had collapsed as a result of Allied victory, thus leaving much of the Middle East up for grabs. After the war it was revealed that even before the war both France and Britain had conspired secretly to carve up Turkey's holdings between themselves. The region's importance to Europe's victorious empires was magnified tremendously when oil was discovered in Persia (present day Iran) shortly before 1914. Given its vast quantities oil was cheaper than coal. As the competition between Germany and Britain had heated up and as inventions in war-making such as submarines and torpedoes had advanced the arms race, the British came to realize that oil-powered vessels could be made much faster, and thus be strategically better.[31] Geological evidence more than suggested that the entire Middle East lay over a vast reservoir of oil. In short order the entire western way of life, and especially the automobile 'civilization' of the United States, would come to depend utterly on access to this essential fuel. The stage was being set for the wars of the late twentieth and twenty-first centuries.

8
Pearl Harbor: The Spark but not the Cause

Our Bunker Hill of tomorrow will be several thousand miles from Boston.

President Franklin Roosevelt, 1940 (Goodwin, 1994)

If we see that Germany is winning the war we ought to help Russia, and if Russia is winning we ought to help Germany, and in that way let them kill as many as possible.

Senator Harry S. Truman, 1941 (Jones, 2008)

America must not be allowed to pick out the eyes of the British Empire.

John Maynard Keynes (Layne, 2006)

Many thousands of volumes and articles have been written about American involvement in World War II, yet at the popular level it remains the most mythologized of the nation's wars, portrayed, even to this day, in rapturous terms as the 'Good War'. The Japanese attack on Pearl Harbor on 7 December 1941 functions in popular culture as the perfect paradigm for the American way of war. Accordingly, treacherous, devious, cunning enemies are always on the horizon planning their perfidies against the innocent, freedom-loving peoples of the United States and others, against which the American people ride to the rescue. In the conventional fantasy Japan slyly undermined peaceful diplomacy and forced the American people into a war they did not want, whose government had employed every means to avoid. Left with no alternative Americans awakened from their 'isolationism', put their democratic energies and commitment to liberty to work and, with the aid of allies, defeated the monstrous evils of Nazism and Japanese militarism. In the process the US also put an end to the Nazi program of genocide against the Jews and others, saved millions of lives and emerged as the global defender of freedom and human rights.

The real story is hardly so starry-eyed. FDR's assumption of unprecedented wartime powers led directly to what historians today agree has become an 'imperial presidency'. Civil liberties domestically were dealt a severe blow with the incarceration in concentration camps of Japanese-Americans in a wholesale negation of constitutional protections. Though many citizens believe that riding to the rescue of Europe's Jews was at the top of the American agenda, the truth is that the fate of Jews was ignored and even deliberately hidden from the public. Despite popular beliefs that Hitler's death camps were unknown until the last stages of the war, the FDR Administration knew of them as early as 1942. Despite entreaties by American Jewish leaders, FDR refused either to ransom Jews from Nazi occupied Europe, or to bomb the death camps and crematoria in order to thwart Hitler's 'final solution'. There is also the terribly ugly matter of American corporate complicity in the rise of the Nazis before the war and the morally worse employment of Nazi and Japanese war criminals after victory for their use in the new Cold War against the Soviets.

The alliance with the Soviet Union, without which the Nazis could not have been defeated, unraveled immediately at the end of the war when suddenly the public was manipulated to re-envision Stalin as Hitler's replacement. The effort by the US to acquire the world's first atomic weapons led to the atrocities of Hiroshima and Nagasaki, a vicious attack upon a country that American officials knew to be on the verge of surrender. The atomic bombings were perceived as a dire threat and message to the Soviets who immediately stepped up their efforts to acquire nuclear weapons themselves, and both nations squared off in a deadly arms race that threatened the future of human civilization itself. In one of history's inevitable ironies the defeat of Germany and Japan opened the way for communist domination in Eastern Europe and China, paved the way for new full scale wars in Korea and Vietnam and numerous smaller but deadly conflicts all over the globe.

The United States emerged from the war as the most powerful nation in history, yet, despite its claims to have served as the arsenal and vanguard of democracy, it began to ally with and prop up right-wing dictatorships on every continent and to suppress independent nationalist movements of all stripes, including democratic ones.

In the final analysis the US entered World War II by stealth, not to redress the crimes committed by Axis powers such as saving Jews, liberating enslaved peoples and fostering democracy, but to preserve the mainstay of American foreign policy – the Open Door to the resources, markets and labor power of the territories that were threatened with closure. Popular culture maintains that the oft-repeated ideals were the nation's primary motivations but the genuine circumstances surrounding the war's outcome belie such mythology.

DAY OF INFAMY – OR DECEPTION?

We did not go to war because we were attacked at Pearl Harbor. I hold rather that we were attacked at Pearl Harbor because we had gone to war.

Arthur Sulzberger, Publisher, *New York Times*, 1941

President Roosevelt was like the physician who has to tell his patient lies for the patient's own good.

Thomas E. Bailey, American Historian

The standard interpretation of US entry into the war begins with the Japanese attack on Pearl Harbor. Yet the US policy of neutrality from 1935 on was constantly undermined and after 1938 FDR's policies amounted to acts of war. The full embargo of oil and steel to Japan and the covert but very real naval war in the North Atlantic against the Nazis in 1941 were but the strongest examples and were certainly taken by the Axis as evidence of American intent to enter the war.

Japan's attack on the American bases in Hawaii has become the legendary archetype of the 'American way of war' which holds that the US departs from the path of peace only when the misdeeds of others leave no alternative. The historical record clearly indicates that the Roosevelt Administration followed policies that effectively left Japan with two choices, what Yale political scientist Bruce Russet, called Japan's 'Hobson's choice'.[1] The island nation could accept permanent subordinate status to the western powers in the international arena and thereby give up the efforts of a half-century to meet the west on equal economic and military terms, or go to war.

The first option was not really possible since the Japanese military would never have accepted such a humiliation, and Washington policy-makers understood this. Therefore, war was essentially inevitable, and desired. When the president froze Japanese assets in the US, then embargoed vital oil and steel exports, then in August 1941, and again even more harshly just ten days before Pearl Harbor, issued an ultimatum to Japan to withdraw its troops from China and Indochina,[2] Japan's government concluded the US left a choice either to accede, and then suffer the certainty of a military coup, or go to war to protect the gains made over the previous decade. No serious politician could entertain any doubt about the choice Japan would make.

JAPAN'S EMPIRE THREATENS WESTERN COLONIALISM

By the late 1930s, despite diplomatic niceties, most American policies aimed at forcing Japan to cease its expansionist efforts in Asia, not because they were brutal and defied all codes of morality (which they did, but so had British, French, and Dutch imperialism), but because Japanese imperialism interfered with American and European development plans for the region. Secretary of State Henry Stimson condemned the Japanese invasion of Manchuria in 1931 in clarion terms, yet he simultaneously belittled and averted the Philippines' call for independence.[3] As Treasury Secretary Henry Morgenthau put matters: 'It's an international battle between Great Britain, Japan and ourselves and China is the bone in the middle.'[4] There was deep hostility in Washington toward Japan's slogan 'Asia for the Asiatics'.

Racism also played its long-standing traditional role. After the Japanese annexation of Manchuria (renamed Manchukuo), analysts in the US State Department worried that:

> white prestige throughout Asia would be dangerously shaken... and the underlying instinct of the Anglo-Saxons is to preserve the Anglo-Saxon breed against the rising tide of color....the common British and American attitude toward people of other colors is a fundamental factor in the present situation.[5]

Of course the Japanese weren't doing anything that British, French, Dutch and American colonialists had not done themselves. The issue was that Japan was attempting to displace the European and American empires. The wars in Asia and Europe were to be, fundamentally, a contest for dominance among imperial powers. While the FDR Administration much preferred Japanese capitulation to American demands, Japan's elites, especially the military, were definitely unwilling to accept the second-class status on the world stage that such acquiescence implied, and FDR knew this.

The US and Japan had been on a collision course since Commodore Perry's naval squadron first appeared on Japan's horizon in 1853 and employed the threat of force to acquire a commercial treaty with Japanese shoguns, thereby impelling Japan to undergo a profound internal restructuring in order to beat western imperialists at their own game for her own protection. Japan's lightning rise to power in East Asia was startling and frightening to the US, given the primacy of the Open Door policy. By 1940 the US was definitely pushing Japan into a 'Hobson's choice', either to submit to rigid American demands to withdraw its army from East Asia or face the military might of what Admiral Isoruko Yamamoto recognized as a 'sleeping giant'.[6] For reasons well understood in official Washington, Japanese leaders could not capitulate to American demands for fear that their imperial system would be toppled in a military coup.

ADMIRAL RICHARDSON WARNS FDR THAT HIS MEASURES THREATEN WAR

In 1939 Admiral James O. Richardson, Commander of the Pacific Fleet, was ordered by FDR to move the fleet from San Diego to Pearl Harbor. Simultaneously, American air and sea forces were beefed up in the Philippines, within striking distance of Japanese bases in Formosa (present day Taiwan). Both Richardson, and other navy and army officials, immediately warned that these actions would be seen as a grave provocation by the Japanese to which they might respond preemptively. Indeed, Admiral Kanji Kato, a former Japanese chief of staff, declared that American actions were like 'drawing a sword before a neighbor's house'.[7]

In his book, published after the war, Richardson detailed the conversation he had with FDR. To the Admiral's warning about the threat of war FDR responded, 'Sooner or later the Japanese would commit an overt act against the United States and the nation would be willing to enter the war.'[8] Because of his frank opposition to his commander-in-chief's policies Richardson was replaced by Admiral Husband Kimmel. But Richardson was not alone in his assessment of the president. FDR's own Secretary of War, Henry Stimson, confided to his diary that 'the President shows evidence of waiting for the accidental shot of some irresponsible captain on either side to be the occasion of his going to war'.[9]

Japan did indeed take the measures employed against it as an indication that the US fully intended to find a way to thwart its growing empire. When ordered to develop plans to attack the American base at Pearl Harbor Admiral Yamamoto told his superiors that Japan could not hope to win the war sure to ensue, the US was too large and powerful and could draw upon seemingly inexhaustible resources. The best outcome, he said, was a long shot. If Japan could succeed in destroying the American fleet it might be able to buy time to build Pacific defenses strong enough to raise doubts among American military planners as to whether the costs of war might be prohibitive and thus Japan might negotiate a favorable settlement with the US.[10]

As events proved, even Yamamoto underestimated the determination of the American interventionists to wage war despite the potential level of casualties. In the end the US sacrificed nearly 400,000 lives in both theaters of war to achieve its aims. To be sure this was a relatively miniscule number compared to the 30 million lives lost in the Soviet Union, or in Britain, France, Germany and Japan. But in no other war than the American Civil War have so many Americans sacrificed their lives to achieve goals decided in Washington and on Wall Street.

AMERICAN MILITARY OFFICIALS LONG UNDERSTOOD THAT PEARL HARBOR WAS VULNERABLE TO SURPRISE ATTACK

When the US Navy began to draw up War Plan Orange after Japan's stunning defeats of China in 1895 and of Russia in 1905, it was clear to both sides that the newly acquired US base at Pearl Harbor would be the key to the outcome. Therefore, American commanders had always known that Pearl Harbor could be, and probably would be, the target of a surprise attack.[11] The Japanese had initiated war with Russia in 1904 in just that manner. Admiral Richardson had warned that 'The Navy had been expecting and planning for a Japanese surprise attack for many years.'[12] In January 1941 Richardson's superior, Admiral Harold Stark, Chief of Naval Operations, declared: 'If war eventuates with Japan, it is believed easily possible that hostilities would be initiated by a surprise attack upon the Fleet or at the naval base at Pearl Harbor.'[13] Army and navy brass were well aware of these concerns, so at least twice during the 1930s the base's defenses were tested in mock air raids conducted by US warplanes. In each case the base failed the test. Nevertheless, adequate defenses against a real attack were never prepared. After returning from his inspection of facilities at Pearl Harbor in 1939, General 'Hap' Arnold, commander of the Army Air Force, said the defenses were inadequate, 'the target presented was an airman's dream – a concentration difficult to miss'.[14] On the eve of war, Chief of Staff General George Marshall observed that the Japanese would be 'stupid' to attack the base. If the Japanese believed that war was inevitable, and that they had extremely limited options, what other target would have served to inflict the kind of damage to the American fleet that they believed necessary? It is difficult to imagine that the highest military figures did not contemplate this question.

We now know that the code-decrypting system known as 'MAGIC' was providing substantial information on Japanese plans and decisions in the period immediately preceding the attack on Pearl Harbor.[15] In 1941 only the Japanese diplomatic code had been fully broken but that source provided plenty of vital information. Additionally, parts of the Japanese naval code were deciphered. On 15 November 1941, after swearing them to secrecy, General Marshall informed a key group of Washington newsmen that 'We are preparing a defensive war against Japan, whereas the Japs believe we are preparing only to defend the Philippines...We know what they know about us and they don't know we know it.'[16] Of course the preparations hardly involved 'defensive' war. According to Secretary Stimson, FDR told his top advisers on 25 November 'that we were likely to be attacked perhaps as soon as next Monday (December 1) and the question raised was how we should maneuver them into the position of firing the first shot without too much danger to ourselves'.[17]

ELECTRONIC INTERCEPTS AND RADIO DIRECTION FINDERS INDICATE JAPAN'S INTENT

Washington also knew from MAGIC intercepts that Japan would not accept the ultimatum to withdraw its troops from East Asia issued by Secretary Hull on FDR's orders in late November 1941, and that the Japanese had decided that war was their only solution. As a consequence all US Pacific commanders were issued a 'war warning' on 27 November when intelligence informed the US government that the Japanese carrier fleet had left home waters. Admiral Stark issued the following statement to all navy commanders in the Pacific: 'Negotiations with Japan have ceased, and an aggressive move by Japan is expected within the next few days.' General Marshall dispatched similar warnings to army commanders, adding, 'The United States desires that Japan commit the first overt act.'[18]

Until quite recently official accounts of the Pearl Harbor attack, echoed by many historians, insisted that the track of the Japanese fleet could not be followed because it maintained strict radio silence. Recent scholarship lays this claim to rest. The US maintained numerous tracking stations throughout the Pacific employing the best contemporary technology in radio direction finding. According to the testimony of numerous former navy specialists in the craft of radio direction finding (RDFs), critical information about the track of the Japanese fleet was dispatched to Washington. Though the Japanese fleet was instructed to maintain radio silence, at a few key junctures in its Pacific transit it was forced to communicate via radio between warships and refueling vessels and this allowed RDFs to focus in on the location of the radio transmission and show that the fleet was sailing due east.[19] Those responsible for defense might have reasoned that the fleet had orders to attack the US facilities at Midway or Wake Island, but logic dictated that an attack on those bases would serve no military purpose. Any attack on US forces would have brought war but only one target possessed strategic military value. If Admiral Yamamoto's gamble was to be realized, the US fleet would have to be destroyed, and it was based at Pearl Harbor.

In addition, the FBI and Office of Naval Intelligence had known for over a year that spies were operating out of the Japanese Consulate in Honolulu, maintaining careful surveillance on the islands' military facilities. They were transmitting key information back to Tokyo constantly, including detailed information about the berths of the carriers and battleships. Throughout 1941 the chief Japanese spy in Honolulu sent numerous reports to Tokyo providing clear maps and other information about the berths of US warships in Pearl Harbor. All of these transmissions were monitored by the FBI and naval intelligence.

FBI director, J. Edgar Hoover, wanted to arrest the spies but was deterred by Assistant Secretary of State Adolf Berle, who emphasized that such detention would reveal the fact that Japanese codes had been broken. 'No expulsion is possible as any charge leading to ouster would reveal American crytographic success to Japan.'[20] As events proved, the American ability to read all Japanese codes (after 1942) was an enormous and decisive strategic advantage.[21] Critically, in the first six days of December these spies sent messages to Japan that ominously spoke of a forthcoming sneak attack. On 2 December one intercept said: 'All American personnel given shore leave as usual. Pearl Harbor not on alert.' The following day Tokyo issued orders to all diplomats across the world to 'burn your code books', for fear they would fall into American or British hands when war came, not realizing how many of their codes were already broken. On 6 December the spies' final transmission stated, 'All clear...no barrage balloons [air defenses] are up...there is an opportunity for a surprise attack against these places'.[22] That same evening, upon reading a separate and key Japanese transmission, FDR told his closest aide, Harry Hopkins, 'This means war.'

And yet neither Admiral Kimmel nor General Short were allowed the clearances necessary to read such transmissions themselves, even though a decoding station was in Hawaii itself. Instead these messages were sent directly to Washington. Both Kimmel and Short believed that if Japanese communications indicated an attack on Hawaii they would be duly notified. The result was that even though the war warning applied to all Pacific commands, both Hawaiian commanders were led to believe the expected attack would occur against the Philippines. Though the Japanese did attack the American bases in the Philippines, *only* to have attacked these bases would have been militarily illogical and useless.

These are critical issues. Had the real motivation been to *prevent* an attack at Pearl Harbor then any and all measures necessary ought to have been taken. When the US embargoed oil and steel, froze Japanese assets and then on 26 November issued an ultimatum to Japan to withdraw all forces from China and Indochina, it was throwing down the gauntlet. Washington's effort at breaking and reading Japanese codes, and especially the desire to protect the knowledge, is a key indicator of an official belief that war was sooner or later to be inevitable. Preventing Japan from gaining knowledge of American cryptographic success by not arresting its spies known to be reconnoitering for an attack speaks of a long-range plan to wage just such a war, and to maintain the all-important strategic and tactical advantages of such a tool. In the event, the US naval victory at Midway, only six months after Pearl Harbor, was made possible by MAGIC. Later, MAGIC's ability to decipher and read Japanese plans led American air forces to kill Admiral Yamamoto in mid-flight, thus depriving Japan of what was probably her best strategic thinker. Never, in three and a half years of war, did Japan learn of American code-breaking advantages.

To their credit, after receiving the war warning of 27 November, the senior navy and army commanders on Hawaii, Admiral Husband Kimmel and General Walter Short, attempted to protect their respective bases using tactics that made basic sense. Kimmel wanted to deploy his carriers to patrol waters to the west of Hawaii, anticipating correctly that any attack would come from that direction. Washington ordered him not to place his fleet in a position that would 'precipitate Japanese action'. Then he was ordered by Washington instead to use these vessels to dispatch army aircraft to Wake and Midway (a third aircraft carrier was sent to San

Diego for repairs), a move that removed the vital carriers from Pearl Harbor and reinforced strategically useless mid-Pacific bases. Short was led to believe that sabotage in Hawaii was the main problem so he kept his army aircraft in concentrated airstrips with increased ground security. Both of these men knew that US cryptographers had broken some vital Japanese codes and they had been privy to some messages, but both senior officers took official counter-measures from their superiors to mean that Washington did not seriously anticipate an attack at Pearl Harbor. They assumed that if their superiors had intelligence that an attack was forthcoming they would be warned directly. That is one reason the island's defenses were down that fateful morning of 7 December 1941, though given the general war admonition better defensive and precautionary measures should have been in place.

Short's air force was destroyed on the ground as planes sat wingtip to wingtip. Kimmel's carrier airplanes were no longer present. The official explanation for the absence of the carriers has always been that Washington wished to beef up defenses elsewhere in the Pacific, but that line of argument makes no sense given that if Japan had attacked those tiny bases she would still be at war with the US but without having inflicted the crippling blow Yamamoto said was necessary for Japan's strategy to be fulfilled. One thing is certain: two of those three carriers were present at the critical Battle of Midway six months later, where intelligence gathered by MAGIC allowed the US to draw the main fleet of the Japanese into a trap and into a resounding defeat that broke the back of Japan's entire strategic offensive. Washington was in possession of critical information indicating an attack at Pearl Harbor. Was a decision made to ensure the critical carriers would survive? Naval warfare had changed radically. Most naval battles were to be won or lost by sea-launched airpower. After Midway, where the carriers spared in Hawaii played a crucial role, Japan's strategic offensive was halted. Thereafter it waged an entirely defensive war, though it would take three more years and tens of thousands of American lives to dislodge Japanese forces from their Pacific island redoubts.[23]

PHILIPPINES LEFT VULNERABLE BY GENERAL MACARTHUR

Another extremely curious set of facts involves the events in the Philippines only eight hours after Pearl Harbor was attacked. Once Oahu was bombed an all-out alert was transmitted so it was certain that US forces in the Philippines knew that the US was at war. Their commander was General Douglas MacArthur, who had for years been in charge of preparing the islands' defenses. His orders, in the event of war with Japan but never carried out, were to bomb Japanese bases in Formosa, Indochina, and China. When the Japanese attacked the Philippines only eight hours after events at Pearl Harbor his subordinates begged him to get US aircraft off the ground to counterattack. For reasons never explained, MacArthur refused to give these orders and the American air forces in the Philippines were destroyed on the ground where they were concentrated like those at Hawaii, wingtip to wingtip.

These forces may not have been able to stop the Japanese takeover of the Philippines but no attempt was made. Nor did they attempt to carry out the mission assigned – to bomb Japanese airbases in range. As a result of the Japanese victory in the Philippines, tens of thousands of American and Filipino troops were taken prisoner in what has come to be called the Bataan Death March, many of them to die horrible deaths from beatings and starvation, in what became the worst single defeat in American military history in terms of loss of life, worse even than Pearl Harbor. Yet, not only was MacArthur not punished or humiliated, as both Kimmel and Short were, he was promoted and given the Congressional Medal of Honor, though his lieutenants at the scene said that MacArthur had never emerged from his fortified command center into the line of fire, the ostensible requirement for the honor.[24]

The attack by Japan on the American base at Pearl Harbor was hardly the 'surprise' of the popular mythology but nevertheless presented the ripe opportunity, anticipated since the end of the first global war in 1919, for the US to employ its vast economic and military power to assume leadership of the capitalist world system and restore it to 'order'. By entering the war at the right time and then waging it under circumstances of its own choosing, the US was certain to incur the least damage and emerge the most powerful nation ever to exist.

NEITHER GERMANY NOR JAPAN CAPABLE OF ATTACKING THE CONTINENTAL US

One of the most deeply entrenched myths of World War II is that Germany had the potential to assume such overlordship itself, or that both Germany and Japan together could have 'taken over the world'. A widely viewed 1942 propaganda film using trick footage by noted Hollywood director Frank Capra actually depicted Japanese troops marching down Constitution Avenue in Washington.[25] This was simply nonsense but very much in the mold of employing fear and panic to mobilize public opinion. But both Axis allies could have, and certainly intended to, foster separate autarkic blocs in Europe – the US's primary market – and in Asia, the long foreseen new American economic frontier. Thus, instead of a unitary global system there would have been competing centers of power in a multi-polar world. Internationalists around Roosevelt believed that for capitalism to survive in America the world would have to be re-ordered to the requirements of American capitalism. Otherwise, they reasoned, in calamitous economic straits, facing severe domestic unrest and tariff obstructions imposed by other nations, the US faced a potential future of economic and political restructuring out of its control, possibilities that themselves presaged even more disorder. Interventionist American elites seized the moment.

The American public majority was clearly against intervention either in Europe or Asia before the 'day of infamy' at Pearl Harbor. Interventionists employed rhetoric much like their forebears before World War I, focusing their arguments on the real and terrible atrocities being committed by the Nazis and Japanese military, employing traditional platitudes about freedom of the seas, free trade and free markets and emphasizing that only the United States could be an 'arsenal of democracy' to avert a future of global totali-tarianism. President Franklin Roosevelt had been ardently in the interventionist camp in 1917 but as the most pragmatic of politicians he could not ignore the deep and widespread public opposition to intervening in the European or Asian wars. A clear majority of Americans believed that the US had achieved nothing except a long casualty list from its participation in World War I. Many believed that Wall Street and industrialists had spurred US entry in order to profit themselves. As a result of a congressional investigation into arms profiteering during the first war, the term 'merchants of death' entered the American lexicon to describe the most prominent American corporations. Roosevelt's policies, many of them secret, show him to be clearly moving toward direct intervention in Europe but he could not show his hand overtly. He constantly reassured the public that 'Your boys are not going to be sent into any foreign wars', even as his policies moved inexorably toward that outcome. Behind the scenes he clearly manipulated policies and events in such a way as to move the nation ever closer to a cause for war.

This assertion is vigorously denied by FDR's defenders but the record, as it has progressively come to light, clearly indicates a desire for war on the part of the nation's elites, of whom Roosevelt was a hereditary member and whose interests he had served throughout his career. The only germane question is 'Why did the American establishment desire war when there was clearly no military threat to the national security of the United States?'

The essential answer is that those driving intervention believed that to preserve 'free market' capitalism at home, to restore something like full employment, to prevent the collapse of existing political institutions, the US would have to re-establish domestic prosperity and to do that it would be necessary to reorder the global system. The goals of both the Nazis' 'New Order' in Europe, and the Japanese 'Greater East Asia Co-Prosperity Sphere' were in flat out contradiction to the maintenance of American foreign trade and investment on American terms and to the American system domestically. If the long range goal of American foreign policy was to be realized, an Open Door to the markets, resources and labor requisite for corporate profits, the entire global system would have to be 'Americanized'.[26] To do so effectively the US would enter the war at just the right time, on American stipulations and timetable, and rely primarily on its vast technological array of war machines, thus to enjoy every advantage. The US would suffer no continental devastation like much of Europe and Asia and would be able to draw on virtually inexhaustible resources, including oil, since in 1941 the US was the world's largest exporter of the vital substance without which war machines did not move. Nor would the US incur politically unacceptable casualty levels. While the US did suffer somewhat more than 400,000 dead, this was, in relative terms, slight compared to all the other combatants, but especially the USSR which suffered approximately 25–30 million dead. By the time the war ended in August 1945 the American public had shown no signs of withdrawing support for it. The US would not have entered the war had its leaders not been convinced that victory was the likely outcome. At war's end, with its economy stronger than ever and both its enemies and allies broken or severely weakened, the US, interventionists believed, would possess the golden moment to restructure the global economy and polity under terms most favorable to the requirements and desires of American financial and industrial interests.

In 1940, at FDR's urging, the democratically-controlled Congress implemented a fiercely unpopular conscription law, initiated a program of massive ship and aircraft construction, and amended neutrality laws to allow FDR's Lend-Lease program to Britain. The

Neutrality Act was passed in 1935 to ensure that the US would not follow the path of 1914–1917. By 1939, after Hitler launched his blitzkrieg across western Europe, Roosevelt's actions moving the US away from neutrality, indeed toward undeclared warfare, gave Germany much the same grounds for open war as had the American pretense at neutrality in 1917.

Unable to pay for American arms Britain's Prime Minister Churchill begged for credit, claiming falsely that if the British Isles fell the Royal Navy would fall into Hitler's hands, thus giving him mastery of the Atlantic.[27] FDR asserted that the US must become 'the great arsenal of democracy'. When the Lend-Lease bill passed Churchill called it 'the most unsordid act in history', but privately resented the terms that in the post-war would shackle and subordinate the British economy to Wall Street, which indeed occurred.[28]

Lend-Lease bound the US and Britain in a *de facto* alliance and in August 1941, meeting secretly with Churchill aboard a navy vessel in the North Atlantic, Roosevelt gave his blessing to an armed alliance. With the connivance of Democratic leaders, President Franklin Roosevelt secretly ordered the US Navy to conduct a covert war in the North Atlantic against Nazi Germany, ordering the navy to 'shoot on sight' any German U-boats encountered and assist British warships to attack German submarines, thereby hoping to initiate a pretext that would spark public outrage and overcome popular opposition to entering the European war. Though Nazi submarines did fire on American vessels, killing American servicemen, it was soon revealed that Americans had fired first, and this produced a backlash from those against entering the war.[29]

This dishonest stratagem failed. Only the all-out Japanese attack on Hawaii overturned American opposition to entering the war. This 'Day of Infamy' was certainly a surprise to the public, but the attack was anticipated in official Washington.

Neither Germany nor Japan had the remotest chance to invade, much less occupy, the US. Former Secretary of the Navy, Josephus Daniels said that 'I can hardly believe that it would be possible for any man to be crazy enough to invade this hemisphere.'[30] The chief of naval operations, Admiral William H. Standley, stated that while Japan's navy could enforce discrimination against American commerce in Asia it had no power to threaten the continental mainland.[31] In May 1941 Adolf Berle, Assistant Secretary of State, declared that 'a naval invasion of the Western Hemisphere is out of the question'. *Fortune* magazine acknowledged that 'the danger of a direct attack upon our shores is relatively remote'.[32] The military correspondent at the *New York Times*, Hanson Baldwin, wrote that 'No air power now assembled is capable of bringing that kind of power against the United States.'[33] No long range bomber existed that could reach the US across either the Pacific or Atlantic, nor were there intercontinental ballistic missiles, and neither Germany nor Japan could get within range of the American mainland with anything remotely resembling an invasion force. As events showed, the US had the naval resources to embark more than 1.5 million of its own and allied troops to invade Europe and another million into the Pacific, but neither Hitler nor Tojo could do the same to the US.

IF THE AXIS POSED NO MILITARY THREAT TO THE US WHAT WAS THE REAL WORRY?

FDR continually emphasized that a Germany in control of the territory and resources of the European heartland, and friendly trading partners or allies in Latin America, might at some future point become a military threat. The claim, however, that the British navy would surrender its ships was false; measures had already been taken to remove it to the western hemisphere should England itself have fallen to Nazi invasion. More importantly, in the air war over the English Channel known as the Battle of Britain, occurring in the summer of 1940, more than a full year before Pearl Harbor, the Royal Air Force roundly defeated Nazi air power, thereby ensuring that no invasion of Britain could take place. Having failed to cross about 30 nautical miles to invade a small island, Hitler was hardly capable of transiting 3,000 miles of the Atlantic to fall upon New York or Washington.

The US continental territory was under no direct military menace from either of the two most powerful Axis nations. Nor did Germany or Japan desire war with the US. Nazi leaders certainly remembered that Germany had been forced to seek the adverse armistice in World War I because of late American entry into that war and that had led to German collapse. Japanese officials were also well aware of the strength of the US; that was the primary reason they resorted to what they hoped would be a 'surprise' attack when they came to believe that their only choice was capitulation to American demands or war. The ensuing conflict resulted from a definition of national security primarily in economic terms and military strategies designed to support that economic agenda, as defined by elites, including

FDR, a Columbia-trained Wall Street attorney and former Under-secretary of the Navy.

Japan's rise to modernity had been meteoric, spurred by fear of conquest and subordination by the western powers, including the US. Japan's humiliation of Russia in 1904–1905 alarmed American naval officials, leading them to draw up 'War Plan Orange' and bolster military bases in Hawaii and the Philippines, measures Japan saw as threatening. Both sides drew up contingency plans for a Pacific war and both recognized the US base at Pearl Harbor, where the American fleet would be concentrated, as the key to victory.[34] After World War I the US and Britain insulted Japan by minimizing her role as an ally against Germany, limiting her island acquisitions in the Pacific and later levering her into accepting an inferior naval force. Between 1931 and 1932, Japan invaded and annexed Manchuria, withdrew from the League of Nations and for the remainder of the decade progressively took over coastal China; in 1941 Japan invaded French Indochina. Japan's announced goal was a 'Monroe Doctrine for Asia',[35] but this came directly into conflict with the overriding goal of American foreign policy, the Open Door.

The Open Door originally envisioned untrammeled access to the resources, labor and markets of East Asia. But Japan closed the door to American trade in Manchuria in 1932. While many Americans decried Japanese atrocities in China, neither these nor the breakup of China's territory were at the heart of policy concerns. In 1935 President Franklin Roosevelt declared that 'the American people would not go to war to preserve the integrity of China' but the US would go to war to maintain 'their right to trade with China'.[36] As long as the US could continue to buy and sell in China, it would matter little who controlled its government, or whether its territory was divided. But negating American access was exactly what Japan wished to do. In November 1938 Tokyo announced its intention to create the Greater East Asia Co-Prosperity Sphere and would close all markets throughout this empire, thereby attempting to dominate the same sort of economic sphere that the US had previously enjoyed throughout the western hemisphere, but which was now threatened by German barter policies.

If these setbacks for US policy were not bad enough, worse things were transpiring: Europe as a whole encompassed the bulk of American trade and Germany was the largest trading partner. As one response to the Great Depression, newly elected President Franklin Roosevelt hoped to open new markets for American exports and renew older ones. He considered 'foreign markets as vitally important to the successful function of corporate capitalism'. But Germany was negatively affected by the global depression too and because of its unfavorable trade balance with the US and severe weakness of its currency, the *Reichmark*, adopted bilateral barter agreements with its other trading partners. By the mid-1930s such agreements with Brazil, Chile, Argentina and Uruguay had, said Secretary of State Cordell Hull, 'artificially displaced our Latin American trade'.[37] Between 1933 and 1935 American exports to Germany were cut by half as Germany increasingly bought from her barter partners. In 1935 Germany terminated its most favored nation agreement with the US, signaling in effect that it no longer needed the US as a trading partner. In 1940, continental markets were effectively closed when Hitler overran central and western Europe and declared 'America for the Americans. Europe for the Europeans.'

Hitler's potential control over much of the European continent was deeply troubling to American financiers and industrialists, though Wall Street itself had provided the plans and capital for Germany's renascence after World War I in the vain hope that Germany would become, in effect, a junior partner with the US in an integrated economy, and some even contributed to Hitler's election campaign in 1932.[38] Until 1933 German financial and industrial elites had been closely allied with their counterparts in America, but Hitler's move toward continental autarky spelled trouble for the US's emergence from the Great Depression. Germany's plan to dominate the European heartland, however, did not pose any military threat to the US even in the relative long-term. This was demonstrated by early 1941 during the Battle of Britain when Hitler signally failed to cross the English Channel and then made the fatal error of invading the Soviet Union. As the *Magazine of Wall Street* put it: 'If Hitler cannot cross the English Channel, how can he cross the Atlantic Ocean?'[39] This view was shared by most military general officers and analysts.

By war's end Germany had made great progress in developing its V-2 rocket, the prototype for what would eventually evolve into intercontinental ballistic missiles, and these had wreaked havoc on London and other cities in Britain. But by no means were these capable of reaching across the ocean. As events showed that was not achieved until 1957 by the Soviets, and even then they were 'contained' by superior American forces.

By the late 1930s the nation's financial elite reasoned that the real threat to American security lay elsewhere. Analysts at the Council on Foreign Relations stressed that 'Only by preserving a trade area that is even wider than the Western hemisphere and Britain can our economy face the future with assurance.'[40] Treasury Secretary Morganthau said: 'The Germans will form a sort of overall trading corporation and what are we to do about our cotton and wheat?' Assistant Secretary of State Breckinridge Long stated that, 'If Germany wins this war and subordinates Europe every commercial order will be routed to Berlin and filled under its orders somewhere in Europe rather than in the United States.'[41] Jesse Jones, Commerce Secretary, said 'maybe we can't be invaded but we might become isolated economically'.[42] *Barron's* magazine, a major business publication, editorialized that 'The great danger facing the Western Hemisphere in the event of a totalitarian victory is not the threat of armed invasion, but rather the threat of trade aggression.'[43] A major lord of Wall Street, Bernard Baruch, spoke for many:

> Germany does not have to conquer us in a military sense. By enslaving her own labor and that of the conquered countries, she can place in the markets of the world products at a price with which we could not compete. This will destroy our standards of living and shake to its depths our moral and physical fiber, already strained to the breaking point.[44]

Baruch's point was affirmed by Thomas Lamont of the First National City Bank of New York: 'Under a Hitler victory we should find ourselves in the midst of a country-wide depression so deep and so profound as to make the worst of the last ten years look like a happy and bountiful time.'[45]

Hitler's economic policies had been successful in thwarting FDR's hopes for expansion of foreign markets as one solution to the Great Depression. Not until the war production ordered by FDR in 1940 took hold did the depression begin to wane.

There were some influential analysts within FDR's circle of advisers, like Vice President Henry Wallace, who argued that the US could reorganize its economy toward hemispheric self-sufficiency with Canada and the British imperial markets, but that would have entailed draconian state control over economic life. That potentiality was anathema to the majority of policy-makers.

FDR's repeated circumventions of the Neutrality Act clearly favored the British and French again, as in World War I, although certainly not for altruistic reasons, as the reduction of both nations virtually to vassal states after World War II showed. In 1941 Roosevelt secretly ordered the American Navy to begin actively assisting British warships in their military actions against German submarines. At first such activities were confined to helping British ships locate the submarines, but before long the US vessels were firing on the German ships too. The result was that a number of US Navy vessels engaged in open combat in the North Atlantic with Germany, leading to the loss of American life. Roosevelt called the subs the 'rattlesnakes of the sea' and attempted to persuade the public that Germany had attacked first. However, he was undermined by his own Navy Secretary who told the *New York Times* the truth; it was US vessels that had violated American neutrality. Harold Stark, Chief of Naval Operations, wrote to a subordinate: 'The Navy is already in the war in the Atlantic, but the country doesn't seem to realize it...Whether the country knows it or not, we are at war.'[46]

FDR's actions were clearly intended to provoke Germany into retaliation that would then cause a hostile reaction in American public opinion. While they failed to impel the US into war, the forays persuaded Hitler that FDR fully intended to find a way into war with Germany, just as the US had in World War I. Fear of this was central to the Axis pact that tied Germany, Japan and Italy in a defensive alliance designed to deter a US strike against any one of these nations. Undoubtedly, when Hitler declared war against the US only a few days after the attack by the Japanese on Pearl Harbor, erroneously believing that the Japanese had inflicted a mortal blow to the American fleet, he hoped to force the US to fight on two fronts, and thus be weakened considerably in a war he and the Japanese believed the US was intent to enter.

While the president's and the nation's financiers' attention was fixed upon Europe's markets as the largest source of America's export dollars, the great China market remained of vital concern. Insisting that Japan's Greater East Asian Co-Prosperity Sphere must be stopped, Morgenthau declared:

> As our own population becomes more intense, as we feel increasingly the need of foreign markets, our definite concern for open markets will be more widely felt among our people and our desire for and insistence upon free opportunity to trade with and among the peoples of the Far East will be intensified. For in that region lie the great potential markets of the future.[47]

As Japan continued its East Asian conquests *Fortune* magazine editorialized:

> With a population of more than 400 million China is the biggest single potential market in the world. A strong China, able and willing to protect the principle of the open market in the Far East, would be worth billions of dollars to the United States.[48]

Most such arguments were made behind the closed, mahogany paneled doors of Washington or Wall Street. The most public argument for American intervention throughout the troubled world, and perhaps the most influential in business circles, was made in the nation's most popular magazine by Henry R. Luce. In his essay, *The American Century,* the very title of which revealed the telling agenda of the financial elites his media outlets represented, Luce declared:

> And the cure [for failure in US foreign policy] is this: to accept wholeheartedly our duty and our opportunity as the most powerful and vital nation in the world and in consequence to exert upon the world the full impact of our influence, *for such purposes as we see fit and by such means as we see fit...*
> Our thinking of world trade today is on ridiculously small terms. For example, we think of Asia as being worth only a few hundred millions a year to us. Actually, in the decades to come Asia will be worth to us exactly zero – or else it will be worth to us four, five, ten billions of dollars a year. And the latter are the terms we must think in, or else confess a pitiful impotence.[49] [author's emphasis]

AMERICA AND THE HOLOCAUST: NOT RESCUING JEWS

In the annals of wartime suffering and atrocity, the Holocaust and atomic bombings are at the top of the list. As a university teacher I often encounter young students who have been taught that one of the primary motivations for the US to enter the war was to 'save the Jews', and also that the atomic bombings were necessary to save American lives in a land invasion planned for November. These beliefs do not stand up to evidence.

American Jewish leaders struggled constantly to keep the plight of their European kin in the public eye. Throughout the Great Depression American public opinion was steadfastly opposed to allowing immigration for Nazi refugees, ostensibly on the rationale that they would compete with Americans for scarce jobs and resources. Yet British refugees, especially children, were admitted, while Jewish children were denied. In the particularly tragic and well-known case of the SS *St. Louis* over 1,200 Jewish refugees actually arrived just off American shores begging Congress to amend immigration restrictions and quotas, only to be turned back to Germany. Subsequent research showed that most were later interned in death camps, including 300 children.

The American population at that time was primarily of European origin and many European immigrants brought their traditional anti-Semitism with them to American shores, so the sort of prejudice abounding in Europe existed in the US as well. State Department posts were filled with people from the traditionally Anglo-Saxon upper classes of American society who believed fervently in the racial superiority of 'Nordic' peoples, and many high officials deliberately blocked proposals to aid or rescue Jews in Nazi occupied territories, and even in neutral countries. Yet as early as 1941 the outlines of what the Nazis termed the 'final solution' were clear and mass killings had already begun in occupied Poland and Ukraine. In that year at least 700,000 Jews had been killed, mainly by firing squad. Private individuals confirmed the establishment of the death camps and this information was relayed to the US State Department.

Roosevelt himself, who showed no personal anti-Jewish bias and had appointed Jews to high positions in the US government, temporized so as not to inflame anti-Semitic sentiment that would injure his political fortunes. Jewish leaders proposed ransoming Jews but this was denied with the argument that giving money to Hitler would only help his cause. Proposals were made to bomb the death camps arguing that since inmates would die anyway, the destruction of the railways leading to camps, the gas chambers and crematoria would probably result in more lives saved than lost. Military officials claimed that aircraft could not be spared from military objectives but many bombing campaigns were conducted against oil refineries and other targets near the more infamous camps, especially Auschwitz, yet no bombs were spared to destroy gas chambers. It was not until the last year of the war that the US government made any moves that resulted in saving Jews. These came in Hungary and Rumania primarily where Nazi defeats made this possible. Of the millions who were facing death, only perhaps 200,000 Jews were ultimately rescued by these late measures though earlier actions probably would have saved many more. Even after the war, when American popular magazines reported on the atrocities with grim photos, public opinion remained opposed to increasing the level of Jewish immigration. Of the number actually rescued only about 21,000 were admitted to the US. Jewish leaders in Congress who proposed measures allowing many more thousands to enter the US were vilified and condemned for taking the part of 'refujews'. Some of their congressional opponents spewed anti-Semitic vitriol on the very floor of the House of Representatives and appealed to public opinion to ensure that Jewish refugees would not enter the US or Britain in great numbers. One reason that the state of Israel was supported and created by allied post-war leaders was precisely to prevent large numbers from settling in the United States and England.[50]

THE ATOMIC BOMBINGS: TO SAVE LIVES OR TO INTIMIDATE COMMUNISTS?

A central tenet of American ideology surrounding World War II is that the atomic bombings were necessary to save American lives and end the war without having to invade the Japanese home islands. President Harry Truman, who replaced FDR upon his death on 12 April 1945, declared as much when he informed the American people of the bombing of Hiroshima on 6 August 1945. In subsequent years he and former Secretary of War Henry Stimson were to state that upwards of 1 million American lives had been saved by the use of the A-bombs. At Hiroshima and Nagasaki at least 170,000 civilians died almost instantly and another 200,000, perhaps many more, died later from their injuries or radiation poisoning.

No documentary evidence ever existed to support the claims made about American lives. Most American soldiers and citizens were being led to believe that, like the invasion of Europe, landings in Japan itself would be likely. While there were contingency plans to invade Japan in November 1945, and possibly again in March 1946, the Japanese were on the verge of surrender in the summer of 1945. The most pessimistic estimates of American casualties potentially resulting from these possible invasions were lower than the claims made by Truman and others, though no one at the time desired any casualties. But in the last phase of the war MAGIC intercepts confirmed Japanese recognition of defeat and a desire to capitulate under what they considered to be honorable terms. The main obstacle to conceding defeat was the American insistence on 'unconditional surrender'. To the Japanese this meant that the emperor would be subject to trial and execution as a war criminal. Many American military leaders believed that dropping the demand for unconditional surrender and guaranteeing the safety and continued reign of the emperor would have ended the war as early as June 1945. They also believed that insistence upon the demand prolonged the war, thereby leading to continuing American casualties. Joseph Grew, the former ambassador to Japan, who was then Acting Secretary of State, said candidly that 'our intention to try the emperor as a war criminal will insure prolongation of the war and cost a large number of human lives'. Admiral William Leahy, the highest ranking officer and Truman's Chief of Staff, said that 'insistence on unconditional surrender would result only in making the Japanese desperate and thereby increase our casualty lists'. Even Army Chief of Staff, General George Marshall, warned against crystallizing the 'phraseology "unconditional surrender"'.

A careful analysis of attitudes prevalent at the time among all officials close to the decision to use the bombs shows clearly that the military general staff did not believe the bombs were necessary for victory, and many of the most prominent, including General Dwight Eisenhower and Leahy, thought that their employment was 'barbaric' and 'inhuman'. Even General Curtis Lemay, the leader of the infamous attack on Tokyo in March 1945 in which napalm firebombs destroyed half the city and killed at least 100,000 people, stated that 'the atomic bomb had nothing to do with the end of the war'. It was civilian decision-makers, more concerned about how the bomb could be used as a tool to shape the post-war order, who insisted on its use.[51]

A special committee comprising a few key politicians, military men and scientists ultimately made the decision to use the bombs on 'workers dwellings', taking the position that there were 'no civilians' any longer in Japan since they claimed the entire country was mobilized against invasion. While the US had made contingency plans for an invasion of Japan these were not to be put in motion until November 1945, if necessary. MAGIC intercepts already indicated the Japanese High Command was willing to surrender if accommodation for the emperor could be assured. MAGIC also informed Washington that the Japanese military had deduced where an American army might land and had concentrated great masses of troops at that location.[52] Here was an opportunity for the US to deliver a fatal blow to the troops guarding the homeland, but no record exists of any discussion to drop the atomic bombs on soldiers. If the bomb was developed as a *military weapon* why was it deliberately used on civilians? Japan's industrial capacity was already destroyed. Its forces on the Asian mainland were being routed by Soviet troops and its navy and air force no longer existed. While the headquarters of Japan's Second Army was outside Hiroshima it was not targeted; rather, 'ground zero' was the heart of both Nagasaki and Hiroshima. This was the first American demonstration of 'shock and awe'. The message such an action implied to the entire world was momentous, and chilling. It was not lost on Stalin.

DOWNFALL

As war neared its culmination, the issue of Soviet entry into the war against Japan began to obsess key American leaders. Roosevelt had always believed he could deal with Stalin, but Truman was reflexively anti-communist and surrounded himself with men equally, or more, hostile to the Soviet Union. The war against Nazi Germany had ended in early May and the US and USSR were already at loggerheads over the division of Europe's territory, and the possibility that the same dispute would occur in East Asia loomed menacingly. Having fought Japan over China and East Asia in general, American leaders had reluctantly accepted the necessity of Soviet entry, since that would surely end Japanese resistance and save American lives. But they were not happy at having to share the spoils with the communists. Circumstances changed fundamentally when scientists in the US Manhattan Project informed Truman and his advisers that they had successfully tested the world's first atomic bomb. Now the US had the most devastating weapon in history to end the war on its terms, without the necessity of Soviet participation; now they could induce Japan to surrender before the Red Army could overrun much of northern China and Korea, and, most especially, before it could occupy parts of Japan itself.[53]

When word came of the atomic success in the desert of New Mexico Truman was in Potsdam, a suburb of Berlin in occupied Germany, at his first major conference with Stalin and Churchill over the spoils of war. Until the A-bomb was tested the US was under duress to accept Soviet territorial and other demands in the Far East as compensation for their entry into war against Japan. A number of Truman's advisers were also willing to alter terms for Japanese surrender. However, the A-bomb, in the words of Stimson, gave the US its 'ace in the hole', and his soon to be Secretary of State, James Byrnes, insisted that Soviet goals in Asia had to be thwarted. It was Byrnes more than any other figure who insisted that the Potsdam Declaration re-affirm the demand for

Japan's unconditional surrender and that Japan be scorched with atomic fire, in great part as a message to Stalin. 'Demonstration of the bomb might impress Russia with America's military might,' said Byrnes, later adding: 'I believed the atomic bomb would be successful and would force the Japanese to accept surrender on our terms. I feared what would happen when the Red Army entered Manchuria.' When the Potsdam Declaration was issued to the Japanese they realized there was to be no guarantee of the emperor's safety and continued rule, so they continued their refusal to surrender; that repudiation became the official rationale for using the new and cataclysmic weapons.

New research has shown that the Soviets very much desired to occupy the northern part of Japan as vengeance for the humiliating defeat of 1905, when Japan annexed Russian territories in the Far East, and to benefit their strategic position.[54] Thus the devastation caused at Hiroshima and Nagasaki induced the Japanese to accept surrender before Soviet troops could land in Japan itself, thereby avoiding the division of that conquered nation that would bedevil American objectives to foster a new order in Asia in the aftermath of World War II, just as the Soviet occupation of eastern Europe and the division of Germany was doing at the time on that continent. In what would be a supreme irony, though, the very defeat of Japan would unleash domestic Chinese communists. Having maneuvered ruthlessly to be in the dominant position to shape the post-war fate of China and East Asia, the US would soon lose the prize, not to Japan or the Soviets, but to the Chinese themselves.

Stalin declared to his associates that he was shocked by the A-bombings. Since his spies knew that the atomic program existed this seems curious. As one of history's most brutal dictators one would think that little could shock such a man. He seems to have been taken aback by the use of the weapons upon an already defeated nation, on helpless civilians, because now he knew that the US could be as ruthless as himself. The atomic bombings at Hiroshima and Nagasaki certainly ended World War II but they were also the first round in the coming Cold War. One nation now possessed a weapon of awesome and terrifying power. No other nation at odds with the US could fail to be intimidated by the lessons of Hiroshima and Nagasaki. The Soviets, for their part, immediately stepped up all efforts to acquire nuclear weapons themselves and the most dangerous arms race in history was on.

Thus did history's most destructive war end. Though nearly 400,000 Americans died in World War II, this was by far the lowest casualty rate of any of the major combatants, owing in part to the enormous advantages of US firepower. A striking example of this is the ratio of American combat deaths at Iwo Jima, 7,500 to 20,000 Japanese deaths. It took the US approximately 25,000 rounds of ammunition, ranging from M-1 bullets to 18 inch naval shells, to kill one Japanese soldier in that month-long battle.

In the Atlantic theater of war the US also fought in such a way as to ensure that its allies did most of the fighting – and dying. To be sure, the US entered the war late and was not yet fully mobilized. Meanwhile, Britain and especially the USSR were on their own as far as combat troops were concerned, but were supplied with vital trucks, weapons and food by Lend-Lease. Stalin urgently desired that a European front be opened by British and American troops as soon as possible in order to alleviate the terrible burdens faced by the Red Army. More than two-thirds of Hitler's legions were concentrated against the Soviet Union. These troops constituted the best of Nazi forces and the USSR soundly defeated them without the direct combat assistance of American or British forces. However, the costs and consequences to the USSR were profound.

The primary motivation for US entry into the war was the prospect that Germany would dominate most of the European continent and the oil reserves of the Middle East, and establish a closed continental system that would exclude most American trade and investment, a 'nightmare' scenario from the perspective of American policy-makers. Yet there was no possibility of defeating Hitler without an alliance with the Soviet Union. The American public forgets, or the reality has been consistently downplayed, that the Soviets did most of the dying to defeat Hitler. Had the Red Army not bogged down the bulk of Nazi legions in a desperate struggle in eastern Europe there would have been absolutely no prospect of the invasion of western Europe on the beaches of Normandy by American and allied forces. This meant that at war's end the Soviets, with a system as antithetical to US objectives as the Nazi program had been, would be in control of much territory that Washington wanted liberated from Hitler's grasp. This eventuality was not lost on planners, and much evidence abounds that official Washington was preparing for a showdown with its erstwhile ally well before the war ended.

Unlike its allies and enemies alike, the US suffered no devastation to its territory; it also endured by far the fewest casualties. Indeed, at the war's end the US was far richer than when it entered, and because all others had spent themselves, it emerged as the dominant power on the planet. As such the United States moved rapidly to reconstruct a global order to serve the long-standing goal of an Open Door to world resources and markets. There were at least two major obstacles to this goal: the opposition of the communists to the expansion of western capitalism and the worldwide revolt of the defeated imperial colonies.

There were domestic issues too. Even before the end of the war the specter of mass unemployment and a return to depression surfaced again. In 1944, Charles Wilson, former chief of General Electric, and FDR's wartime production tsar, had worried about the 16 million GIs who would shortly return to civilian life. Would breadlines await them?[55] War production was manifestly the only real factor that had ended the Great Depression, but even so it had absorbed only a fraction of those formerly unemployed. The bulk of young would-be workers were now wearing military uniforms. Wilson's answer was a 'permanent war economy'. But for that a permanent enemy, or enemies, would be required.

9
Cold War: The Clash of Ideology or of Empires?

The United States was master of the earth. No England, no France, no Germany, no Japan left to dispute the Republic's will. Only the mysterious Soviet would survive to act as the balance in the scale of power.

Gore Vidal (Vidal, 1967)

There was never from about two weeks from the time I took charge of this project any illusion on my part but that Russia was our enemy and the project was conducted on that basis.

General Leslie Groves, Military Director
of the Manhattan Project, 1942 (Takaki, 1995)

I do not know any responsible official, military or civilian, in this government or any government, who believes that the Soviet government now plans conquest by open military aggression.

John Foster Dulles, 1949 (Lens and Zinn, 2003)

The geo-political struggle and arms race with the communist world known as the Cold War lasted so long (1945–1991), and was so fraught with existential danger to human civilization, that it is often forgotten that the United States and Soviet Union had been allies against Nazi Germany. Strategic as it was, this alliance came down to a marriage of expediency and no sooner had the dust of war settled than the erstwhile confederates confronted each other over the spoils of victory. At war's end the United States' continental territory was untouched and it was by far the wealthiest and most powerful nation on the planet. The Soviet Union, where most of the European fighting had been waged, lay in ashes with 30 million dead. With their common enemies prostrate the two allies briefly had a positive opportunity for a workable compromise over military and economic issues, and thus for a more peaceful future. But peace was not on the horizon.

After World War II anti-communism became the watchword of the day and the Soviets were demonized as entirely responsible for the state of tension that unfolded dangerously and rapidly. Neither side was blameless but the record clearly shows more effort at conciliation by Moscow than by Washington. Unwilling to acknowledge that the USSR had vital national security issues far more pressing than their own, advocates of a permanent military establishment and Open Door to the markets of Eastern Europe and East Asia claimed that the Soviets and Chinese communists had replaced the Nazis and imperial Japan as the threats to the 'American way of life'. On the basis of this claim they militarized American society as never before.

SOVIETS INDISPENSABLE TO DEFEAT OF HITLER

In American popular culture World War II is seen as the victory of democracy over German and Japanese dictatorship, with the United States playing the major role. There is no denying that US military firepower defeated Japan. Indeed, American war planners never doubted victory. Americans have been loath, however, to accept less than full credit for triumph over Nazi Germany. Certainly the American Lend-Lease program provided Britain and the Soviet Union with essential resources, including arms, and the massive American and British aerial bombardment of German factories and cities contributed to Hitler's downfall. But in terms of ground combat and the defeat of millions of Nazi soldiers, the Soviet Red Army was indisputably central. The war on Europe's eastern front was far more destructive and savage than in the west and millions of soldiers and civilians on both sides perished. More than two-thirds of Hitler's legions were concentrated against the Soviets, where they fought a desperate and losing effort to keep the Red Army at bay. When German forces entered the Soviet Union in 1941 they committed atrocities on a colossal scale, including the roundup and systematic extermination of Jews, and the slaughter of many other civilians. By late 1942 the Red Army had reversed Germany's fortunes and in 1945 broke through into Germany itself and began to exact an equally atrocious retribution.

It is often forgotten too, deliberately omitted, that when the Nazis conquered states in Eastern Europe they subordinated their governments and forged military alliances with these puppet regimes. The result was that Hungarian, Ukrainian, Romanian and other pro-Nazi troops invaded Soviet Russia alongside the Germans as partners.[1] Thus, it was on the basis that these regimes had waged war against the USSR that the Red Army occupied these nations after driving the Nazis back, eventually to total defeat. In the popular view of the Cold War the Reds had occupied innocent nations illegitimately. But this was false. The Soviets planted themselves in Eastern Europe for much the same reasons that the US occupied western Germany and Japan. It is true that the smaller nations of Eastern Europe were pawns but they were bargaining chips to each side. Both the US and USSR wished Europe to be reconstructed along lines beneficial to their specific economic and security interests. In terms of physical security there was no doubt as to which nation had the greater claim.

The overwhelming majority of Hitler's best troops had been locked in mortal struggle in the east. Thus, when the US finally, in the last year of war, was able to employ its vast wealth of resources to mount the largest seaborne invasion force in history on the north coast of France, the effort succeeded *only* because the least combat experienced, and fewest, Nazi troops were there as defenders. Had the bulk of Nazi forces not been bogged down in the east they would have been on the beaches of France and therefore no such invasion would have been possible or even considered. Hitler could not have been defeated without the Soviet Union. Had he confined his effort to conquering western Europe, and not attacked Russia, Europe's recent history would be very different.

But Hitler had made it supremely clear in his book *Mein Kampf* that he intended to extend German living space (*lebensraum*) to the Slavic east and to defeat communism once and for all. The Soviet system had only recently been stabilized after years of civil war and internal communist party purges. Stalin feared that the western European powers might align with Germany against him. Since he desired no such war he allied with Hitler in 1939.[2] This certainly disappointed the British and US bitterly. But then in the late summer of 1941 Hitler reneged on his pact with Stalin and invaded the USSR. By this time the US was in an undeclared but *de facto* naval war with Germany. Once full-scale declared war broke out both Britain and the United States understood that Germany could only be defeated with the aid of the Soviets. This posed a very difficult problem for American goals. If US foreign policy was predicated upon keeping an Open Door for American business enterprise to the resources, markets and labor power of Europe as a whole, and the Nazis had to be prevented from shutting that portal, this goal could only be achieved with the indispensable assistance of a regime that had been equally hostile to the Open Door. At best only half the loaf of American war aims could be attained. Instead of Nazi autarky throughout Eastern Europe, Soviet communism would prevail, and whatever access American corporations might have to trade with this bloc it would not be on American terms. The cold hard fact was that at war's end the Russians occupied the same territory in Europe's east as had the Nazis.

Some historians argue that if Roosevelt had been younger, healthier and able to continue he might have arranged a favorable agreement with Stalin that may have benefited both nations. FDR would have faced the same bitter opposition his successor faced domestically, but he was far more sophisticated a politician and more of a realist. The Soviets had been portrayed in heroic terms by the US press and Hollywood while the war was still ongoing, but rightists and anti-communists in the US were already in 1945 accusing Roosevelt of having lost Eastern Europe to the hated Reds, though the region was hardly America's to lose. In any case Roosevelt died just as the war was ending and his place was taken by an inexperienced and easily manipulated, at least initially, Harry S. Truman, who was himself reflexively anti-communist and who almost immediately went on the political and ideological offensive against yesterday's ally.

YESTERDAY'S ESSENTIAL ALLY BECOMES THE NEW THREAT

In short order the Truman Administration claimed that the Soviets had now replaced the Nazis as the principal threat to global order and American national security. Less than three months after Japan's surrender on 2 September 1945 the enormously influential *Life* magazine startled readers with graphic depictions of a Soviet atomic missile attack on US cities, though pointedly the Soviets did not possess an atomic bomb, and intercontinental missiles did not exist and would not until 1957. Most mainstream publications followed suit with lurid depictions of what the USSR could do to the US despite its obvious weakness.[3] In 1946 Admiral Chester Nimitz, hero of the Pacific War, declared, with no evidence whatever, that the Soviets were preparing to bomb England and launch submarine attacks against American coastal cities. Presidential adviser Clark Clifford claimed that the communist threat was so dire 'the United States must be prepared to wage atomic and biological warfare'. Only five months after Germany surrendered, the Joint Chiefs of Staff issued a report calling for the atomic bombing of 20 cities in the USSR if that country 'developed *either a means of defense against our attack* or the capacity for an eventual attack on the

United States' (author's emphasis).[4] All this despite the fact that the USSR had suffered the greatest devastation to its national territory of any belligerent, worse even than atomically desolated Japan, and had not the remotest possibility of attacking the United States. Nor did it have such an intention.

All of European Russia's major cities and towns, estimated at 70,000, were destroyed, its roads, and railways in ruins, its crops and livestock dead or stolen, and at least 30 million of its soldiers and civilians dead.[5] Though the Red Army was immense, and its soldiers extremely combat-hardened, it showed no signs of moving beyond the territories it had wrested from the Nazis with so much blood. Nor did it seek territorial gains in Western Europe or the Middle East. Yet, the American public was indoctrinated to believe that Soviet-led communism was on the march with the goal of 'world conquest'. This was exactly the propaganda employed about the Nazis and Japanese. The permanent enemy required for a permanent war economy had miraculously materialized.

This is not to say that Soviet communism lived up to its promises, or functioned as a benevolent regime. Far from it. Russia was behaving as Russia had always behaved, and still does. The Soviet victory enabled Stalin to re-extend control over some of what had been lost to Russia's empire during World War I and what he deemed Tsarist Russia's natural sphere. After two devastating invasions in a quarter century the Soviet general staff obsessed over territorial security. The Yalta Accords of 1945 reflected the realities of war. The Soviet Union occupied Eastern Europe as a result of its overwhelming victory over the Nazis. This enormous contribution to Nazi defeat had to be acknowledged. Yalta also accorded the Soviets territories in East Asia, some of which had been forcibly taken from Russia in its war against Japan from 1904 to 1905. At the time the accords were signed then Secretary of War Henry Stimson acknowledged they recognized the USSR's vital concerns for future security. The same Joint Chiefs who planned a sneak attack on Russia out of fear of its military power also said in another position paper that the USSR's policy was defensive in nature and aimed merely 'to establish a Soviet Monroe Doctrine for the area under her shadow, primarily and urgently for security'.[6]

Harry S. Truman's ascension to the presidency on the sudden death of FDR in April 1945 brought about a sea change in the US's relationship with the USSR. Demonizing the Soviets quickly became the major component in the campaign to assert the newfound power in Washington's hand to reconstruct and stabilize the global capitalist economy. Therefore, in order to gain the American people's support for the remilitarization and increased tax burden that would be required to confront this new enemy, the highly positive image of the Soviets, that portrayed Stalin and the Red Army as noble allies in the war against Nazism induced by American propaganda, had to be reversed.[7]

A hopeful moment thus became a tragic one, yet entirely in keeping with the historical thrust of American development and foreign policy. Though the seeds of both world wars were planted in Europe, the United States entered each war knowing that European empires and Japan would be sapped, if not finished. By 1940 a golden opening had arisen for Washington to intervene at the right moment, replace many of its rivals at the pinnacle of global power and reconfigure global order. Already, the phrase 'American century' had entered the public vocabulary. [8]

The major problem for American post-war plans was that though the war had been a pyrrhic victory for Russia it still remained a great power, and it straddled much of Europe. Despite no navy to speak of and no airforce capable of crossing oceans, the USSR had the largest, most-bloodied, most combat experienced army on earth. Even so, though it occupied much of the very region the US had wanted freed from German rule and opened to American enterprise, it was not capable, nor did it desire, to occupy Western Europe.

Uppermost on Stalin's agenda was rebuilding an utterly devastated nation and ensuring that invasion by a foreign enemy could never take place again. For Soviet foreign policy maintaining control of Eastern Europe as a bulwark, a *cordon sanitaire*, was indispensable against any possibility of incursion from the west. To safeguard their country and their rule the Soviets were more than willing to modify the doctrines of communism and world revolution. Had the Truman Administration been willing to acknowledge this profound need on the part of the Soviets, and to work with them to guarantee their security, the possibilities for subsequent cooperation might have proved invaluable to both nations. Genuinely frightened by American actions in the early Cold War, the Russians were goaded to intensify their own acquisition of atomic weapons, thereby ensuring that Soviet nuclear capabilities would become the very threat, and the *only such threat*, to American national security that propaganda had claimed but which had been utterly false.

THE ATOMIC ARMS RACE BEGINS

As American officials intended, the atomic bombings of Japan had badly unnerved the Soviets. Not only were the bombings of Hiroshima and Nagasaki a warning that such destruction of entire cities and ruthlessness against helpless civilians could be visited elsewhere, they also ended the war abruptly on American terms, forestalling the USSR's occupation of Japan, to prevent any repeat of the problems inherent in the division of Germany.

The future of atomic weapons thus lay at the center of both nations' critical concerns. Many Americans, including leading atomic scientists who developed the bomb, had worried that nuclear weapons in the hands of one nation would induce a terrifying arms race that portended the annihilation of human civilization. The Soviets demanded the destruction of all existing atomic weapons, though no American official believed they would stop their own program. To mollify domestic critics the Truman Administration created a special committee headed by Undersecretary of State Dean Acheson to advance policies for the control of such armaments and atomic energy in general. When this committee's proposals were deemed too soft, its recommendations were replaced by those of Wall Street baron, Barnard Baruch. The Baruch Plan demanded that the Soviets submit to international inspections and end their A-bomb project, then in its early stage, while the US would retain its atomic monopoly until satisfied no Soviet bomb would or could be created. Then, and only then, would the US reconsider whether or not to destroy its own bomb making capacity. It was, as a Baruch staff member conceded, 'obviously unacceptable to the Soviets with the full realization that they would reject it'. Acheson himself said that the Baruch Plan would guarantee the failure of international control of atomic weapons. The Joint Chiefs of Staff wanted only one dimension of control. 'The bomb should continue to be at the heart of America's arsenal, and a system of controls should be established that would prevent the Russians from developing the weapon.' The nuclear arms race, that on more than one occasion would bring the world to the brink of Armageddon, was on.[9]

SOVIETS WITHDRAW VOLUNTARILY FROM CONQUERED AREAS

In early 1946 Winston Churchill made his famous 'Iron Curtain' speech[10] in the US in which he described what he termed the barbaric and illegitimate domination of Eastern Europe by the Soviets. Yet, as prime minister of Britain, and Stalin's ally, he had cut a bargain with the Soviet dictator himself by which Britain would recognize Soviet mastery throughout the east in return for Stalin's acknowledgement of Britain's continued sphere in Greece, a bargain Stalin kept.[11] The real record of Soviet actions in the immediate post-war period demonstrated a genuine willingness to cooperate with the US and its allies. Austria had been annexed by Germany in 1938 and so had also participated in the invasion of Russia. At war's end the Red Army occupied about half of Austria, but it withdrew voluntarily.

Similarly, the Soviets also withdrew from Chinese territory occupied when the Red Army declared war on Japan in 1945. In 1947 Truman issued his famous doctrine in which he accused the Soviets of intervening in Greece's civil war waged between native Greek communists and right-wing forces that had collaborated with the Nazis, and who were then also supported by Britain. But Stalin kept his word with Churchill and gave no aid to the Greek communists. That is precisely why the Greek communists were defeated.

In yet another case both Russia and Britain had occupied Iran and Azerbaijan in order to keep immense reserves of oil from Nazi control. FDR had assured Stalin that Russia could obtain Iranian oil for necessary reconstruction after the war. The Soviets agreed to withdraw from this area by March 1946, yet when the time came they balked; not because they wished to annex the region but to ensure that Iran would provide the USSR with oil. Initially the Truman Administration urged the Iranians to broker such an oil deal. At this early stage of American power Washington was already maneuvering to create a buffer between the USSR and Middle East oil, and saw Iran as pivotal. So, after the Soviets did withdraw Washington then told Iran to renege.[12]

In every one of these cases there was nothing the US could have done had Russia actually behaved in the manner that American propaganda falsely claimed, that is, with military force. In the case of Iran even the A-bomb was useless since that would have irradiated and poisoned (or utterly destroyed) the oil wells. In fact, Russian actions belied the claim that they were relentlessly pursuing new conquests. No evidence existed of any Soviet desire to move militarily beyond the areas occupied during the rout of Nazi Germany. By contrast Britain still had its imperial armies all over the globe, as did the US. None of this meant that Stalin did not remain a despot; it meant that the Soviet leadership was committed to traditional Russian concerns of security and dominance within its perceived sphere. To ensure their security the Soviets were willing to meet the US approximately half way. George F. Kennan of the State Department, the very architect of early American Cold War policy of containing the Soviet Union, nevertheless continued to insist that 'Our first aim with respect to Russia in time of peace, is to encourage and promote by means short of war the retraction of undue Russian power and influence from the present satellite area.'[13]

Ever the pragmatist and realist FDR recognized that the Red Army occupied Eastern Europe and could not be removed, as did Churchill despite his later hypocrisy. The Yalta Accords, agreed in April 1945 between the US, Britain, and the Soviet Union, not only reflected the real balance of power at that moment but affirmed the division of Europe with the possibility for future mutual cooperation. Months later the balance of power would be altered exponentially by the American atomic bomb.

It is true that communist parties in western Europe, especially in France and Italy, were very strong and posed an electoral threat to the American reconstruction agenda in that region. Communists could rise to power there democratically and showed every sign of doing so, owing to widespread dissatisfaction with the regimes that had brought on war and ruin. Certainly the Soviets aided such political movements where they could, but given the Soviets' own domestic problems such assistance was minimal. The American response was to deploy the newly established Central Intelligence Agency to areas where electoral communist success was possible, there to employ every dirty trick available, including bribery, vote fraud and even assassination to prevent communist electoral success. In both France and Italy the CIA worked openly with organized crime to intimidate organized labor. Ironically the US accused the Soviets of thuggery. If democracy was to result in communist gains then democracy had to be jettisoned.

CAPITALISM AND COMMUNISM VIE FOR THE LOYALTIES OF THE DEFEATED EMPIRES' COLONIES

Americans are educated to take capitalism for granted as the only rational system of social and economic organization. The brutal and unjust history of capitalist evolution is all but censored. Indeed, while communist nations were usually derided as slave states, the fact that slavery and mass slaughter were indispensable ingredients of western capitalism's rise is not open for discussion, at least in mainstream forums. When communist ideas began to percolate into society they were both an intellectual and grass roots response to the very real depredations of capitalism. Clearly communist revolutions did not succeed in creating better societies for their peoples, as capitalist societies claim they do for their own. Soviet rule over its satellites was brutal. But if the capitalist west prospers greatly today it does so directly as an historical legacy of the early western conquest of much of the planet, a system erected as a result of genocide and slavery at its dawn and maintained by exploitation and war to this day. The west can and does vilify communist crimes. But there is nothing in the communist record not matched by capitalist societies in terms of crimes against humanity.

The record of capitalist larceny is why so many colonized peoples struggling for independence from western rule turned toward communist and socialist ideas in the aftermath of World War II; that, and their recognition that the European empires, and Japan, were finished. As victims they had first hand knowledge of the west's hypocrisy and its claims to bring the benefits of civilization to the benighted denizens of what was condescendingly termed the 'Third World'. They knew that western nations prospered at their expense. Nationalists like Vietnam's Ho Chi Minh had seen first hand the beneficence of French capitalism and rejected it utterly. European colonizers employed noble rhetoric and platitudes but the realities involved plantations and mines that paid slave wages, a system backed by prisons and executions. The widely held notion that the US opposed communism on moral grounds is flatly contradicted by the fact that throughout the Cold War Washington overthrew numerous democracies because they pursued policies in opposition to US intentions. In many cases the US filled these power vacuums with bloody dictatorships every bit as brutish and criminal as anything to be found in the communist world.

American policy-makers understood that World War II's costs in lives and treasure would all but bankrupt western Europe's empires, and Japan's, presenting the long anticipated opening to replace them, if not in exactly the same way. So the stage was set for a titanic struggle between the United States and the Soviet Union for the loyalties of the former colonial subjects. This contest was one of the cardinal issues at the heart of American opposition to the communist world. Throughout the post-war era, until the collapse of the USSR in 1991, both sides would square off and on too many occasions would stand at the brink of nuclear war. At other times the two opponents would arm proxies such as Koreans, Vietnamese, Cubans, Angolans, Ethiopians and many others, and foster wars all over the planet such that by the end of the twentieth century almost as many people would die of these so-called 'savage wars of peace' as had been killed in World War II.[14]

The Great Depression in the US had been caused by speculation in stock markets, overproduction, restriction of credit, collapsed purchasing power and the closure of overseas markets by countries reverting to economic nationalism, or autarky, especially Britain, Germany and Japan. The USSR already impeded capitalist penetration on American terms. In the decade before the war most foreign markets were off limits to American goods and services. Then the war itself shattered the global capitalist system. This was the deepest crisis facing American political, social and economic stability at home immediately in the post-war years. There was absolutely no military threat from any corner of the globe. American analysts reasoned that the only way to avert a return to stagnation was through the economic and financial reconstruction of the global order on American terms.

THE THREAT OF A CLOSED WORLD REMAINS: GERMANY BECOMES A NEW AXIS

American policy faced a four-pronged threat: the ruined nations of Europe and Asia – both friends and former foes – might revert to the economic nationalism and closure of markets that had characterized the pre-war years. Post-war impoverishment in these regions might lead populations toward communism and socialism. Ruined nations could not buy American goods owing to their lack of dollars. Finally, the colonies were in revolt, threatening to align themselves with Moscow, or in nationalist directions otherwise independent of US desires.[15]

So the key to post-war American strategy focused fundamentally on economic security, not the claimed military threat from communism. The 'closed world' that had preceded the war, with restrictions on market access and discriminatory trade practices such as tariffs, was a major factor in the depth of the Great Depression.[16] In order 'to maintain a world economic order based on free trade and currency convertibility' the US hosted the Bretton Woods conference of 1944 at which the American dollar was pegged as the standard, backed by the world's greatest gold reserves, against which all other currencies would exchange. This gave the US economy preponderant leverage over the evolution of the new global system.[17]

Germany was the key to reconstruction strategy as the new 'axis' of an integrated European market. At the end of the war Germany had been co-occupied by the US, Britain and the USSR. The issue of the shape of Germany's reunification had been left open by the big three powers. Russia occupied about one-third of the nation, the largely agricultural eastern sector, while the US and Britain ruled the industrial west. This posed an immediate problem for US–Soviet cooperation since Russia wanted to carry off Germany's remaining industrial plants as part of the exacting indemnity it desired and as a measure to cripple any future re-industrialization that could lead to Germany's remilitarization. This came directly into conflict with American goals. As Stalin saw matters, the issue revolved around Russian need for security versus American desire for gain. The question of Germany's future would ultimately be the root of Washington's decision to militarize the Cold War.

US ambassador to the newly created United Nations, John Foster Dulles, said 'a healthy Europe' could not be 'divided into small compartments'. It had to be organized into 'an integrated market big enough to justify modern methods of mass production for mass consumption'.[18] An early draft of the Truman Doctrine had declared that:

> Two great wars and an intervening world depression have weakened the system almost everywhere except in the United States...if, by default, we permit free enterprise to disappear in other countries of the world, the very existence of our democracy will be gravely threatened.[19]

Envisioning a global 'America, Inc.' Washington policy-makers would anoint defeated Germany and Japan as junior partners with management rights over many of the areas formerly comprising the very empires they had sought to rule. In order to renew capitalist prosperity the US would ally with its former enemies to thwart the opposition of both communists and any economic nationalists (any who put their national economic interests before American corporate interests) on the scene. What Truman, a Democrat, and Dulles, a Republican, feared above all was any return to self-contained economic blocs that would freeze American enterprise out. Whether this took the form of Stalinism, Chinese communism, state socialism or Arab nationalism, any type of economic autarky anywhere was unacceptable to official Washington. In 1904 Teddy Roosevelt had extended the Monroe Doctrine and American dominance throughout the western hemisphere; now Truman, in his famous doctrine of 1947, would extend it to the planet.

CONTROL OF OIL BECOMES THE LINCHPIN OF AMERICAN POLICY

Fundamental to American management of capitalist economies, and the military power to back it up, was control of the resource necessary to fuel the system. In the words of the US State Department oil had become 'a stupendous source of strategic power, and one of the greatest material prizes in world history'. James Forrestal, who had directed the Navy Department during the war and would soon become the nation's first Secretary of Defense, put matters quite baldly. 'Whoever sits on the valve of Middle East oil may control the destiny of Europe.'[20] George Kennan, architect of early anti-communist policy, wrote that 'US control over Japanese oil imports would help provide "veto power" over Japan's military and industrial policies.'[21] In another position paper the State Department declared:

> *Our petroleum policy is predicated on a mutual recognition of a very extensive joint interest and upon control...of the great bulk of the petroleum resources of the world...*US–UK agreement upon the broad, forward-looking pattern of the development and utilization of petroleum resources under the control of the two countries is of the highest strategic and commercial importance. [author's emphasis][22]

The inclusion of the British government in this proposed condominium was quite disingenuous, since American policy all along had been to displace Britain at the top of the system, to remake it on American terms: to play Rome to Britain's Athens.

As we have seen, the Middle East had been cynically carved up and occupied by Britain and France after World War I. Owing to the shock and cost of World War II both nations were losing their empires. Having ascended to the pinnacle of the system that had evolved by conquest, the US would shortly, in the name of countering communists but really in order to maintain its new position, be forced to intervene in the Middle East for strategic reasons and to ensure its access to and control over the disposition of vital oil.

Solving these problems would require outlays of US tax revenues that would dwarf the costs incurred by the war itself, and if not managed tightly could lead back to depression.

The Truman Doctrine of 1947 committed the US to provide assistance to any nation at risk from communist movements or insurgencies, but it was also a major response to the economic uncertainties facing reconstruction of the global system. The capitalist British Empire had been the greatest impediment to American hegemony in the pre-war system. In another of history's ironies Prime Minister Churchill had allied with the US in order to save his nation's empire, only to see it bankrupted by victory. Britain had succumbed to classic 'imperial overstretch',[23] and the main beneficiary of this precipitous decline was its ally and rival. In desperate need of loans from the only nation with funds, London agreed to convert its currency, the pound sterling, to dollars, thereby transferring economic management at home and economic control of its dominions to the US. The imperial roles had been reversed, a goal sought by Washington and Wall Street for half a century. But the US had also now adopted Britain's role as enforcer in the empire she was losing. The first stop was Greece, formerly London's satellite, now in danger of succumbing to home-grown communists.

The anti-communist propaganda of the Truman Doctrine also prepared the American public and Congress for even greater outlays of American dollars. Truman's message emphasized the communist threat to Greece, Turkey and the oil of the Middle East, but this was not entirely honest. Its deeper goal was to overcome political reluctance to extend massive loans for European recovery. As noted, Stalin was not interfering in the Greek civil war between communists and rightists. The aid thus extended by Truman defeated the Greek communists and lined the US up with a reactionary and dictatorial regime. There was no evidence that the Soviets were interfering in Turkey and that Muslim nations' communists were a weak minority in any case. As Chairman Arthur Vandenburg of the powerful Senate Foreign Relations Committee told Truman, if he wanted Congress to put up the money he would have 'to scare hell out of the American people'.[24] Thus an equally massive distortion and deception campaign about Russia's proclaimed threat was set in motion to match the enormous outlays of funds that would be necessary to rebuild Europe's shattered economies to suit the American agenda of a world open to American corporate penetration. Communism was on the march the public was told; only the United States stood in its path.

THE 'MARTIAL PLAN'

Named after Secretary of State George C. Marshall, the European Recovery Program is often presented as an impeccable example of American generosity towards war-ruined nations, including former enemies. But the plan was crafted primarily as a measure to resolve the 'dollar gap' crisis and restore the US economy and international trade. Prior to the depression and war, Europe and Japan had exported their products to the US and been paid in dollars, which these nations then used to import American products. In the post-war period European currencies and the Japanese yen were essentially worthless. In the absence of dollars to buy American goods, global trade could not be re-established and the US was in danger of falling back into depression, mass unemployment and social instability. The plan envisioned ultimately an integrated European Common Market, with a re-industrialized Germany at its core and a common currency easily converted into dollars. Billions of tax dollars would be pumped into ruined Europe (with a similar plan for Japan) and then be re-circulated back into the US to purchase reconstruction services and materials from American companies. The war-devastated nations would be rebuilt and American prosperity would return.

The key to European recovery, said American analysts, was Germany. Secretary Marshall declared that 'the restoration of Europe required the restoration of Germany. Without a revival of Germany's production there can be no revival of Europe's economy.' The chairman of General Motors, then the largest corporation in the world, said that without German integration into a common European market 'there is nothing that could convince us in General Motors that it was either sound or desirable or worthwhile to undertake an operation of any consequence in a country like France'.

France itself was adamantly opposed to re-industrializing the neighbor that had invaded it twice that century but was induced to accept the plan when it realized that the enormous reparations it desired from Germany could only be obtained if German industry was resurrected. France also fervently wanted to hold on to its empire, especially in North Africa and Indochina. To have any hope of success it would have to depend on the United States and would therefore be required to go along with the Marshall Plan.

Russia, however, was a very different case. Under no circumstances could the Soviet Union accept a reunified Germany reconstructed along the lines that had enabled its rise as a military power in the first place. Germany had also twice invaded Russian territory in one generation, with consequences far more extreme than for France. The USSR desperately needed aid, even more than the nations of western Europe, and at the final allied conference at Potsdam had asked Truman for a $10 billion loan, having previously been promised $6 billion by FDR. Stalin took measures to cooperate with the US, such as allowing non-communists to share rule in strategic Poland and Czechoslovakia, by withdrawing troops from Austria, Manchuria and Iran, and by refraining to support communist movements in China, Greece and elsewhere. Washington had continued to dangle the possibility of the loan to Moscow without making any concrete guarantees. It never did extend the money.

In 1948 the US offered Marshall Plan aid to Czechoslovakia which had fallen under Nazi rule during the war when its puppet government had allied with Hitler. Nevertheless, that nation was allowed by Stalin to have elections in which non-communists shared power. Czechoslovakia straddled east and west and sought good relations with both sides. But it was clear that acceptance of Marshall Plan aid would tie the small nation's economy to the west and erode the *cordon sanitaire* that Soviet foreign policy saw as key to its national security. Rather than allow Czechoslovakia out of its orbit the Soviets ruthlessly toppled the non-communist government of Edward Benes and occupied the country. This was the first military foray conducted by the Soviets after World War II, and it occurred in a nation that had been an enemy, and had previously been occupied by the Red Army. This move against the Czechs hardly portended the global conquest that Washington's propaganda insisted was the Soviet goal.

Had Italy at the time elected a communist government and showed signs of lining up with the USSR the United States would have overthrown that government (actually it would never have allowed any communists, elected or not, in the first place). Nevertheless, Washington seized upon the Czech overthrow as perfect evidence of its own propaganda. The Reds were relentlessly seeking world conquest and would have to be 'contained'. The die was cast. The USSR would be denied reconstruction aid, it would be banned from the renewed global economic system and its proclaimed menace would be employed to justify rearmament in the US and Western Europe.

Critics of the European Recovery Plan in the US, like FDR's former vice-president Henry Wallace, dubbed it the 'Martial Plan'.[25]

Wallace, who was running for president in the 1948 election, argued strenuously that Truman's policies were deliberately fostering mistrust, a dangerous arms race and potential future war. Like FDR he believed that mutual cooperation between Washington and Moscow could be worked out favorably to both nations, if only the US would take seriously Russia's genuine security concerns. He and many others doubted Truman's professed humanitarian motives for the plan, believing it was calculated primarily to profit large corporations, especially many war industries that had grown to gargantuan proportions as a result of wartime contracts with guaranteed profits. What would the workforce's share be? If a new war should come who would do the dying?[26]

In response to the dispute over the Marshall Plan big business established the Committee for the Marshall Plan. Massively funded by concerns like Chase Bank, General Motors, Westinghouse, Standard Oil and numerous Wall Street law firms and brokerage houses, the public was saturated with media ads touting the benefits the economy would reap. Simultaneously, critics were portrayed as communists or communist sympathizers. New epithets entered the political vocabulary. Opponents of the plan, or of Truman's anti-communist policies in general, were now derided as 'stalinoids', 'parlor pinkos' and communist 'fellow travelers'. The most conservative elements in the American Federation of Labor (AFL) and the Congress of Industrial Organizations (CIO) were enlisted to line the unions up with corporate America. The Truman Administration also mandated the Federal Employee Loyalty Program requiring millions of federal employees to take a loyalty oath. This energized the extreme right wing in American politics since it more than implied that the administration had allowed itself to be infiltrated by 'subversives' and fed the witch hunt against any critics of US foreign policy that followed. Wallace himself, whom FDR had trusted as he had never trusted Truman, was depicted in the popular press as Stalin's 'stooge'. The former Vice-President's interest in eastern religions was ridiculed and condemned as a betrayal of America's 'Christian heritage'. The strongest political link to FDR's New Deal, Wallace and his bid for the presidency, was derailed by such caricatures. An age of irrationality, intolerance, censorship and militarized anti-communism had dawned and would dominate American domestic politics almost for half a century.

THE FUTURE OF GERMANY FURTHER POLARIZES THE COLD WAR

The years 1948–1950 were critical to the evolution of American Cold War policies and the future of American democracy. The crucial issue of Germany heated nearly to atomic warfare over the capital city of Berlin; the Chinese communists overthrew the regime the US had propped up against Japan; the Soviets exploded their first atomic bomb; war in Korea broke out suddenly, and across the globe the colonies were in open revolt. Panic gripped the Truman Administration while its right-wing opponents mounted a hysterical condemnation of the government's policies. Owing to its unpopularity, the draft laws of World War II had been allowed to lapse but on 24 June 1948 Congress instituted a new Selective Service Act that would conscript able-bodied males for compulsory military service, not to defend American shores but once again to be deployed thousands of miles from home.[27] The militarization of the Cold War and the creation of the 'permanent war economy' was now becoming law. The National Security State, what President Dwight Eisenhower would later call the 'military-industrial complex', was now unremittingly fastened on to American life, adding new branches to the republican form of government, neither elected nor seemingly subordinate to the original three prescribed by the Constitution. (The Constitution prescribes a legislative branch, an executive and a judicial. The new National Security State involved the creation of the Central Intelligence Agency and the National Security Council which effectively acted as new branches unelected by anyone.) Coupled with the rising power of the Central Intelligence Agency this 'secret government', operating behind the scenes and in the shadows of American political life, would maneuver ceaselessly to reduce government 'by the people' to political theater once and for all.

The fate of Germany, split between the capitalist west and Soviet east, polarized the issues between the US and USSR. By 1948 it was clear that no compromise on Germany's reunification could be reached that satisfied either side. When the US announced that it had created a separate currency for West Germany the Soviets decided to close the border between their zone, East Germany, and the West, halting any progress toward reunification. The American intent was to foster re-industrialization and economic stability in West Germany such that it could begin importing American and western European products. This flatly rendered null the agreement made at Yalta for Russian reparations from the wealthier, industrialized western zone of Germany. The Soviets announced that the mutual co-government of Germany had come to a halt. The critical issue was Berlin, Germany's capital deep in the Soviet zone that had also been co-occupied and governed by the allies. Now the Soviets shut the access roads and rails leading to Berlin from the west. The US wanted German reunification on terms that would make it an ally and stalwart economic partner. The Soviets wanted Germany rendered militarily impotent and that meant severe limits to German industrial capacity.

Rather than assent to what amounted to the permanent division of Germany, Washington initiated a risky airlift to Berlin to supply its forces and peoples in the western zone. American officials knew that Russia might take military action but reasoned that the US atomic monopoly would inhibit that possibility. General Lucius Clay, High Commissioner of the American zone, stated baldly that 'It is our view that they are bluffing and that their hand can and should be called now. They are definitely afraid of our air might.'[28] Two squadrons of B-29 bombers, the same aircraft that had dropped the Hiroshima and Nagasaki bombs, were deployed to bases in England, within striking distance of Moscow and Leningrad.[29]

As the world held its breath the American calculation proved correct. The Soviets backed down owing to their absolute weakness. But in the face of nuclear blackmail they ratcheted up the production of their own A-bomb, detonating it in August 1949. For the first time in this deadly post-war geo-strategic chess game the US found itself checked. Though the USSR still had no capacity to bomb the US, it could now attack Paris or London if growing political conflict were to lead to war. In that case the American objective of reconstructing Europe to benefit the US would come to worse than nothing. Rather than attempt to halt what would become the most dangerous arms race in the history of the human species the Truman Administration, and its successor, would deliberately escalate the peril by launching the H-bomb project, calculating with the arrogance of power that they could manage the risk of thermonuclear war.

BUILDING THE PERMANENT WAR ECONOMY

The North Atlantic Treaty Organization (NATO) was the first formal treaty binding the United States to a military alliance with a foreign power, in this case numerous nations. Originally publicized as a means to contain the possibility of German resurgence, it was really a multi-pronged element in American post-war strategy for reconstructing a new global order, as well as confronting the USSR. As such it was the 'logical corollary to the Marshall Plan'.[30] First on the agenda was the military coalition against the USSR encompassing the major western European nations and the US. Reassuring France that Germany could not again pose a threat was a major part of the overall design, but harnessing the industrial strength of West Germany, and eventually its military, as guardian to an integrated western European economy was crucial. Without the prosperity such an economic union could foster, the European side of NATO could not afford the arms necessary for the military strength of the alliance.

Such arms would for the foreseeable future be manufactured in the US by corporations which had produced armaments during the war and which had grown to gargantuan proportions as a result of tax-funded war contracts. Reliant on guaranteed profits from government during the war these companies now faced insolvency owing to the disappearance of demand for massive quantities of ships, aircraft, tanks, trucks and a myriad of other products. Yet these very firms, and the satellite industries that fed them, had become integral to the American economy and the maintenance of full employment. With 16 million former servicemen looking for work, the downsizing or bankruptcy of major industrial companies posed the danger of a return to depression. Unless the demand could be re-invigorated.[31]

While American officials worked to reconstruct capitalism in Europe and Asia as an impediment to the spread of communism, or socialism, or independent nationalism of any sort, others decided, ironically, to foster what amounted to military socialism at home. Though American policy-makers asserted that *laissez-faire* principles continued to drive the economy, and decried state management of the economies in the communist world, the marriage of political Washington to the industrial-financial sectors created a similar model in the US, with the critical difference that public investments would result not in social returns but in private profit. Sometimes called the 'welfare-warfare state' American prosperity would be maintained via a permanent war economy. Massive government outlays and tax and debt funded contracts would continue to underpin major sectors of the industrial and financial economy especially for maintaining and upgrading the arms industry, but also for the most pressing and politically sensitive social needs, like veterans services. Management of the political, military and economic systems would require a revolving door wherein executives would move easily from one sector to the other.

Key among public investments would be a massive 'G.I. Bill' that would provide free tuition and generous stipends for veterans to attend universities, colleges and technical institutions and thereby upgrade the skills and educational levels of millions, essential for future innovations and economic prosperity. This would go a long way towards warding off a return to mass unemployment and widespread discontent among those whose sacrifices had sustained the war. Simultaneously the same veterans would receive below market loans for mortgages. The 'baby boom' of the post-war years was rendering an already dilapidated and scarce housing stock insufficient. An immediate result was the growth of the construction industry and the overnight invention of suburbia. Such stimuli would foster numerous new industries to absorb the workforce and maintain American productivity, and ensure domestic tranquility, while the overseas restoration of capitalism would also ensure mutuality of trade. Since the keystone of the structure was the new politico-military-industrial complex, all that was needed to ensure perpetuation was to maintain permanent enemies.

LOSING CHINA TO THE CHINESE

Washington had already turned Russia deliberately from ally to foe. Then in 1949 the Chinese communists drove the regime of Jiang Jieshi to the offshore island of Formosa (today Taiwan). Immediately Washington declared that this had been orchestrated in Moscow and was evidence of the international communist conspiracy to conquer the world. Now there were two Red Armies.

Well before entering the war itself, US military aid (including American pilots) to Jiang's corrupt regime against Japan, was a principal link in the chain of events leading up to Pearl Harbor. Jiang's Kuomintang army spent more time robbing their fellow Chinese, and living well off American funds, than engaging the Japanese invaders. The only genuine resistance to the Japanese in China came from the communists, a fact not lost on the Chinese masses.[32] Chinese communists came to power as a result of their wartime resistance to Japan, which won them the backing of millions, not because they were the puppets of Stalin, and Washington knew this although officials and their propagandists lied to the American public in order to 'scare hell out of them'.

FDR had agreed at Yalta that the Soviets could retake Sakhalin, which the Japanese had annexed from Russia in 1905, and the Kurile Islands north of Japan, establish a naval base at Port Arthur and maintain rail links to the port of Dairen. The matter of Japan itself was left open. For his part Stalin renounced assistance to the Chinese communists and acknowledged Jiang's sovereignty over Manchuria.[33]

The Soviet Union went to war with Japan only in May 1945 after Germany's surrender. The Soviets desired payback for the humiliation suffered at the hands of Japan in 1905 and also wished to co-occupy Japan with the US. By mid-summer the Red Army had overrun Manchuria and northern China, easily crushing Japanese resistance. Because bitter conflict over the spoils of the European war had already begun, Washington wanted to end the war before the Russians could enter Japan itself. This was made possible on 16 July when the US successfully detonated the world's first atomic bomb. As Secretary Stimson told Truman, 'with our new weapon we would not need the assistance of the Russians to conquer Japan'.[34] With his new 'ace in the hole' Truman could abrogate the Yalta Agreements, claiming falsely that the Soviets were not entitled to the gains in Manchuria that had been agreed by FDR, and which the Russians now actually possessed. Truman even considered sending US marines to beat the Red Army to the areas promised them, but retracted when he realized they would be seriously endangered.

Having fought the Japanese to prevent them from controlling Chinese resources and markets, and closing the American Open Door, the Truman Administration now claimed that the Soviets were on the verge of succeeding where Japan had failed. In fact, Washington had little to fear from Moscow in the region. Having wrested the prize of China from the grasp of the Japanese the US was now about to lose China to the Chinese.

Despite what were clearly American betrayals of wartime agreements, Stalin did keep his promise not to aid the Chinese communists, actually supporting the Kuomintang, their bitter enemies. This was an effort to draw Jiang into the Soviet orbit and away from the Americans. Stalin also did withdraw his forces from most of Manchuria and north China in 1946, even though these regions bordered the Soviet Union and he had every reason to believe the US desired its own dominance in the region. Because Soviet worries focused on national security issues and not on the export of communist ideology, and Eastern Europe was central to those concerns, they were willing to back off in north-east Asia.

The Chinese communists, however, were not bound by any of this and moved against the regime they blamed for China's 14-year occupation by the Japanese, and for its very real exploitation of China's peasants. On 3 September 1945, one day after Japan formally surrendered, two divisions of US marines were landed along coastal China to occupy seaports, guard railways, secure coal mines and otherwise help to revive China's economy. Armed Japanese soldiers were ordered by the marines to assist them in these occupations.[35] General George Marshall was dispatched to China with orders to broker a peace between the communists and Kuomintang, a measure that failed. By early 1946 as tensions heated up between Washington and Moscow, the Soviet Army withdrew. Seizing vast stores of stockpiled Japanese arms, the Chinese communists with an iron disciplined army backed by four-fifths of the population, some 600 million people, began their takeover of power.[36]

The Chinese communists could draw on Chinese nationalism going back to Britain's Opium Wars of the mid-nineteenth century, western incursions into China during the Boxer Rebellion, as well as Japan's recent invasion. When China closed the Open Door in 1949, expelling most westerners, it did so in light of its own interests, not Russia's. Realistic policy analysts understood that deep fissures existed between Stalin and Mao Jedong, the Chinese communist leader. Nevertheless American policy-makers, and especially the Republican right-wing, deliberately contrived to persuade the public that the 'yellow peril' was now even more dangerous than before. In another year the US would be embroiled in yet another war in Asia.

10
Cold War/Hot War: Savage Wars of Peace?

There are aggressive forces in the world coming from the Soviet Union which are just as destructive as Hitler was, and I think are a greater menace than Hitler was.

> Averell Harriman, Former Ambassador to the USSR; Senior Partner,
> Brown Bros. and Harriman Bank, 1948 (Powaski, 1991)

Korea does not really matter now. I had never heard of the bloody place until I was seventy-four. Its importance lies in the fact that it has led to the re-arming of America.

> Winston Churchill, 1953 (Ford with Soyoung, 2007)

United States policy throughout the Cold War was framed in the name of containing communism and fostering democracy. Yet Washington overthrew legitimately elected governments, rigged elections, assassinated or abetted the murder of political figures and propped up criminal dictatorships that in moral terms were equivalent to anything to be found in the communist camp. The reasons are simple: the contest for global leadership was no morality play. George F. Kennan, the early architect of American Cold War strategy, put matters in the starkest terms:

> We should cease to talk about vague…and unreal objectives such as human rights, the raising of living standards, and democratization. The day is not far off when we are going to have to deal in straight power concepts. The less we are hampered by idealistic slogans, the better.

American propaganda blamed the rebellion of Europe's colonies on communism too, though the real reason for global de-colonization was imperial tyranny in the first place, and the collapse of European power after World War II. Communism served well as the bogey to be used to counteract any opposition to the goal of an American-led world order. By 1950 the US ruling elite had committed the nation's people and resources to confront these threats.

In 1950, as a response to the shocks of the Russian atomic bomb and the Chinese communist revolution, Washington chose to intervene in a civil war in Korea to prevent a takeover by native communists. From that moment on, the world over, the US and communists remained locked in mortal struggle, ensnaring many who wished to take neither side. Though the US never dared to attack Russia after it acquired the means to retaliate with nuclear weapons, the 'cold' conflict took the form of many hot wars by proxy in Korea, Vietnam, Laos, Cambodia, East Timor, Afghanistan, Central America, the horn of Africa, Angola and Mozambique. Beyond these horrific wars, numerous other covert interventions, coups, assassinations and other crimes resulted in a death toll approaching the losses of World War II itself and the majority of casualties were civilians. These wars and forays sometimes were sanctioned by the United Nations but most constituted violations of the very international law to which the US and Soviets had pledged their support in order to avert the atrocity of war. None was declared by the Congress of the United States as prescribed by the US Constitution. And in every one the US public was whipsawed by lies and deceptions into initial support.

The Soviet A-bomb and the 'fall' of China sent shockwaves through the Truman Administration and intensified the manufactured paranoia rippling through the politics of the nation. The most reactionary elements, soon to be known as 'McCarthyites' after Senator Joseph McCarthy of Wisconsin, accused Truman of having 'lost' China and demanded more bellicose responses to communism. These extremists eventually claimed that American policies were actually steered by communists who had infiltrated the administration and were undermining the foundations of the republic like red termites.

CREATING THE WARFARE STATE

In short order the Truman Administration moved to the right and completely reorganized the executive branch of government, giving it powers even FDR had never assumed. The imperial presidency was permanently grafted on to the American system. The National Security Act of 1949 created the National Security Council (NSC) and the Central Intelligence Agency (CIA). The NSC rapidly delegated to itself foreign policy prerogatives formerly the province of the State Department, while CIA's prime mandate from Congress was to analyze data to ferret out 'threats' and leave other

US agencies to develop policies to meet them. The 'Company' as its members called it, soon engaged in illegal assassinations and coups against governments opposing US interests. Policies pursued by both the NSC and CIA would create security threats where none had previously existed. Before long these new agencies would act virtually as un-elected branches of government, believing the president worked for them, not the opposite. A new and shadowy 'secret government' was slowly entrenching itself.

On March 10, 1950 President Truman authorized a secret program to develop the hydrogen bomb, hoping to trump the Soviet A-bomb. Needless to say the Russians immediately responded with their own H-bomb project. With explosive energy thousands of times more powerful than the atomic bomb, this new weapon foreshadowed Armageddon.

In April the newly created NSC issued National Security Paper No. 68 (NSC-68), at that time the most far-reaching policy document in American history (it would be exceeded only by the manifesto of the neo-conservatives in 2000, 'Rebuilding America's Defenses'). This extraordinary top-secret document asserted that communism across the planet was a monolithic movement directed from Moscow and that American defenses had become 'dangerously inadequate', thus, major changes were required and failure would result in loss of strength to the USSR. The Reds were animated by a 'fanatical faith antithetical to our own' and desired to establish 'absolute authority over the rest of the world'. To meet this unprecedented threat, major financial and economic sacrifices would be necessary, including tripling the defense budget to the detriment of social programs. The 'absence of order among nations was becoming intolerable'.[1]

NSC-68 emphasized that the USSR was allocating disproportionate resources to heavy industry and arms production that the US must outstrip. This was a classic case of 'guns vs. butter' because of the Soviets' own perceived weakness *vis-à-vis* overwhelming American advantages. Nevertheless, the report continued, the US must not vacillate for fear that the Soviets might precipitate global war. 'Only if we had overwhelming atomic superiority and obtained command of the air might the USSR be deterred from employing its atomic weapons *as we progressed toward the fulfillment of our objectives*' (author's emphasis).[2] An already deadly arms race was now moving into potentially catastrophic territory.

While the dangerous extravagance of NSC-68 provoked no debate within the new National Security State, Congress and the American people were another matter. Significant numbers of law-makers and citizens believed their government was manufacturing hysteria and infecting the public with paranoia. The success of NSC-68's objectives could not be assured without major tax increases and gigantic new defense expenditures so opposition was silenced by the anti-communist witch hunts of the late 1940s and 50s that labeled all opposition as communist, or soft on communism. Even so in 1950 it appeared that efforts to raise taxes and enlarge the Pentagon would fail in Congress. As one anonymous aide to Acheson (perhaps Acheson himself) put it: 'We were really sweating it, and then, thank God, Korea came along!'[3]

To police the world, to risk nuclear war, to eradicate the creed of communism, all in the name of national defense, the new national security priesthood would wage bloody war in Korea and Vietnam, overthrow the democratically elected governments of Iran, Guatemala, and Chile, assassinate the elected president of Congo, nearly come to nuclear war over Cuba, foster civil wars throughout Africa, topple the regime in Indonesia and enable reigns of terror by right-wing death squads throughout Central America. While it is certainly true that communist regimes brutalized their own peoples, they infrequently carried out military offensives outside their borders. The US did so in numbers literally too many to list.

After 1945 the US intervened in Greece and Turkey, attempted a covert overthrow of the communist regime in Ukraine with right-wing Ukrainians who had collaborated with the Nazis, went to war in Korea and against China, overthrew the legitimate governments of Iran and Guatemala, aided attempts to assassinate the leaders of Egypt and Iraq, sent marines into Lebanon, attempted the overthrow of Castro in Cuba, initiated war with Vietnam, Laos and Cambodia, invaded the Dominican Republic, overthrew Lumumba in Congo and Sukarno in Indonesia, aided right-wing death squads in Guatemala and El Salvador, attempted the overthrow of the elected government of Nicaragua, aided Saddam Hussein to wage war with Iran and vice-versa, armed Islamic militants from across the Muslim world to wage jihad against the Soviets in Afghanistan, invaded Panama, waged Operation Desert Storm to drive Iraq from Kuwait, bombed Serbia and invaded Iraq and Afghanistan. And this litany barely scratches the surface.

What follows covers only the most major operations undertaken by the US government during the Cold War.

KOREA

We are fighting in Korea so we won't have to fight in Wichita, or in Chicago, or in New Orleans, or in San Francisco Bay.

President Harry S. Truman, October 1952

I would say that the entire, almost the entire Korean peninsula, is just a terrible mess. Everything is destroyed. There is nothing standing worthy of the name...there were no more targets in Korea.

General Emmett O'Donnell, U.S. Bomber Command, Far East

The War was fought without regard for the South Koreans, and their unfortunate country was regarded as an arena rather than a country to be liberated...the South Korean was regarded as a 'gook' like his cousins North.

The Armed Forces Yearbook, 1951

The Korean War is the most forgotten and least understood conflict fought by Americans in the twentieth century. It stemmed from the overriding goal of American policy to ensure that East Asia remained within the Open Door framework. Having fought Japan for primacy in the region the US, in the inevitable irony of history, had lost China to the Chinese. After that the US was loathe to allow any Asian nation to slip from the western orbit.

Korea was often called the 'hermit kingdom' with good reason since it was a small nation with a unique culture that was no threat to any of its neighbors. It became the victim of an immense calamity caused by great power rivalries. American pilots returning to their bases in the last year of war reported that there were no targets left to bomb in the north because vast tracts of Korean territory had been turned into a veritable wasteland. When an armistice was signed the nation was still split along exactly the same frontier as when the war began three years earlier, but Korea would never be the same again. It remains divided to this day. Both Koreas bristle with nuclear weapons and a large American force remains on standby. North Korea is probably the most militarized and regimented nation on earth because its rulers decided grimly and resolutely that they would never again allow a foreign nation to ravage it as the US did from 1950 to 1953.

Korea divided by US and USSR in 1945

Korea bordered Russia's traditional Far Eastern provinces in Siberia. One reason Russia had gone to war with Japan in 1904 was over Korea. The rivalry between Russia and Japan, and the penetration of East Asia by Britain and Germany, had led the US to issue the Open Door Notes (see Chapter 7), lest the entire area be closed to American enterprise. In 1909 Japan occupied Korea, exploited it as a colony, and remained until Japanese defeat after World War II in 1945. When the Soviet Army entered the war against Japan in May 1945 it easily swept the Japanese aside and quickly occupied northern China. It could easily have occupied all of Korea at the time but it had entered into an informal agreement at Yalta to occupy only the north and let the US to do the same in the south. Roosevelt had proposed a trusteeship for Korea and the Soviets were open to the idea but feared it was a tactic to incorporate the country as part of a permanent American presence in their own sphere of influence. So Korea's future remained an open question. The agreement between Stalin and FDR had come before the atomic bomb when US–Soviet relations were still somewhat amicable and while the US still believed Soviet assistance against Japan was militarily necessary. By 1948 the wartime alliance had morphed into bitter enmity. As the Cold War heated up, the Truman Administration tried to outmaneuver the Russians, pretending that there had been no Yalta agreement on Korea.[4]

Just as the future of Germany within the new American global order was crucial, so was it necessary that Japan play a similar role in the Far East. For Japan's economy to be rebuilt and re-integrated into the system as the 'workshop of Asia', and the prime American trading partner in the region, it would require access to the resources and labor power of the very colonies it had just lost in the war, though now it would be a subsidiary under American supervision. Korea's extractive and manufacturing industries had been financed by Japan and were critical to its economic resurrection.

The Russian Revolution of 1917 inspired communist/nationalist movements throughout the colonized world. Just as communism thrived in China so it increasingly won popular support in Korea against Japanese occupiers. Throughout World War II the Korean communists led the primary resistance to the Japanese and were, even before the Red Army arrived in 1945, the most powerful political entity throughout the entire peninsula, and had a highly disciplined armed force. As a result, Korean communists believed they had won the right to a major role in an independent Korea.[5]

A majority of Koreans favor full independence and national unity

Few Koreans of any political stripe favored trusteeship and the vast majority wanted full independence. A minority was bitterly opposed to communist rule. The American commander in southern Korea, General John Hodge, wrote to Washington that 'southern Korea can best be described as a powder keg ready to explode at the application of a spark'.[6] In the absence of any promises of independence the communists might seize power. Hodge hoped to thwart this outcome by cultivating the traditional Korean elite, who had collaborated with the Japanese in order to maintain their own privileged positions, and the bitterly anti-communist nationalists led by Syngman Rhee.

Employing Korean soldiers and police who had helped the Japanese rule over their compatriots, Hodge ensured that civil war would become even more reactionary and vicious than it already was. Between 1946 and the outbreak of the Korean War at least 100,000 Koreans had already died as a result of this civil war. Even Hodge admitted that the South Korean government was essentially a fascist regime, much like Nazism.[7] Just as the Nazis moved first against the communists, so too did South Korea's regime. For example, on the island of Cheju, a clear majority was loyal to the communists but, as Hodge noted, they were not under the influence of the Soviets but had banded together against the Japanese. By 1949 the Republic of Korea (ROK) Army had killed about 33,000 inhabitants, about 12 per cent of the population, and removed the rest.[8]

At this point the Truman Doctrine was promising aid to nations struggling against communism, even if the communists had the support of clear-cut majorities, as was the case in Korea (and Vietnam). While the US State Department insisted that whatever was salvageable in north-east Asia must not be allowed to remain outside the Open Door, the American military insisted that security issues in Europe were of far graver urgency and thereby hoped to withdraw US forces from Korea for use there. Even General Douglas MacArthur, who would soon command all UN forces in Korea, warned against the US getting bogged down in a land war in Asia. In 1948, as Soviet troops withdrew from North Korea as promised, the US balked at its own departure, moving to bolster South Korean armed forces. The future of Korea was turned over to the United

Nations which called for elections to be held in each zone, followed by the establishment of a National Assembly composed proportionally of members from each side. American officials reasoned that because two-thirds of Korea's population lived in the south this would result in a non-communist majority, but they couldn't bring themselves to believe that communists had actually won the support of most of the people.[9] As it turned out elections (rigged) were held only in the south, where the anti-communist Rhee won overwhelmingly despite the fact that a majority of the population favored the communists.

It has long been an article of faith among anti-communist true believers that the Soviets instigated the sudden cross-border attack by communist forces from the north in June 1950 that started the Korean War. The Soviets did not instigate the war. The North Koreans, led by Kim Il-Sung, had been armed by the Soviets, but Syngman Rhee's regime had been armed by the US. In fact, the US was constantly trying to restrain the South Koreans from attacking the North. The war began at Kim's initiative.[10] Indeed, if the Soviets had wanted to protect the North Korean communists they could have blocked the American effort to intervene by rushing back to the UN Security Council to veto the American resolution authorizing troops to take the lead in halting 'aggression' in Korea. The Soviets had been boycotting the UN over the issue of its refusal to seat communist China in the General Assembly. The UN recognized the rump government of Jiang on the island of Taiwan (Formosa) as the government of China until Nixon made his opening to China in the 1970s. For their part communists in China had just come to power and hardly wanted such a war on its borders.[11]

American officials write Korea out of the US 'Defense Perimeter'

One possible reason for the North's attack may have been statements made by General Douglas MacArthur in 1949 and repeated by Secretary of State, Dean Acheson, just five months before the outbreak of war:

> Our defensive dispositions against Asiatic aggression used to be based on the West Coast of the American continent. The Pacific was looked upon as the avenue of possible enemy approach. Now the Pacific has become an Anglo-Saxon lake and our line of defense runs through the chain of islands fringing the coast of Asia. It starts from the Philippines and continues through the Ryukyu Archipelago, which includes its main bastion, Okinawa.

Then it bends back through Japan and the Aleutian Island chain to Alaska.[12]

Pointedly this perimeter did not include Korea. Why did a country that had not been of concern in January suddenly become a vital security matter in June? The answer lies in the growing hysteria brought on both by the Truman Administration's own rhetoric, the accusations emanating from the right-wing that the Democrats had 'lost' China and the increasing determination among all factions of the American elite that no more of the resources, markets and immense labor power of Asia be lost. In their own words they were 'drawing the line' in Asia.

Convinced that the attack was a conspiracy among the Soviets, Red China and North Korea, Washington moved troops quickly on to the Korean peninsula to reinforce South Koreans and Americans already there, lest the North Korean communists win in a rout. Truman declared Korea to be 'the Greece of Asia. If we are tough enough now, if we stand up to them like we did in Greece three years ago, they won't take any such steps.'[13]

Willfully blind, or simply dishonest, Truman ignored the fact that in each case the Soviets took a hands-off stance. So too, for the moment, did the Chinese, who had far more pressing problems on their hands.

The sudden attack in June 1950 caught the South Korean and US armies off guard and a rout followed. Taking advantage of the Soviet absence in the UN Security Council, the US used the UN to ratify the decision that Acheson and Truman had already made, though the president emphasized that the US desired only 'to restore peace… and the border'.[14] To get around the constitutional requirement of a formal declaration of war by Congress, Truman acted unilaterally and labeled American efforts as a 'police action'.[15]

The war began very badly for both South Koreans and Americans. North Korean forces overwhelmed defenses and pushed south rapidly capturing Seoul, South Korea's capital. Fighting quickly led to atrocities on both sides. American forces were now fighting guerrillas, very different from the uniformed soldiers American GIs faced in World War II. Coupled with their traditionally indoctrinated racism toward 'gooks', unable to distinguish insurgents among panicked refugees, American troops began firing indiscriminately on civilians. One American correspondent wrote 'It is not a time to be a Korean, for the Yankees are shooting them all.' A British newsman reported that GIs 'never spoke of the enemy as if they were people, but as one might speak of apes'.[16] Another British journalist said of the prison camps where South Koreans whose loyalties were suspect had been rounded up willy-nilly, 'I had seen Belsen, but this was worse.'[17] North Koreans retaliated in kind.

The dire military situation prompted MacArthur to say 'I see here a unique use for the atomic bomb.' Only two weeks into the war the Joint Chiefs of Staff considered whether A-bombs should be made available to the general.[18]

By September enough American troops had been deployed so that the bomb was put on hold. In that month the 1st Marine Division conducted landings behind North Korean forces at the port of Inchon and, in tandem with army units, reversed the military conditions and drove the northerners back across the 38th Parallel. This was the mission the UN had authorized – the restoration of the pre-war political and military status quo, before the North Korean incursion. This tactical victory would be the last time MacArthur displayed his avowed military genius. The *New York Times* exulted that the final phase of the war was at hand.[19]

Rather than face overwhelming American firepower, particularly from the air, North Korean regulars dispersed to fight another day. Meanwhile MacArthur still faced a powerful guerrilla force in the south that continued to bleed Americans. MacArthur concluded that only by punishing and occupying the North could the southern war be brought under control. Hence, in November the commander ordered that a wasteland be created between the front and the Chinese border, destroying from the air every 'installation, factory, city, and village' over thousands of square miles.[20] After what amounted to a genocidal assault on helpless civilians the general then launched what he termed a 'reconnaissance in force' but which was really an effort to conquer North Korea entirely and unify Korea on American terms. Now, hundreds of thousands of American and South Korean forces poured into North Korea virtually on the border of China.

China enters the war

The victory of China's communists had occurred only a year previously and their leaders viewed their hold on power as tenuous, given the implacable hostility of the US and its western allies. Thus, MacArthur's march to the Yalu River, China's border with Korea, was seen as an acute threat to the revolution. The head of the CIA, General Walter Bedell Smith, had warned that the Chinese would 'probably genuinely fear an invasion of Manchuria' itself and would establish a *cordon sanitaire* 'regardless of the increased risk of general war'.[21] Zhou En-Lai, China's premier and foreign minister, told numerous foreign ambassadors that 'the Chinese people...will not supinely tolerate seeing their neighbors savagely invaded by the imperialists'. China would never 'tolerate American soldiers crossing the parallel', the artificial boundary line created by both the US and USSR separating northern and southern Korea.[22] MacArthur sneered at such claims saying 'We are no longer fearful of their intervention. They have no air force...if the Chinese tried to get down to Pyongyang there would be a great slaughter...we are the best.'[23]

On November 27 approximately 400,000 Chinese plunged into North Korea and 'chopped the U.N. forces to pieces'.[24] Only three days earlier MacArthur had declared his own 'end-the-war offensive' and told his troops he would have them 'home by Christmas'.[25] American forces are in Korea to this day.

The Soviet boundary was very close to Korea's and though they had not instigated the war, and were already at odds with communist China, they would not have accepted the defeat of China or an American army so close to their territory either. Having ignored intelligence warnings that China would aid the North Koreans MacArthur was badly outmaneuvered and US forces began to retreat largely in disorganized and chaotic fashion. Before long communist forces had regained the territory lost earlier. Acheson declared the rout the 'worst defeat of U.S. forces since Bull Run', saying later 'the defeat of U.S. forces in Korea in December [1950] was an incalculable defeat to U.S. foreign policy'.[26]

Truman threatens to use the atomic bomb

With panic gripping Washington Truman used the atomic threat, stating publicly that the use of the bomb was under 'active consideration'. The Strategic Air Command was put on alert 'to dispatch without delay medium bomb groups to the Far East...this augmentation should include atomic capabilities'.[27] On December 9 MacArthur formally requested authority to employ A-bombs against China itself, though his request was denied. In later interviews he said his strategy would have won the war in ten days. 'I would have dropped between thirty and fifty atomic bombs...strung across the neck of Manchuria then spread behind us – from the Sea of Japan to the Yellow Sea – a belt of radioactive cobalt...it has an active life of between sixty and 120 years.'[28] Since North Korea also bordered the Soviet Union, the USSR at this point dispatched aircraft and pilots to defend the airspace over North Korea and China. The world stared into the abyss of World War III.

The Joint Chiefs sent word to MacArthur that China had the capacity to force his troops out of Korea but that he should take no measures that would lead to general war.[29] However, after driving South Korean and American forces across the border the Chinese People's Army stopped and pulled back to the 38th Parallel. Russian pilots were ordered not to venture south of that line. The communists were signaling a willingness to negotiate peace terms that would have restored the pre-war status quo. A golden opportunity existed to stop the killing and destruction but Truman decided at that point to prolong the war. At stake was the tripling of taxation to implement NSC-68 and thereby the entire policy of containment.[30] American and UN forces continued to use air power and naval shelling to devastate northern cities even as Chinese forces pushed MacArthur's army south. In retreat MacArthur adopted a scorched earth policy 'to leave no facility standing which the enemy might use'.[31] Simultaneously the CIA stepped up covert operations against China's coastal cities, though it took special care to make it appear that the Kuomintang forces on Taiwan were responsible.[32] The ROK continued rounding up all those suspected of disloyalty and undertook mass executions, often with the blessing or indifference of American forces.

The war grinds to a stalemate

Despite the tremendous loss of life and desolation, by the summer of 1951 the war had essentially ground to a stalemate. The Chinese were unwilling to provoke a wider war and MacArthur constantly reproved his commander-in-chief for his unwillingness to attack Chinese territory directly, leading Truman to relieve him of command. Though the general was greeted enthusiastically by massive crowds upon his return to the US, the public was actually growing weary of the war and Washington was beginning to realize that all out war with China would mean war with the Soviet Union, and any escalation would lead to World War III. Thus the 'limited' war in Korea could not be won. Now Truman reverted to the original UN mandate to restore the status quo.[33] Truce negotiations between all sides began in the summer of 1951, yet while talks continued so did the war. At the same time the US initiated a giant bombing campaign code-named 'Operation Strangle'. North Koreans began digging underground shelters and living in them, leading one British observer to note that the population was living a 'troglodyte existence'.[34]

Meanwhile the US had signed its final peace treaty with Japan, aided the re-establishment of its armed forces and, against the very constitution the US had written for its vanquished enemy, actually deployed Japanese minesweepers against North Korea.[35] Given that Korea, China and Russia had all been victimized by Japanese militarism this was a grievous affront and caused the communists to dig in and hold their positions. Shortly thereafter the Chinese accused Washington of germ warfare. By this time it was known that Washington had put captured Japanese and Nazi germ warfare experts to work in its own bacteriological programs. The issue was further complicated by 'confessions' by American prisoners of war that they had participated in germ warfare. Washington rejected these out of hand as having been forced by torture. A voluntary scientific group visited North Korea to investigate and concluded the charges were true based on evidence they saw that closely paralleled the actual methods used by the Japanese during World War II. They also pointed to diseases such as hemorrhagic fever that had never been seen in temperate regions before, and live flies in below-zero weather. The fact that the US government lied about its employment of captured enemy scientists, and its own chemical and germ warfare program, raises suspicions in and of itself. Nevertheless, the accusations remain unproved, though disturbing.[36]

Amidst talk of truce atrocities increase

In late 1952 Dwight D. Eisenhower was elected president largely on the strength of his promise that 'I shall go to Korea', which the public interpreted to mean he would end the war. Most historians now conclude that Eisenhower secretly sent word to the Chinese that he would use nuclear weapons. This dire threat led the Chinese to seek a nuclear guarantee from Stalin in return. Then almost miraculously Stalin died unexpectedly and a thawed political climate appeared rapidly in Moscow where new leaders pressured the North Koreans to come to terms. By April 1953 agreement was reached to release sick and wounded prisoners on all sides, but these talks soon broke down over whether communist prisoners would be forcibly returned. Many did not desire to return to China or utterly devastated North Korea. Communists captured by the South Korean Army were forcibly tattooed with anti-communist slogans under the eyes of Americans. Such marks would be seen as treasonous to either the North Korean or Chinese governments thus precluding the prisoners' return later.[37] According to Admiral Turner Joy, who led the American team negotiating truce, communist prisoners who desired repatriation were 'either beaten black and blue or killed'.[38]

For their part American officials accused the communists of torture and 'brainwashing', arguing that numerous 'Manchurian candidates' had been essentially hypnotized into treasonous activities. Approximately 2,700 American POWs died in communist captivity, most in the first year of war when frigid conditions and lack of food were the lot of their captors too, and POWs were frequently marched from one location to another to avoid bombs. No one knows how many American prisoners died from 'friendly fire'. In truth the conditions of the war were so abominable that atrocities on both sides became inevitable. The standard accounts of the Korean War emphasize communist brutality. Few American chroniclers describe their own nation's conduct honestly. American camps housing communists were guarded by South Koreans who exacted terrible retributions from their northern kin. On a number of occasions when communist prisoners rebelled at their treatment, Americans sent in tanks and flamethrowers to put resistance down, usually killing hundreds at a time. According to the British defense chief, 'The U.N. prisoners in Chinese hands, although subject to "re-education" processes of varying intensity...were certainly better off in every way than any held by the Americans...' The communists released all Americans but a few chose to stay behind. In American minds these were the brainwashed. In the UN camps violence was employed to prevent repatriation by communists in a propaganda effort to convince the world that prisoners rejected communism.[39]

The last full year of war was the most brutal on all sides. Eisenhower knew that the unpopularity of the war had infected the troops as well. In the final week of war the UN forces suffered 29,629 casualties, while the communists endured over 72,000. By 1953 desertions had quintupled in the US armed forces and, according to a study late in the war, 90 per cent of troops hospitalized were there for self-inflicted wounds. In an effort to force the North Koreans to come to terms acceptable to Washington, the US Air Force began massive bombing of the north's dams and dikes only two months before the armistice was signed. These dams were absolutely essential for agriculture and their destruction unleashed devastating floods that wiped out entire villages and destroyed crops for the year, thereby leading to starvation for many. The revision of the so-called 'rules of war' in the Geneva Convention after World War II forbids the deliberate bombing of targets essential to the lives of civilian populations. When the Nazis had destroyed the

Netherlands' dikes in 1944 and killed many thousands of civilians, those responsible were tried as war criminals at Nuremburg.[40]

At end of war 3 million dead and Korea reverts to original division

For Koreans the war was hardly limited. Nearly one in every seven lost their lives, and many principal cities were as devastated as Hiroshima or Nagasaki. Even MacArthur, who had directed much of the destruction, said 'I have seen, I guess, as much blood and disaster as any living man, and it just curdled my stomach the last time I was there.' The Korean War set in stone the militarization of American society that had been proposed by the creators of NSC-68. By 1952 arms expenditures reached 67 per cent of the Defense budget, and the Pentagon and CIA were collaborating on numerous interventions against regimes – some communist, most not – all over the world. Both political parties had whipped up paranoia on the falsehood that Soviet communism posed an imminent military threat to the US. Their real fears stemmed from awareness that communist regimes blocked access by American capital to vast areas of the globe, and was limited also by the growing nationalism and desire for independence by the colonies of the now defeated empires. It was far easier to mobilize public support for the new crusade by emphasizing the liability to the 'American way of life', inflating the gravity of the real problem and shifting the blame to a bogeyman. By choosing to militarize the Cold War American policy-makers engendered fear in both the USSR and China. In what the CIA would later term 'blowback', American actions led both nations to intensify or develop their own nuclear arsenals, thereby creating the only genuine threat to American national security. Should this delicate balance of terror tip one way or another a holocaust like none before could follow.

VIETNAM

We sure are pleased with those backroom boys at Dow. The original product wasn't so hot – if the gooks were quick they could scrape it off. So the boys started adding polystyrene – now it sticks like shit to a blanket...It'll even burn under water now...it'll keep on burning right down to the bone so they die anyway of phosphorous poisoning.

(Anonymous American pilot)

I call it the madman theory, Bob...I want the North Vietnamese to believe I've reached the point where I might do anything to stop the war. We'll just slip the

word to them that 'for God's sake you know Nixon is obsessed about communists'.
We can't restrain him when he's angry – and he has his hand on the nuclear button
– and Ho Chi Minh himself will be in Paris in two days begging for peace.

(President Richard Nixon)

If they want to make war for 20 years then we shall make war for 20 years. If
they want to make peace then we shall make peace and then invite them to tea
afterwards.

(Ho Chi Minh, 1966)

No sooner had the US extricated itself from an enormously costly
stalemate in Korea, with a loss of 54,000 American lives, than
it stepped deliberately into another conflict in Indochina. The
Vietnamese forces, known as the Viet Minh and led by Ho Chi
Minh, had just delivered France its most humiliating defeat ever.
The decisive victory of Vietnamese forces at Dien Bien Phu broke
the French public's will to continue the French–Indochina war.
It had been one thing for the French to be soundly defeated by
Germans in World War II, it was quite another to suffer a rout by
colonial 'inferiors'. The sudden collapse of French rule in Indochina
sent shock waves around the planet. If the Vietnamese could so
effectively take advantage of France's diminished imperial power
and free themselves, then so might the many other colonies of
Europe and America throughout Africa, Asia and Latin America.
The Viet Minh victory inspired other subject peoples and accelerated
the de-colonization of all Europe's subjects.

Just as they were meeting in Geneva, Switzerland, to validate the
armistice in Korea, the great powers also agreed to formulate an
end to the French–Indochina war. The Geneva Accords provided
for the *temporary* division of Vietnam in order to facilitate the
orderly withdrawal of French forces into the south and the forces
of the Viet Minh into the north. After a two-year cooling-off period,
elections would be held across all of Vietnam, French forces would
leave and the newly independent nation would emerge under the
government of its choice. Because the Central Intelligence Agency
knew that the communist party of Ho Chi Minh would win these
prescribed elections overwhelmingly, US Secretary of State John
Foster Dulles refused to sign the accords and the CIA immediately
began to subvert them by sponsoring a handpicked candidate, Ngo
Dinh Diem, for an election to be held only in the south of Vietnam
in which only Diem ran, and by creating an armed force, the Army
of the Republic of Vietnam (ARVN) to protect his regime. Thus

Washington attempted to render the 'temporary' division of Vietnam into a permanent status. The independence of Vietnam under a government of its people's choice was thereby nullified.

The result for Vietnam and all of Indochina was a tragedy of vast proportions. In the end the United States withdrew from Vietnam in 1975 after losing more than 58,000 lives. Vietnam, Laos and Cambodia lost at least 4 million dead and innumerable wounded, orphaned and widowed. Toxic herbicides like Agent Orange were sprayed over an area the size of New Mexico and still contaminate Vietnam's water and soil. That nation now has the greatest proportion of birth defects in the world.

Most tragically, after years of continuing the war by embargo the US 'normalized' relations with its former enemy in 1995 on terms that could essentially have been achieved with no loss of life in 1954, had the American people not succumbed to the paranoid propaganda that all nationalists and professed communists were puppets of Moscow and, therefore, enemies of the US.

Vietnamese communists as American allies

American involvement in Vietnam began during World War II when the forces of the Viet Minh allied with American soldiers under the command of the Office of Strategic Services (OSS). The Viet Minh was organized by the Vietnamese communist party led by Ho Chi Minh in response to the Japanese takeover of Vietnam in 1941. Ho saw how easily the French had been toppled and believed that if the Japanese could also be defeated then Vietnam's independence would be at hand. When the US declared war on Japan, the Vietnamese liberation forces understood that their new enemy would undoubtedly be defeated by the US and let it be known that they stood ready to help by providing intelligence, aiding downed American flyers and locating Japanese bases. By 1944 OSS forces were in the jungles of Vietnam alongside the Viet Minh.

On the very day that Japan formally surrendered to the US, September 2, 1945, Ho stood before a massive crowd in Hanoi and read the Vietnamese Declaration of Independence in words substantially borrowed from Thomas Jefferson. At his side stood American OSS officers. The American flag graced the stage and an American B-24 flew overhead in honor of the occasion. OSS officers wrote to their commanders that the Viet Minh were led by communists but were primarily nationalists, more interested in independence than anything else. The US they said could scarcely find a better ally in south-east Asia than the Vietnamese and urged Washington to recognize their independence.[41]

Truman takes the side of France to re-conquer Vietnam

Despite the *de facto* aid provided by the Viet Minh, the Truman Administration turned its back and promptly aided the French to retake their colony. American ships ferried troops to Vietnam and the US remained silent as French naval vessels bombarded the port of Haiphong, killing 6,000 civilians.[42]

The explanation for Truman's defection lies in the overarching American strategy to reconstruct and re-integrate Europe into a new global order envisioned by Washington, and its determination to contain the primary obstacle, communism, or any 'ism' in opposition to this goal. The renewal of Germany's industry, and its military, would be essential and France (not to mention the USSR) was profoundly displeased and fearful. To win French support for the pro-German restoration of Europe's economies, the US promised to assist France to re-conquer Vietnam, and thereby deny any new outpost to communism. By 1949, after the success of the communist revolution in China, the US frantically wished to draw the line in Asia as well, and determined to stifle Vietnamese nationalism. Ho was never the puppet of either Russia or communist China and his potential as a friend to the US was ignored.

The outcome of the 1946–1954 French–Indochina war ought to have served as a dire warning to Washington, but traditional attitudes that the US could always do what others could not prevailed. The war went badly for the French from the beginning. The Viet Minh forces swelled from about 2,000 in 1946 to over 350,000 by 1954, as well as hundreds of thousands of people organized into support groups to wage 'people's war'.[43] After eight years of brutal warfare they humiliated the French at the historic battle of Dien Bien Phu. The game was up for France and its empire.

By 1952 the US was paying for about 80 per cent of France's war and had built up a vested interest in its outcome. Thus, when the Geneva Accords provided for an independent communist-led Vietnam, Washington moved to undermine the provision for the temporary division of Vietnam and moved to make it permanent by leading the American public to believe that there were really two Vietnams: one democratic and in need of American defense, the other communist and intent on undermining its neighbor. To ratchet up the anxiety already produced by Cold War indoctrination the 'domino theory' was formulated, claiming that if Indochina fell then all of southern Asia would topple into the hands of communists. Revelations later showed that even the CIA did not believe this assertion but it served to frighten the public.[44]

France defeated: The US steps into the breach

It is often believed that, as in Korea, the US intervened in an ongoing civil war. In fact, after France's defeat the US created the civil war. The minority of Vietnamese who took the side of France, and then the US, did so primarily because their collaboration with foreigners benefited them, and they feared the loss of special privileges under a communist regime. Ultimately most lost everything. Had the Geneva Accords been followed there would have been no war, and also no casualty list numbering in the millions.

The Geneva mandated elections were perverted when the US moved to make the division of Vietnam permanent by handpicking Ngo Dinh Diem to be president of South Vietnam and held rigged elections in which the only candidate claimed to win by 98 per cent of the vote. Diem had lived in Washington for years, was largely unknown to southern Vietnamese and was Catholic, unlike most Vietnamese. To provide the political base Diem did not possess, the CIA stirred rumors in the North of a coming persecution of Catholics by the communists. The agency then aided a boatlift of nearly 1 million northern Vietnamese Catholics to the south to settle around Saigon where they received privileged status and came into conflict with local Buddhists.

In immediate response to the imposition of what they considered another foreign puppet regime, communist leaders urged popular rebellion. Viet Minh who had gone north when the Geneva Accords temporarily divided Vietnam, had by now returned to their ancestral southern villages *en masse* and established the National Front for the Liberation of Vietnam (NLF) basing this in the pre-existing village organization that had undone the French.

One reason the Viet Minh had won popular support was the fact that they had expropriated landlords and redistributed land to peasants. The Diem regime confiscated these lands and gave them back to landlords who had largely sided with the French. Diem conscripted villagers into a new Army of the Republic of Vietnam (ARVN) and attempted to repress the rebellion of the very people his government claimed to represent democratically. When villagers continued to aid the NLF he imprisoned them in 'strategic hamlets', guarded compounds where individuals were monitored closely. The NLF, whom Diem derisively called the 'Viet Cong', mounted a fierce resistance despite the advantages the ARVN possessed in terms of advanced weapons and American special forces who trained them and accompanied them on operations. Diem, in turn, stepped up his repression, jailing all dissidents, most of whom were Buddhists, and was soon seen in Washington as a liability, since his rule could no longer be construed as democratic. In early October 1963, only weeks before his own assassination, President John F. Kennedy approved a coup by Diem's own generals in which Diem and his brother were murdered. They were shortly replaced by a series of military dictatorships, each of which Washington tried to portray as representing South Vietnamese democracy. In fact popular revolution led by the NLF intensified against the perceived puppet regime. Despite every conceivable military advantage the ARVN enjoyed in weapons provided by the US the South Vietnamese government was about to fall to the people it falsely claimed to represent. To prevent this Washington employed a pretext to insert American armed forces.

No change in personnel could alter the fact that the government of South Vietnam was a creation of foreigners that was clearly designed to thwart Vietnamese independence and was opposed by the majority of the people it claimed to rule. Although President Lyndon Johnson and his advisers claimed the southern insurgency was orchestrated in Hanoi, all intelligence agencies agreed that it was overwhelmingly indigenous.[45] Realizing that the regime the US had created to stop communism in south-east Asia was about to fall to the very citizens it purported to represent, Johnson's only hope of preventing that lay in inserting American troops.

On August 2, 1964 Johnson suddenly interrupted television broadcasting with a live speech to the American public charging North Vietnamese communists with an attack on a naval vessel, the USS *Maddox*, in international waters. Two days later he charged them with an attack on another ship, though both charges were false.[46] In response Johnson ordered the first bombing of North Vietnam and won from Congress the Tonkin Gulf Resolution effectively giving him a blank check to wage war in Vietnam. Most Americans reflexively believed their president.

But Johnson was lying. American naval vessels had long been assisting South Vietnamese ARVN and naval forces to attack northern coastal facilities and were thus violating North Vietnam's territorial waters under international law. The North Vietnamese were simply defending their territory and wanted to create an incident that would demonstrate that the US was covertly waging war against their regime. Most historians agree that LBJ did not want to get sucked into a war in Asian jungles but he was a captive of the anti-communist doctrine. Above all he did not wish to be the first president to lose a war.[47] His administration had been looking for a pretext to bring American firepower to bear and got it by falsifying what had really occurred in the Gulf of Tonkin, and he was aided and abetted by the American press which reported only his version of events. Many in Congress had contacts in the navy who reported the truth, but most voted as the president desired, afraid a no vote would tarnish them as insufficiently anti-communist. LBJ was then in the middle of his re-election campaign and promised American mothers that he 'would not send American boys to do what Asian boys should be doing for themselves'. In fact the full-scale buildup for war was commencing as he spoke.

Two US senators, Wayne Morse of Oregon and Ernest Gruening of Alaska, voted against the Tonkin Gulf Resolution arguing to the American people that their president was being dishonest, and warning that it would draw the US into a long-term quagmire and tragedy. Their patriotism was openly questioned. They were proven correct.

In March 1965 LBJ committed the first ground combat troops from the Marine Corps, rapidly followed by the deployment of Army divisions. By 1968 over 550,000 troops were in Vietnam.

Prior to Tonkin, the communist regime in the north had provided minimal assistance to the southern based NLF, not wanting to engage the mightiest armed forces on the planet. Once the bombing of North Vietnam began, though, it was clear the US believed the key to its success would be the destruction of the northern communist regime. So hundreds of thousands of regular forces from the Peoples' Army of Vietnam (PAVN) began to infiltrate into the south via Laos and Cambodia along what came to be called the 'Ho Chi Minh Trail'.

American firepower devastates Vietnam but fails to root out resistance

American firepower was vastly superior to anything either the NLF or the PAVN could muster. Yet, though the US enjoyed a vastly numerically superior 'kill ratio' it could not root out or stem the resistance. So LBJ and his Secretary of Defense, Robert McNamara, increased the ferocity of the air war. By 1967 the Joint Chiefs declared there were no more major targets left to destroy in the north.[48] The vast majority of US bombing, however, occurred in the south, the very region Washington claimed to be rescuing, and the toll on the civilian population was staggering.

The US treated Vietnam as a laboratory for testing its growing arsenal of new weapons, demonstrating their terrifying lethality to potential enemies as well. 'The genius of American applied science flourished in the exploration of new ways to kill or inflict injury.'[49] Most were anti-personnel weapons designed mainly to terrorize the civilian population, leading high profile dissenters like Martin Luther King to compare them to German testing on civilians during World War II.[50]

Under no illusion that they could inflict a wound like Dien Bien Phu on the US, the northern communists and NLF devised a go-for-broke tactic that they calculated might break the American public's support for the war. In December 1967, on the eve of the Vietnamese New Year of Tet, the PAVN attacked and surrounded the US base at Khe Sanh along the Demilitarized Zone between North and South Vietnam, placing the marines there under siege. Fearing a disaster, the US rushed 50,000 troops to the area but this left southern positions vulnerable, exactly as communist strategists hoped. In January 1968 the NLF attacked every major southern city simultaneously, sending American and ARVN troops reeling. Even the American Embassy in Saigon, previously thought invulnerable, was overrun briefly.

Though the US eventually crushed the Tet Offensive, the US public had reached a psychological breaking point. Having been told for three years that there was 'light at the end of the tunnel' and that victory was near, facts on the ground proved otherwise. After the Tet Offensive a majority of Americans wished some kind of end to the war. When Secretary McNamara resigned in a state of nervous collapse his replacement, Clark Clifford, soon told LBJ that the war could not be won. With hundreds of thousands of protesters regularly outside the White House chanting 'Hey, hey, LBJ. How many kids did you kill today?' and growing congressional attention to his mendacious account of the attacks in the Gulf of Tonkin in 1964, Johnson suddenly withdrew his name for re-election. Though Republican candidate Richard Nixon immediately announced that he would end the war 'with honor', a new phase of conflict was about to ensue.

The infamous massacre of 500 civilians at the South Vietnamese hamlet of My Lai occurred during the Tet Offensive, although it was not revealed until more than a year later. It had initially been reported as a great victory over the NLF. But a disaffected American

GI wrote to Congress to reveal what had really happened and an investigation was launched. Even so the massacre was blamed on poor leadership in order to hide the greater atrocity of the war itself. Simultaneously, and for the first time in American history, veterans emerged at anti-war rallies to recount many other horrific atrocities that were a daily part of the war. Indeed, many avowed that massacres such as took place at My Lai occurred every week, and implored their fellow citizens to stop the conflict from which they had just returned.[51] Many citizens who had been sitting on the fence concluded that if soldiers dissented then something must be truly amiss in Vietnam.

Having pledged to end the war Nixon widens it

Nixon won the presidency largely on his pledges to end the war and to restore 'law and order' to the streets which were rife with anti-war and civil rights protests. Yet he retained the goal of an anti-communist South Vietnam. This could not be ensured without American firepower. Nixon's quandary was how to make war and peace at the same time. He would withdraw American troops and the ARVN would take over the fighting. Since it was the very incapacity of the ARVN that had occasioned the US intervention in the first place Nixon's 'Vietnamization' policy was inherently illogical, but it did reduce American casualties and diminished protest.

Only the continual application of American airpower could sustain such a strategy and Nixon reasoned that if the Ho Chi Minh Trail and communist sanctuaries in nearby Laos and Cambodia could be cut then the US might be able to dry up the flood of volunteers constantly infiltrating into the south. In reality, secret bombing of both Laos and Cambodia had been ongoing for years, deliberately unreported in the US media. Nixon intensified the onslaught. Then in May 1970 he shocked the nation by invading Cambodia. Instead of ending the war Nixon was widening it. This led immediately to massive street protests and student walkouts at one-third of American university campuses, and resulted in the infamous Kent State and Jackson State killings of students. (Kent State was a public university in Ohio where armed National Guardsmen fired on demonstrating students, killing four. Ten days later at the all-black Jackson State College in Mississippi two students were killed by police, though this got much less attention than the killings of white, middle-class students.) In February 1971 ARVN units and some US forces moved into Laos but suffered a severe defeat and were forced to withdraw.

By this time the war was spawning serious inflation and the business classes were growing worried about the long term costs to the economy. As early as 1967 a 10 per cent surcharge on individual and corporate taxes had been levied to finance the war, leading to an immediate spike in opposition to the war. While the war initially stimulated the economy, most business executives not profiting directly as arms purveyors saw the war as a net drain.[52]

Nixon was aware of these concerns and surprised the nation further by normalizing relations with China in order to open what would soon be massive trade relations. Since Nixon had made his political reputation as a strident anti-communist, especially against China, this was a radical departure but one that highlighted the growing economic weakness caused by the war. From their side the Chinese insisted on an end to the war on their border. Nixon also made new enemies when the burglary of the Democratic National Committee headquarters at the Watergate complex, and his own role in attempting to cover it up, was revealed.

Though formal peace discussions had been held between the US and communists in Paris since 1968 they had achieved nothing because American negotiators insisted that the North Vietnamese accept the division of their homeland, and recognize the government of South Vietnam, something absolutely unacceptable to them. When Nixon entered office about 30,000 Americans had died. Four years later almost as many had perished on his watch. With his re-election in 1972 looming Nixon authorized secret meetings outside the Paris framework between Henry Kissinger and Le Duc Tho of North Vietnam. Anxious to take credit for a peace accord, Kissinger dropped the earlier demand for the removal of all PAVN troops from the south and offered a cease fire in return for the release of American prisoners of war. The prime minister of South Vietnam, Nguyen Van Thieu, immediately accused the US of a sellout causing Kissinger to revise the offer he had made to the north. Le Duc Tho rejected these changes, so to punish North Vietnam one last time Nixon unleashed the most intense and destructive bombing of the entire war. Now known infamously as the 'Christmas Bombing', this air assault over Hanoi and Haiphong only weeks before the peace treaty was signed killed thousands of civilians and stained the already ignominious global reputation of the United States even more.

Costs and consequences

Vietnam had been one of the world's poorest countries even before the war. Afterwards the nation had to cope with approximately 3 million dead (there were another million and a half in Cambodia and Laos), millions of widows and orphans and about 10 million refugees, while epidemic disease coupled with the destruction of health care services was rampant. Exposure to toxic herbicides would soon bring huge numbers of cancers and birth defects. Even to this day the sheer numbers of unexploded bombs, and mines long hidden, continue to kill and maim. It is no exaggeration to say that Vietnam, Laos and Cambodia are among the most war ravaged nations in history.[53]

In the war's aftermath hawks argued that the 'loss' of Indochina was a 'stab in the back' by disloyal Americans. They pointed primarily to the deeper tragedy in Cambodia that followed the peace accords when the communist Khmer Rouge took over that small nation from the right-wing military dictatorship that had been sponsored by the US. Yet the secret and long-term American bombing of Cambodia had killed hundreds of thousands of civilians and utterly uprooted the peasant economy, leading many villagers into the arms of the Khmer Rouge. Unable to take action against the US aerial assault, the Khmer Rouge and its uneducated peasant followers sought retribution from their fellow Cambodians, whom they accused of having either collaborated with the American enemy directly, or having betrayed Khmer identity by adopting western values and lifestyles. While the Khmer Rouge must bear the brunt of responsibility for the murder of perhaps 2 million of their fellow Cambodians, they would not have won the support they did had it not been for the massive air assault carried out by the US which so alienated the Cambodian peasantry. The United States thus bears significant accountability as well.[54]

The cost of the war to the US was enormous. At the top were the more than 58,000 lives lost, and approximately 300,000 wounded, followed by the early subsequent deaths of thousands by suicide and drug and alcohol abuse as the ravages of Post Traumatic Stress Disorder set in. Agent Orange, containing the deadly poison dioxin, had also been sprayed on American soldiers and led to exotic cancers among them and birth defects in their children. At least $150 billion was spent directly on the war and this sum could have funded a national health care program, subsidized new energy research, fostered affordable home loan programs or many other pressing social needs.

For the 'victorious' Vietnamese the war was a catastrophe that impedes their nation's development to this day.

In the presidential campaign of 1980 Ronald Reagan sought to re-awaken Cold War animosities by claiming that the war in Vietnam had been a 'noble cause' betrayed by disloyal Americans. The movement against the war in Vietnam was by far the greatest in US history, mobilizing the largest street demonstrations ever and bringing great numbers of Vietnam veterans, as well as veterans of World War II and Korea into opposition. 'Nobility' was present in the millions of Americans who believed that the lies for which so many Americans and Indochinese had died were in fact perversions of the American creed.

Yet domestic political and economic factors and geo-political circumstances also contributed to ending the Vietnam War. Revelations in the 'Pentagon Papers', top-secret documents released by former defense analyst Daniel Ellsberg, showed clearly that five consecutive administrations had lied about the war in order to maintain public support.[55] The near impeachment and resignation of Nixon also soured public opinion. In the mid-1970s, senatorial investigations revealed long-standing connections between the CIA and organized crime, and illegal plots to assassinate foreign leaders. For a time it seemed the American people were determined that the nation take a radically different turn.

In the immediate aftermath of the Vietnam War the Cold War mentality cooled noticeably. The domino theory was abandoned. The imperial presidency came into disrepute. The conflation of the anti-war movement with the parallel Civil Rights and Women's movements contributed to more social equality. Militarism was recognized and challenged. Attempts were made to rein in the CIA. The Draft was abandoned in favor of an 'all-volunteer army', though this did not solve the problem that most recruits still came from the bottom half of American society where there was less opportunity for higher education and work. Many Americans believed that the end of forced conscription would hinder new imperial wars from developing. But the nation's elite still championed an American-sponsored world order and scrambled to understand how best to accomplish this agenda in radically changed conditions. The military brass welcomed the transition because they had lost faith that a conscript army could be depended upon to win wars. An all-volunteer army made up of young men (and women) with few other options in the American economy could be highly profession-alized, reliable and deadly, and would be employed readily after the collapse of the Soviet Union in 1991.

THE MIDDLE EAST AND THE COLD WAR

One enormous advantage among many that the US had in waging World War II was its own vast supply of petroleum. American oil fueled the colossal American juggernaut as well as that of many of its allies. By the late stages of the war, however, a critical reality surfaced. US supplies would no longer meet US requirements. If American global predominance was to be maintained, then new foreign sources of the precious substance would have to be located and brought under American protection. Allies would have to be found – or created – and bases constructed. Post-war reconstruction of Europe's economies as vital trading partners also factored into this strategy since the US would also have to guarantee their access to oil on terms effectively structured by Washington and the major oil companies.

The first step came in 1943 when President Franklin Roosevelt left the Cairo Conference of the Allies to meet secretly with King Ibn Saud of Saudi Arabia. No record exists of the agreement the two worked out, but it clearly committed both nations to a symbiotic relationship in which the US would have access to Saudi oil and the Arab nation would be guaranteed American military guardianship. Thus did the US take the first fateful steps toward its own dependence on the world's oil giant, becoming the defender of one of the most corrupt and brutal regimes in the Arab world.[56]

At the same time US officials understood that the sun was setting on the British and French and their rule of the Middle East. While the Soviets also had expansive oil reserves, their wartime ravages limited their abilities to pump and refine enough for themselves, so for some time into the future they would also be forced to seek outside supplies. Moving quickly the US sought to replace the Europeans and limit Soviet access to the region's oil, and thereby ran headlong into mounting Pan-Arabism, Iranian nationalism and resurgent Islam. American support for the newly created state of Israel set amidst the Muslim world also fostered deep resistance to Washington's agenda.

Ironically, prior to World War II the US was viewed favorably in the region owing to its oft-declared opposition to colonialism. But Washington was busy re-inventing the rules of empire and it was not long before antipathy to the US became endemic throughout the region.

Israel

Winston Churchill once said that he had not become the king's first minister to preside over the dissolution of the British Empire. But preside over it he did. In yet another of history's inevitable ironies England was victorious in World War II but because of suffering what famed economist John Maynard Keynes called a 'financial Dunkirk' it eventually lost the very prizes it fought to keep. Reliant on the American Lend-Lease program during the war, England's dire economic straits left it even more dependent afterwards. In very short order Britain lost its 'jewel in the crown', India (and Pakistan), followed by Greece, Suez and Palestine.

Britain had taken over the former Turkish province of Palestine after World War I. Seeking aid against the Ottomans, the UK had promised independence to Arab allies, yet at the same time pledged in the Balfour Declaration that Jewish settlers in Palestine could have a state of their own. Both guarantees were mutually irreconcilable and in any case neither was kept.

Jews had begun migrating out of Europe to Palestine in the late nineteenth century in response to various persecutions. The leader of what would be termed the Zionist Movement, Theodore Herzl, believed that Jews would never be safe or accepted in any European country and therefore needed a state of their own. A return to Zion, or the ancient Jewish homeland, was their solution.[57]

When the first Zionist pioneers entered Turkish-ruled Palestine they got on well with their Arab neighbors, but as desires by both Jews and Arabs for a national homeland on the same territory intensified, so did violence. Even before World War II intense conflict had broken out between Arabs and various factions of the Zionists, and between these groups and the British army. One extreme right-wing Jewish faction, Lehi, bombed the headquarters of the British Army in the King David Hotel, killing numerous civilians as well as soldiers. Jewish extremists also resorted to car bombs targeting Arab opponents, a practice roundly condemned by Israelis today.[58] The Nazi Holocaust had magnified the Zionist cause and justified for many adherents any means to attain their end.

Unwilling to accept Jewish refugees the US fosters the creation of Israel

Both Britain and the United States had thwarted Jewish escape routes from the Nazis and both nations refused mass immigration to their shores. At the end of the war many Americans felt a sense of guilt over their country's failure to do much to rescue Europe's

Jews, especially after the terrible atrocities in the death camps were revealed. Only at the very end of the war did the Roosevelt Administration move to save about 200,000 eastern European Jews, a small number given the 6 million actually murdered. Even then the US allowed only a meager number to enter the US itself.[59]

By 1947 Britain wanted to wash its hands of Palestine and handed the problem to the infant United Nations. The UN plan divided British Palestine into what it proposed would be two separate states, giving more and better land to Jews, with Jerusalem to be the mutual capital of both Jews and Arabs. The Arabs rejected it out of hand. Some Zionists had wanted to occupy all of what they termed *Eretz Yisrael*, or the territory encompassed by ancient Israel, a vastly expanded area which would include Jordan and parts of Egypt, Syria and Iraq. David Ben Gurion, the first prime minister of Israel, was not pleased with the UN partition of Palestine but suggested accepting it temporarily and finding the means to enlarge Israel's territory in the future.[60] Circumstances would allow this expansion much earlier than expected.

In 1948 Jewish leaders declared Israel's independence and statehood. The neighboring Arab states immediately launched a war against the new state of Israel. Many Israelis had served in the British, Canadian and American armies against Hitler and had military skills. The new state had also imported arms from communist Czechoslovakia. Many Zionists were also socialists; some were communists and the Soviets were willing to support Israel to stifle the US. Without much difficulty Israeli forces defeated the Arabs, while at the same time deliberately cleansing Israel itself of hundreds of thousands of Palestinian Arabs, at times employing terror and atrocity, and extending the frontiers of Israel well beyond the lines prescribed by the UN. Over 800,000 Palestinians were now homeless and living in squalid refugee camps in nearby Arab nations.

The problem for the Truman Administration was whether to support the UN plan and then recognize the new state and, if it did, whether to demand that Israel return to the original boundaries and allow refugees the right of return to their villages. Administration officials were split. Truman himself was on record as supporting a Jewish state, but as violence flared before partition he suddenly opposed the plan, calling for a period of UN trusteeship instead, provoking many American Jews. Secretaries of State George Marshall and Dean Acheson feared that Arab anger would jeopardize the American access to oil. They also opposed allowing

Jewish refugees in Europe to enter Palestine in mass numbers, while also opposing their settlement in the US. Public opinion still opposed the immigration of Europe's refugees, including those who had suffered most. One faction led by the president's legal counsel, Clark Clifford, recommended recognition for pragmatic reasons, including the necessity to win the Jewish vote in the election of 1948 in key states like New York. The Joint Chiefs of Staff and Navy Secretary James Forrestal viewed matters purely militarily, emphasizing the need to keep Israel oriented to the west and its armed forces cooperative in the defense of regional oil fields and Anglo-American airfields in Egypt and Turkey.[61]

Once re-elected, Truman recognized Israel. One Democratic insider claimed that contributions to the president's electoral campaign from wealthy American Jews was 'what paid for the state of Israel'.[62]

'A land without people for a people without land?'

Ultimately the claims of Jews to an ancient homeland and similar avowals from Arabs who had lived on the land for hundreds of years proved irreconcilable. Arab–Israeli conflict undoubtedly would have been inevitable even if the original UN plan had been followed to the letter. After all, the UN vote to bifurcate Palestine was opposed by every Arab state, and Palestinian Arabs had no say at all. Seen from the Arab perspective Israel was a western implant designed to keep former colonial subjects in thrall. Individual Arab states also had their own designs on Palestinian territory. Israelis and Jews elsewhere believed that the new state was justified by centuries of persecution that had culminated in the *Shoah* or Holocaust. One thing is certain, the creation of the state of Israel in the midst of what had been Arab and Muslim territory for more than a millennium has been a primary source of tension and conflict throughout the Middle East and Muslim world in general.

In 1956 Israel joined Britain and France in a military effort to wrest control of the Suez Canal from Egypt, which had nationalized the waterway. Gamal Abdul Nasser had overthrown the corrupt, collaborationist monarchy and had called for Arab unity. At that stage the US hoped to win Egyptian and other Arab friendship as part of the larger strategy against communism. Consequently, exercising economic leverage, the Eisenhower Administration forced the British and French and Israelis to withdraw. The Suez Crisis ensured future enmity between Egypt and Israel. It also launched Nasser as the leading prophet of Pan-Arabism, a movement the

US found as obstructive to its grand agenda in the Middle East as communism itself. In yet another of history's inevitable ironies, Nasser's policy of suppressing the Muslim Brotherhood only strengthened Islamic fundamentalism, so that as the US increasingly moved against Pan-Arabism it found Islamic extremists rising to take its place as the principal impediment to the American goals in the region.

The US fairly quickly decided to cement a military and intelligence relationship with Israel, ostensibly to keep the Soviets at bay. Yet, since a more realistic threat to the American post-World War II strategy stemmed from nationalism in the region and opposition from Arab regimes, Israel served as a base of military and covert intelligence operations. It was a 'strategic asset'.[63] After Suez the US began providing the Jewish state with massive military and economic aid, which accelerated after the 1967 Six Day War wherein Israel conducted what it termed a pre-emptive attack against Egypt, Jordan and Syria and seized Egypt's Sinai Peninsula, the Gaza Strip, Syria's Golan heights and the West Bank of the Jordan River, the area comprising what is supposed to be the independent Palestinian state mandated by the UN in 1947. Indeed, Israel receives more aid than any other single nation. The CIA and Israel's intelligence agency, Mossad, have developed close ties, and have collaborated in numerous covert actions against other nations, many outside the Middle East.[64]

Despite the end of the Cold War, the relationship between the US and Israel has intensified because although American support for Israel was premised on developing a Middle East ally against potential Soviet incursion, the deeper reason has always been strategic positioning to control the production and flow of oil against any perceived threat to American dominance. Although the administration of George W. Bush proposed what it called a 'road map' for peace between Israel and Palestinians, nothing substantial has been effected. Israel has allowed hundreds of illegal Jewish settlements to be built in the area known as the West Bank, most of which is supposed to constitute the Palestinian state mandated by the UN in 1947, which Israel occupied after the 1967 war. The Bush plan stipulated abandoning these settlements and turning the land back to Palestinian control. Instead more settlements have been built and the Israeli government has stepped up efforts to build walls between Jewish settlements and Palestinian villages, thus reducing the area for the Palestinian state that has yet to come into existence. Despite years of rhetoric about an eventual independent state of Palestine, the record seems clearly to indicate that Israel and the US intend never to allow such a state to exist. True or not, Palestinians believe this and that is the source of endless violence throughout the region.

Israel a most bizarre ally

Israel and the United States are said to have a 'special relationship' but Israel is certainly the most bizarre ally the US has ever had. Israel has never hesitated to spy on its benefactor, in many cases using American military personnel to steal secrets.[65] One of the most shocking actions taken by this abnormal confederate was the attack by Israeli aircraft on the USS *Liberty* on June 8, 1967. The American ship was a state-of-the-art spy ship itself listening to communications by all sides in the Arab–Israeli Six Day War. It was unmistakably not a ship that resembled anything possessed by the Egyptian navy, was flying the US flag and was in international waters when it was attacked by squads of planes and torpedo boats over a period of hours, killing 34 US seamen and wounding 170. Survivors said that even men in lifeboats were attacked in clear violation of the 'rules of war'. Later investigations turned up evidence that Israeli pilots themselves were aghast at their orders to attack what they reported as an American vessel. The *Liberty* instantly broadcast to its superiors in the US Sixth Fleet on the other side of the Mediterranean that it was under attack. Though jet aircraft could easily have been dispatched to arrive within ten minutes, assistance to the vessel never arrived because it was called off directly by President Johnson. Though the incident occasioned much outrage in the US, both nations' governments closed the matter by claiming it was a tragic error, but that remains impossible to believe.

Numerous theories have emerged to explain why Israel would attack the only real ally it had. One conjecture holds that the Israeli government did not want the US to discover plans to attack and hold the Golan Heights in Syria, which it had promised Washington it would not do. This seems a thin justification. Some speculate that the Israelis wished to cover-up a mass execution and secret burial of Egyptian prisoners in the Sinai desert, a clear transgression of the Geneva Convention.[66] A more sinister reading argues that Washington and Israel colluded to create the impression that it was Egypt that attacked the ship, thus giving the US a pretext to enter the war, but this is also difficult to swallow. Such an intrigue would rest on an assumption that the Soviets themselves would not intervene since they were backing Egypt, and a direct attack on Egyptian forces by the US might have led to World War III. Direct American involvement in the war would also have alienated Arab oil regimes, as was the case six years later during the Yom Kippur War of 1973, begun by Egypt and Syria to recover losses incurred during the Six Day War of 1967, which was followed by the Arab oil embargo. Whatever the truth, the explanation of tragic error implies a mutual cover-up between the US and Israel and more than suggests an alarming and ominous motive.[67]

Considerable evidence exists that Israeli spies stole nuclear secrets from the US to build their own nuclear complex, and that American officials 'winked and nodded' as Israel crossed the nuclear threshold. The Israelis have never publicly admitted they possess nuclear weapons but CIA estimates put their arsenal at between 200 and 300 warheads. Needless to say these weapons frighten Israel's immediate neighbors, who, quite understandably, want to possess such weapons of their own as a 'deterrent' to any strike by the Jewish state. That is one reason that Saddam Hussein fostered Iraq's nuclear program in the early 1980s. In 1983 Israel attacked and destroyed this facility thereby increasing tensions and hatred throughout the region. American policy is overtly committed to a 'nuclear-free Middle East' but has covertly allowed its ally to become the only nuclear power in the region. In fact, Israel has the capacity to vaporize every Muslim capital. With the largest and most modern airforce in the Middle East, and the fourth largest army in the world, Israel has more than enough forces and conventional weapons to satisfy its security requirements. It does not need nuclear weapons for that.

Seymour Hersh, the noted investigative journalist, has revealed that the Israeli nuclear program exists mainly as a last resort, its 'Samson option'. Just as the ancient Hebrew judge of the Old Testament killed all his Philistine enemies along with himself, Israel is prepared to destroy all its enemies should it believe that its very existence is endangered, and it has the means to do so.[68]

American reaction to Israel's nukes is hypocritical at best. Under the Nuclear Non-Proliferation Treaty, which Israel has pointedly not signed, Washington is supposed to enact sanctions against nations that have not endorsed the measure. While the US denounced the proven attempt by Iraq, and later by Pakistan and North Korea, to acquire nuclear weapons, and recently condemned the unproven Iranian weapons program, it silently endorses Israel's (and India's). This imbalance is one reason that Palestinians, and more recently

Lebanese members of Hezbollah, have resorted to the 'unequal' warfare known as terrorism.

Iran

Like Korea, Iran had been no threat to any of its neighbors but had been the victim of the 'Great Game' played out between Russian and British imperialism. Discovery of Iran's oil fields just as World War I broke out led Britain to take advantage of Russian weakness and intensify its control of Iranian politics via the Anglo–Iranian oil company (soon to be the British Petroleum Company).

By 1946, with British weakness evident, the entire Middle East began to gravitate toward what Washington considered the left. Certainly communist parties existed and played to Moscow but the real issue was burgeoning nationalism and the desire by peoples of the Middle East for independence and control over natural resources, of which oil was prime. In 1952 the Iranian parliament named the widely popular Mohammed Mossadegh as prime minister on the strength of his desire to nationalize Iranian oil and take it from British control. This both alarmed Washington and presented an opportunity. Decrying Mossadegh as a tool of the communists who would sell Iranian oil to the USSR and thereby strengthen Stalin's hand, the US moved the CIA into operation to overthrow the prime minister and restore Shah Reza Pahlavi, thereby co-opting Iranian nationalism, as well as the British, and 'starving' Stalin of oil at one fell swoop.

The CIA overthrows the constitutional government of Iran and installs a dictator

The operation was the first successful overthrow of a foreign government by the CIA and became the model for its future actions. Though claiming these measures as necessary to thwart the Soviets, the deeper goal, as part of the American grand strategy, was to acquire effective control over Iranian oil and build up military defenses and bases in the region. The ancient Persians gave us the word *satrap*. In order to make their widespread empire more efficient, Persian kings ruled through local native chieftains. Now a modern Persian had become Washington's puppet and tool.

In short order Washington began to arm its *satrap*'s military forces with some of the most modern weapons then being manufactured by American 'defense' industries. With oil now safely managed by American petroleum giants on a 60:40 ratio to their own great profit, the Iranian treasury also had billions of dollars to inject into

American defense corporations. The federal government abetted this process by selling surplus weapons to Iran, including jet aircraft, tanks, naval vessels etc. and then buying new ones from their defense contractors.

American military personnel were dispatched to Iran to train its armed forces. Simultaneously the CIA managed the training of Iran's secret police, known by its acronym SAVAK, which soon brutally crushed all opposition, engaging in widespread torture, murder and suppression of all dissidents, especially of Fundamentalists. For the next quarter century the Shah's Iran would serve Washington as loyal client and surrogate, ostensibly to stifle Soviet expansion but equally to foil any form of nationalist opposition to the American overarching agenda.

As the Shah 'modernized' Iran he had to suppress the fundamentalist Shia Muslims, most of whom lived outside the metropolis of Tehran in conditions that had not changed in centuries. While the Iranian regime concentrated on raising the living standards of its elites and middle classes, many of whom were becoming progressively secularized, the conditions of the villagers outside the major cities were ignored, and, indeed, worsened. This left them susceptible to the influences of fundamentalist ayatollahs who inveighed constantly against the apostasy and immorality of Iranian rulers and city dwellers, blaming them for the poverty of the countryside. This circumstance, in turn, led the Shah to step up his increasingly brutal repression of the Shia, leading to many clashes between them and his armed forces. At one point, defying an edict that the traditional women's headdress, the *chador*, could no longer be worn in public, tens of thousands of women demonstrated in Tehran wearing the garment. The security forces opened fire, killing dozens and wounding scores. From that moment on the Shah's days were numbered, though the CIA completely missed what was coming.

The Shah overthrown: American sponsored tyranny in Iran leads to Islamic Fundamentalism so the US fosters dictatorship in Iraq

In 1979 the Shah was overthrown during a massive public strike and street violence, leading him to flee the country, ultimately going to the US. When radical students and Muslims demanded that Washington deport him back to Iran to face criminal charges President Carter refused. The result was the takeover of the American embassy in Tehran and the capture and imprisonment for 444 days of American personnel. During this takeover, Iranian militants discovered numerous documents stipulating the degree to which the US had collaborated with the Shah in the brutal suppression of the Iranian people and the overthrow of Prime Minister Mossadegh in 1953. The Iranian regime was taken over by religious figures who became more radically fundamentalist and stridently anti-American. Speaking directly to the deep anti-American resentments of other Muslims in the region, both Shia and Sunni, Iranian militants urged them to rise up against the 'Great Satan'. In short order this uprising materialized, creating panic in the neighboring Muslim nations of Iraq, Egypt and especially Saudi Arabia, where equally repressive and brutal regimes relied on US assistance to rule over their populations.

Washington responded with a punishing embargo of Iranian oil and the seizure of the nation's financial assets in the US. However, these measures were flatly contradicted by the actions the Reagan Administration took when war broke out between Iraq and Iran in 1980. Considerable circumstantial evidence has led numerous analysts to conclude that the Reagan election team made a secret deal with the Iranians not to release the American captives until after the election of 1980, thereby preventing the incumbent, Jimmy Carter, from achieving a major political victory and increasing the likelihood that Reagan would win. In return the Reagan presidency would provide arms to the Iranian regime. Since such traffic with the Iranian enemy had been prohibited by Congress, any arms deliveries would have to be arranged covertly, and they were. At the same time Congress had also forbidden military aid to guerrillas in Nicaragua (known as *Contras*) attempting to overthrow a Marxist government there. To make the end runs around Congress, Reagan operatives secretly bought arms from communist Czechoslovakia, sold them to the *Contras* who paid for them by selling cocaine and then provided them to the Iranians who used them to kill Iraqis.[69]

The US had broken off diplomatic relations with Iraq after it had nationalized its oil reserves but quickly renewed relations with the government of Saddam Hussein as a counterweight to Iran, providing him with weapons, chemicals and vital intelligence so that he could kill Iranians. American strategy seemed to be aimed at weakening both nations. The Iran–Iraq war killed at least 1 million people and devastated both economies. Though the Iran–*Contra* scandal revealed the lies, deceptions and crimes of the Reagan presidency, Reagan's ill-deserved reputation as a great president survived and he remains a mythological figure today. Later, when the administration of George W. Bush invaded Iraq in 2003, one justification was that Saddam had used poison gas on Kurdish Iraqis during the Iran–Iraq War. Absent from virtually all reports was the stark fact that the US had provided Saddam with the chemicals to make the gas, thus becoming an accomplice in this war crime.

Cuba

After the Spanish–American War (see Chapter 6) the US effectively ruled Cuba through a succession of client regimes that fostered American business penetration of the island especially in sugar, tobacco, banking and oil refining. By the 1950s the island was the poorest nation in the western hemisphere though its elites and wealthy Americans lived high and well in what for them was a tropical paradise. In addition to generous profits that American companies extracted, Cuba was also a major source of organized crime's illicit revenues in gambling, drugs and prostitution, all made possible by the ruling regime's cooperation. The most important opposition to that regime came from the movement led by Fidel Castro whose principal goal was to oust the Americans and those who collaborated with them.

Both Washington and the Mafia provided some assistance to Castro early on, believing that any future regime would accommodate US wishes. Although Castro inveighed against the Americans his words were taken as the usual rhetoric of Latin American strongmen who eventually played Washington's game. American officials were wrong about Castro though. He immediately began kicking American corporations out of Cuba, expropriating their properties and driving Cubans who had collaborated with them out of the country.

Numerous American plans to invade Cuba to topple Fidel Castro's regime were formulated but never carried out, and covert plots to assassinate him all failed. Knowing the desire of Washington, business leaders and organized crime to overthrow him, Castro allied himself with the Soviet Union in order to forestall that outcome. In the process the US and USSR moved to the very precipice of nuclear war.

When Fidel Castro took over Cuba in 1959 there was little worry in Washington. The previous dictator, Fulgencio Batista – who had originally been installed by Washington because the previous Cuban ruler had attempted to nullify the Platt Amendment (written into the Cuban constitution by the American Senator Orville Platt, enabling the US to intervene at will militarily in Cuban affairs, see chapter 6) – had become a liability owing to his brutal rule. American officials had every reason to think that

Castro would accommodate himself to the US just as almost all *caudillos* (a Latin-American Spanish term for 'strongman' or 'chieftain') throughout Latin America, and especially in Cuba, had done since the turn of the century. Both the CIA and the Mafia, collaborating closely, had extended some assistance to his revolutionary movement, believing he would enact reforms but otherwise accede to traditional American interests.[70]

As Jose Marti (Cuba's equivalent of George Washington) had feared in 1898, once the US entered Cuba 'who would get it out?' Cuba had become a source of rich sugar and tobacco profits for American companies, an offshore American banking haven free of regulation, an unregulated oil refining platform, a playground for the American rich and a golden goose for the organized crime families of the Mafia.

Although the US had promised to liberate Cuba from the dire conditions fostered by Spain in 1898, the Cuban population had become the poorest in the western hemisphere, with the greatest rates of curable illnesses and highest rates of illiteracy, while the top 10 per cent or so lived in opulence. The Cuban elites largely collaborated with American dominance and received their perquisites in return. Indeed, Castro himself had come from a wealthy landowning family, but he was among the few who chafed under American neo-colonialism.

It wasn't long before American political and financial elites realized that Castro fully intended to keep his promise to obtain full Cuban independence from the US. He expropriated the vast plantations owned by Cubans and made them over into agricultural collectives. He rounded up and jailed many members of the Cuban elite who had committed crimes against ordinary citizens and caused an exodus of the rich to Miami. Then he turned to seizing American sugar and tobacco plantations, closed American oil refineries that had been located in Cuba to avoid American environmental regulations and expelled Mafia gangsters who owned the gambling casinos, drug dens and brothels where desperately poor Cuban women sold themselves to wealthy Americans who flocked to Cuba to enjoy vices unavailable so easily, cheaply and at no legal risk in the US.

The Eisenhower Administration had initiated a series of covert operations against many different types of opponents to US interests on every continent, usually labeling them communist-inspired. One of the more sinister plots to emerge from the National Security State, though never implemented, clearly shows how American policy had become as criminal as anything to be accused of its enemies. *Operation Northwoods* was a plan urged by the Joint Chiefs of Staff that would have sunk an American naval vessel in Cuban waters, or dressed anti-Castro Cuban exiles in Castro's army uniforms to carry out a staged attack on the American naval base at Guantanamo Bay. Such pretexts would then have served for full scale war against Cuba. Another aspect of the plan envisioned setting off terrorist bombs in Miami and then blaming Castro.[71] As later investigations and Senate hearings proved, the CIA secretly allied itself with the Mafia in order to murder Castro. This dark alliance continued under the Kennedy Administration though it seems that both JFK and his brother, Attorney General Robert Kennedy, remained unaware of it, since they were prosecuting mob members in the US at the time.[72] However, JFK allowed an attempt by anti-Castro Cuban exiles to invade the island to overthrow Castro, using much the same plan that had successfully overthrown Jacobo Arbenz in Guatemala in 1954. The attempted landing at the Bay of Pigs in 1961, only three months after JFK took office, was an utter fiasco and a blow to Kennedy's prestige. He felt betrayed and manipulated by the hawks surrounding him.

The Soviets had already extended significant military aid to Castro and their intelligence agency, the KGB, and Castro's, knew of the plan. Recent documents show that the CIA knew that the Cubans and Russians knew, but went ahead anyway, almost certainly to ensure the assault would fail so that a follow-up invasion by American forces would be necessary and the US could seize the island.[73] JFK forbade action by US forces, since that would have violated international law, earning the bitter enmity of many in the CIA and Mafia.

The most dangerous crisis in human history

The USSR had its own reasons for crossing the Atlantic to ally with an anti-American regime only miles from the US, in violation of the Monroe Doctrine and Teddy Roosevelt's corollary. The United States had by that time encircled the Soviet Union with bomber and missile bases rendering it extremely vulnerable to nuclear attack. Thus Castro's defiance of the US provided the Soviets with an opportunity to give Americans a taste of their own medicine. This grew to gravely perilous proportions when Soviet nuclear missiles were installed in Cuba in 1962.

Kennedy understood that the missiles did not constitute any more of a physical threat than did the Soviet missiles in Kazakhstan,

15,000 miles away. Those ICBMs (Inter-Continental Ballistic Missiles) could also vaporize American cities. The threat was primarily political – domestically. The hard right-wing in the US saw the Soviet presence in the American lake as intolerable. The Soviets would back down if confronted, they insisted. The Joint Chiefs of Staff and many in the CIA demanded that JFK attack the missile bases in Cuba.[74]

We who are alive now owe this cheerful fact to JFK's judgment then. Despite his well-known flaws, the decisions he made spared the world from a nuclear holocaust. An attack on the Soviet bases in Cuba, followed by attacks on their naval vessels, would have led to a Soviet attack on American forces in Europe, with immense casualties on both sides. That, in turn, would have sparked the use of the only reserves remaining in each nation's arsenal, nuclear weapons. JFK sent word to Soviet Premier Nikita Khruschev that he was prepared to remove missiles on the USSR's doorstep in Turkey if the Soviets would do so in Cuba. This allowed both nations to save 'face' and was to be followed up with more negotiations aimed at reducing Cold War tensions and nuclear arsenals themselves.

Kennedy fired the top echelon of the CIA, including its long-tenured director, Allen Dulles, pushed the bellicose members of the Joint Chiefs into retirement, began arms reductions, initiated a 'hot line' direct communication with the Soviet premier and began to plan for a withdrawal from Vietnam, where some 15,000 'advisers' were already carrying out operations.[75] Portentously, he vowed to 'smash the CIA into a thousand pieces'.[76] All of these actions struck at the core ideology of the Cold War hard-liners, as well as their economic interests.

Tragically, JFK and Robert Kennedy continued to plot the overthrow of Castro via assassination, though at the same time they also initiated secret talks with Cuban officials to effect a negotiated peace. As recently de-classified documents show, the overthrow plan, code-named *Operation Mongoose*, was infiltrated by Mafia figures, with aid by rogue CIA agents, who used it to assassinate Kennedy himself, knowing that Robert Kennedy would never be able to divulge the original unlawful plot or prosecute the perpetrators without also revealing the level of corruption that had permeated the government.[77] We shall never know whether the plan to end hostilities might have borne success. Just as republican Rome succumbed to empire and the murder of its emperors by those charged with their protection, so the United States in its imperial epoch has hastened down that road as well.

With Kennedy's death the temperature cool-down in the Cold War he initiated halted immediately. In the USSR, Khruschev's own hawks saw him as a feeble cold warrior and cast him out, to be replaced by hard-liners. Rather than withdraw from Vietnam as JFK hoped to do, his successor, LBJ, escalated and intensified the war. The Cold War was back in full with billions of tax dollars again flowing into the Military–Industrial–Congressional–CIA complex.

11
War on Terror

Pick one of those sheikdoms, any of them, and overthrow the government there, as a lesson to the Saudis.

Henry Kissinger, 1975 (Kissinger, 1975)

For America, the chief geo-political prize is Eurasia.

Zbigniew Brzezinski, 1997 (Brzezinski, 1997)

Our policy is to get rid of Saddam, not his regime.

Richard Haas, former Director of Middle East Affairs,
National Security Council, 1991 (Cockburn and Cockburn, 1999)

Having by its bellicose policies transformed the Soviet Union from ally to enemy after World War II, the US spent almost the next 50 years engaging this enemy in numerous cold and hot contests across the globe. The carnage was reckoned in millions of lives lost and blighted, and economies ruined. More than once the two superpowers approached the nuclear abyss. Then suddenly, catching America's intelligence agencies completely by surprise, the 'evil empire' suddenly imploded in 1991 and its satellites rapidly declared independence. No longer would American foreign policy be based on the assumption of a bi-polar world. In terms of military, economic and political strength the US stood alone.

A NEW AMERICAN CENTURY?

Yet the 'paranoid' strain in American political life remained intact. No sooner did the US find itself atop the global hierarchy of power than many of the most hard-line Cold Warriors began to envision new threats, while others saw opportunities. Departing from the post-war consensus within the foreign policy establishment that had emphasized alliance building, a new thrust called for nothing less than a planetary order by American fiat. In 1992, just as the USSR collapsed, Undersecretary of Defense for Policy Paul Wolfowitz crafted a Defense Policy Guidance document that became the policy template for the radical manifesto of the neo-conservatives who came to dominate American foreign policy under George W. Bush. The so-called 'Bush Doctrine' called for actions that would ensure that the US retained its primacy as the lone superpower in order to structure and protect a global system that served American geo-strategic interests. In the absence of the communist counterweight and as the premiere global power, the US should be prepared to act unilaterally and preemptively to prevent any new power or combination of powers to emerge to challenge American hegemony. Since the maintenance of global dominance requires the indispensable fuel for the American economy and the armed forces that would carry out this grand strategy, 'In the Middle East and Southwest Asia, our overall objective is to remain the predominant outside power in the region and preserve U.S. and Western access to the region's oil.'[1]

But the world is not playing according to the new rules. Though Russia has abandoned communism and is now officially a fellow capitalist nation, the US remains locked in dangerous competition with this nuclear power over Caspian Sea oil and natural gas, the loyalties of former Soviet republics in Central Asia and the labor markets and resources of Eastern Europe. Communist China, in its infancy and weak at the dawn of the Cold War, is also now a nuclear power, intent on the restoration of its traditional status as the great hegemon of East Asia, and rapidly becoming an economic superpower in its own right. Other regional powers like India, Pakistan, and Iran and coalitions in Latin America have emerged to challenge American bids for dominance in their zones. Most perilous to the new global order is the ever expanding and intensifying hatred emanating from Islamic fundamentalists that stems directly from American efforts to dominate the Middle East and its oil during the Cold War.

GIVING THE SOVIET UNION ITS VIETNAM WAR

The collapse of Soviet power was hastened by its 1979 invasion of Afghanistan. Long a client state on the border of the USSR, Afghanistan had fallen into civil war between competing Marxist factions. The Soviets intervened in an attempt to stabilize the country but the incursion of 120,000 Red Army troops galvanized the pent up loathing of Afghanistan's tribal population which had long despised the secularization imposed by communist regimes. Meanwhile, in the US, policy-makers claimed the invasion was a

Soviet first move to dominate the Middle East oil fields and pipe lines. Some still lamented the recent defeat in Vietnam which they falsely blamed on the Soviets. President Jimmy Carter declared the so-called 'Carter Doctrine' which announced on January 23, 1980 that the US would protect Middle East states from communist attack, though the Soviets showed no evidence of harboring such aims. National Security Adviser, Zbigniew Brzezinski, put matters frankly. An opportunity had arisen, he said; 'We didn't push the Russians to intervene but we knowingly increased the probability that they would.' On the day the Red Army invaded Afghanistan he exulted, 'Now we can give the USSR its Vietnam War.'[2]

In short order the CIA undertook the largest, costliest covert operation in its history.[3] From across the Muslim world – from Bosnia to Egypt to Saudi Arabia to China's far western province of Xinjiang – the CIA recruited upwards of 50,000 Muslim jihadists, known as the *mujahideen*, to wage holy war in Afghanistan upon the Soviet infidels who had transgressed against Muslim peoples. Some of the funds for this operation came secretly from Congress but the vast bulk came from Saudi Arabia and was funneled to the jihadists through the InterServices Intelligence (ISI) agency of Pakistan, which had sided with the US in the Cold War. Another source of funding came from the lucrative trade in opium, of which the CIA was well aware. In addition to fighters the CIA also provided Stinger missiles – shoulder held, high tech, heat seeking weapons – that could bring down Soviet helicopters and accurately ravage Russian forces.[4]

Even before the Soviet invasion President Carter had extended the Monroe Doctrine further yet by enunciating his own corollary: 'Any attempt by any outside force to gain control of the Persian Gulf region will be regarded as an assault on the vital interests of the United States, and such an assault will be repelled by any means necessary, including military force.' There was no question as to what those vital interests were. Since at least the 1970s, after the shock caused by the Arab oil embargo, the most prominent American policy-makers had entertained fantasies of seizing Middle East oil fields.[5]

The Soviets, however, showed no indication of any move toward Middle East oil reserves. Their primary concern was to stabilize Afghanistan before the strife there could spread to the Muslim republics throughout Central Asia, and thus destabilize the USSR itself. Though the communist bogey was invoked as a threat, Washington's real goal was to foment the breakup of the Soviet Union and hope that the indigenous Muslim peoples of the region would see the US as their ally and cooperate with American desires to tap central Asian oil. But American intervention backfired and fostered conditions for the rise of Islamic fundamentalism in Afghanistan and throughout the Muslim world.

TERRORISTS AS 'FREEDOM FIGHTERS'

The American-sponsored jihadists were called 'freedom fighters' but this was a classic Orwellian designation. These Islamists fostered terror throughout Soviet central Asia and succeeded in stirring up the Muslim populations in Kazakhstan, Kyrgyzstan, Tajikistan, Uzbekistan and Turkmenistan to rebel against Soviet rule, all to the delight of official Washington. Among these *mujahideen* was Osama Bin Laden. In Washington-speak when American sponsored terrorists kill and maim enemies, even civilians, they are 'striking a blow for freedom'. When the enemies do the same to Americans they are magically transformed into demons.

The Soviet misadventure in Afghanistan hastened a process of decay already in evidence, but which hastened the USSR's collapse and departure from the Cold War arena. No sooner had the most formidable foe the US ever faced disappeared than the very terrorists the US had sponsored turned their guns around to inflict as much damage as possible on their former benefactor.

Just as the USSR was disassembling itself, the dictator of Iraq decided he would move against his neighbor and annex its territory, and oil. In his endeavor to seize Kuwait Saddam Hussein had reason to believe that the US would take no position and would refrain from interfering. The American ambassador to Baghdad had said as much herself. Whether this was a trap set for Saddam to provide a pretext for American troops to enter the Middle East in force is open to debate, but there is no question that the subsequent assault on Iraq and the stationing of numerous American troops on Saudi Arabian soil, in proximity to the sacred sites of Islam, set off a wave of anti-American hatred and jihad that has only grown stronger, particularly since the invasion of Iraq in 2003.

Had Saddam succeeded in annexing Kuwait, he would have challenged Saudi Arabia as the world's largest oil producer and been in a position to defy the Organization of Petroleum Exporting Countries (OPEC) and alter the international pricing system, perhaps to topple the dollar as the premiere oil-trading currency in favor of the new Euro.[6] He would probably have been able to sell outside the OPEC cartel and perhaps broker special deals with American rivals like China, or even Germany and Japan, and free them of the control of petroleum that the US had imposed at the end of World War II. Saddam also had fantasies of accomplishing what others before him, like Gamal Abdul Nasser of Egypt, had failed to do – the unification of Greater Arabia against the West. This, said George H.W. Bush, 'shall not stand'.

To stop Saddam Bush launched Operation Desert Storm in January 1991, sending half a million troops into the region and easily defeated Iraq in what can only be described as a 'turkey shoot'. The Iraqi army stood no chance against the high tech weapons and air power of the US. The Iraqi army, composed of ill-trained and poorly armed conscripts, was routed and slaughtered mercilessly. At that point it seemed likely that the US would invade Iraq itself and topple Saddam. But the consequences of such a move were too unpredictable. In the power vacuum left by Saddam's departure the potential that Iraq's majority Shia population could seize control and ally with their religious brethren in Iran was too threatening. Saddam was the devil the US knew very well. While US officials preferred Saddamism without Saddam, at least for the moment, his regime would ensure that Iraq did not succumb to Shi'ite fundamentalism and spread the poison into Saudi Arabia.

TERRORIZING IRAQI CIVILIANS

Most ominously, American air forces attacked Iraq's civilian infrastructure in blatant violation of international law, reducing a country that had been one of the most developed in the Middle East to an 'apocalyptic' condition.[7] A Harvard University study team reported that the bombing 'effectively terminated everything vital to human survival in Iraq – electricity, water, sewage systems, agriculture, industry, health care…'[8] Evidence from the US Defense Department's own website proved that a principal aim of the bombing campaign was precisely to cause rampant epidemic disease. One document dated January 1991 admitted openly that 'Increased incidence of disease will be attributable to degradation of normal preventive medicine, waste disposal, water purification/distribution, electricity, and decreased ability to control disease outbreaks.' Another icily amoral document from February 1991 declares: 'Conditions are favorable for communicable disease outbreaks.'[9] The only possible explanation for such a certifiable war crime is that Washington intended to *terrorize* the Iraqi population and to send a clear message throughout the region and the world.[10] This is what happens when weak nations defy the will and interests of the United States in the new world order.

According to the United Nations at least 1.7 million Iraqis died, not directly from bombs, but from the damage to civilian infrastructure that knocked out power to hospitals and, accompanied by draconian sanctions, prevented medicines and food from reaching the population, thereby worsening disease and hunger. In 1999 70 members of Congress wrote a letter to President Clinton asking him to lift the sanctions on Iraq and end what they termed 'infanticide masquerading as policy'.[11] In an infamous interview with the American television network CBS, Secretary of State Madeleine Albright was asked 'We have heard that a half million children have died. I mean, that's more children than died in Hiroshima. Is the price worth it?' Albright did not hesitate for a moment: 'I think this is a very hard choice, but the price – we think the price is worth it.'[12] This unashamed endorsement of war crimes immediately circulated throughout the Muslim world and is a prime piece of evidence explaining 'why they hate us'.

At the start of the Gulf War Bush asked the Saudi king to allow aircraft and troops to be based in the kingdom, claiming falsely that Saddam also intended to seize Saudi oilfields. At this point one of the most prominent jihadists recruited by the CIA for the holy war in Afghanistan came to the fore with an offer to defend the Islamic holy places of Mecca and Medina from the 'apostate' Saddam Hussein, instead of allowing foreign forces on Saudi soil. When the king did permit American troops to enter Saudi Arabia, Osama Bin Laden turned his considerable fortune – and his CIA sponsored training – toward overthrowing the corrupt Saudi royal family and conducting all out struggle against the westerners who had dominated the Muslim world for nearly a century. As Bin Laden publicly announced, this desecration of Islamic holy places was the final outrage and made the US the number one enemy of fundamentalist Muslims everywhere.[13] Before long, in a series of attacks on American warships and US embassies in East Africa, the organization run by Bin Laden, al Qaeda, proved itself a terrifying threat.

ABANDONING AFGHANISTAN TO WARLORDS AND THE RISE OF THE TALIBAN AND AL QAEDA

As the crisis in the Persian Gulf rolled out in 1990 and the Soviets completed their withdrawal from Afghanistan the US simply washed its hands of any responsibility for the ruin and chaos that had befallen that desolated nation. With their agricultural economy ravaged Afghan farmers quickly turned to cultivating opium poppies and Afghanistan became the world's greatest supplier of heroin. Afghan warlords rapidly fell out with each other, largely along ethnic lines and over the control of the lucrative drug trade. The CIA had been aware that one source of income for the *mujahideen* had been opium and the agency had turned a blind eye, thus playing a substantial role in the expansion of illicit drug trafficking and a rise in addiction globally.[14]

Amidst such disorder the average Afghani's life became intolerable so a substantial majority of the predominant *Pashtun* ethnic group turned toward an Islamic fundamentalist sect calling itself the *Taliban*. Before long the warlords had been routed and the Taliban proceeded to enact a rigid, puritanical and intolerant interpretation of Islamic law (*Sharia*) and brought Afghanistan under their rule. Because Osama Bin Laden had anointed himself the purifier of Islam, and because he proffered generous sums of money, the Taliban offered him safe haven. It was from al Qaeda encampments in Afghanistan that the numerous attacks upon American targets were launched.

On September 11, 2001 al Qaeda, in a classic case of what the CIA terms 'blowback', succeeded in the most destructive act of terrorism on US soil by bringing down the twin towers of the World Trade Center in New York and severely damaging the Pentagon, both of the targets striking symbols of American power.[15]

This horrific atrocity completely astonished the American public and the question 'Why do they hate us?' reverberated across the nation. Some called for a sane and diplomatic solution to the growing problem of international terrorism but that would require an honest appraisal as to why, indeed, there was so much antipathy toward the US, especially in the Muslim world and the role US policies played. That approach has been suppressed as 'unpatriotic' and 'pro-terrorist' by both the government and mainstream media, in favor of assaults and threats against Muslim countries.

DEMONIZING IRAQ FOR THE EVENTS OF 9/11 TO FOSTER HYSTERIA AT HOME

Though no evidence whatsoever indicated that Saddam Hussein had been involved in these attacks, both Vice President Richard Cheney and Defense Secretary Donald Rumsfeld immediately called for action against Iraq.[16] These and other officials falsely claimed that Saddam had plotted with al Qaeda, and possessed weapons of mass destruction (WMD) that he intended to use against his neighbors and the US itself. These charges were preposterous. While there was an al Qaeda affiliated organization in northern Iraq, the *Mujahideen e Khalq*, this group was actually under the protection of American forces in the northern Kurdish sector of Iraq and used Iraqi territory to conduct terrorism against America's enemy, Iran.[17] The hypocrisy was palpable. Since 1991 Iraq had been under an exacting UN sanctions program and the agency had dispatched inspection teams to rid the nation of WMD. Outgoing Defense Secretary William Cohen, a Republican, reported to incoming President Bush on January 10, 2001 that 'Iraq no longer poses a military threat to its neighbors'.[18] The chief weapons inspector until 1998, Scott Ritter, was a former US Marine Corps officer and a lifelong Republican. He reported clearly that Saddam's WMD had been eradicated and flatly contradicted the Bush Administration's claims, saying that 'If I had to quantify Iraq's threat I would say zero.'[19] He was followed by a Swedish diplomat and former head of the International Atomic Energy Agency who categorically denied that Iraq possessed any WMD and insisted that the US war on Iraq was illegal under international law. Numerous former CIA, State Department and arms control officials soundly endorsed these conclusions.

Nevertheless, the Bush Administration exploited and fed the hysteria in the aftermath of 9/11, such that by October 2002, when the US Congress shamefully but predictably caved in to pressure and voted to give Bush authority to invade Iraq, about two-thirds of the American public had come to believe that Saddam had been complicit in the attacks and posed an immediate threat to the US itself. In March 2003, despite personal misgivings that the intelligence was faulty at best, Secretary of State Colin Powell went before the United Nations and asserted flatly, with cartoonish and false 'evidence' that Saddam Hussein did possess biological, chemical weapons and was developing nuclear capacities. Powell also claimed that a 'high level' al Qaeda operative had informed the CIA that there was a close link between Saddam and the jihadists, although he knew that this 'information' had been obtained by intense torture, testimony that the victim later repudiated.[20] A few days later American forces invaded Iraq. Since then not a single WMD or secret weapons lab has been located.

Yet, if Iraq had been disarmed and posed no credible threat to the US and had no hand in the 9/11 attacks, what then was the *real* reason Bush lied to the American people and took them to war?

Condoleezza Rice, then National Security Adviser, put matters obliquely:

> An earthquake of the magnitude of 9/11 can shift the tectonic plates of international politics...the international system has been in flux since the collapse of Soviet power...this is a period not just of grave danger but of enormous opportunity...to create a new balance of power that favored freedom.[21]

Freedom for whom? Opportunity for what?

THE REAL REASONS THE US INVADED IRAQ

Well before Bush took office in January 2001, as a result of a Supreme Court decision and *not* the ballot, numerous former officials of his father's administration, now calling themselves *The Project for a New American Century* (PNAC), submitted a manifesto to the incoming president: 'Rebuilding America's Defenses: Strategy, Forces, and Resources for a New Century', an extension of the 1992 Defense Guidance Document written by Wolfowitz and signed by many of the very people who would soon be driving American foreign policy.[22] A comprehensive and radical revision of the tactics that had been employed for a half-century previously, the document utterly rejected multilateralism. PNAC exulted that a new prospect had arisen with the collapse of communism and called for unilateral global hegemony by the world's only superpower stating baldly that, 'At present the United States faces no global rival. America's grand strategy should aim to preserve and extend this advantageous position as far into the future as possible.' Among many stipulations the document also demanded maintaining global US pre-eminence, precluding the rise of a great power rival, 'a worldwide command and control system' and major military buildups around the globe, especially in the Middle East, even US 'Space Forces'. While decrying the possibility of nuclear proliferation the PNAC agenda also demanded a modernization of the US nuclear arsenal. In a most telling phrase the manifesto asserted that 'The need for a substantial American force presence in the Gulf transcends the issue of the regime of Saddam Hussein.'

Tellingly the PNAC manifesto cautioned that this program could probably not be implemented 'absent a new Pearl Harbor'. Miraculously, that turning point arrived on 11 September 2001.

THE PRIZE

It comes as a surprise to many that before World War II the US was the world's chief supplier of oil. Yet even before the war ended analysts knew that the future would bring growing dependence on foreign oil. That is the reason President Franklin Roosevelt cut his famous deal with the king of Saudi Arabia to provide American military protection to the kingdom in return for access to its vast reserves of oil. By 1945 the State Department had concluded that 'In Saudi Arabia, the oil resources constitute a stupendous source of strategic power, and one of the greatest material prizes in world history.'[23] Today Saudi Arabia alone produces 25 per cent of the world's oil.

Former CIA analyst and NSC staff member, Kenneth Pollack, has noted that 'the global economy built over the last 50 years rests on a foundation of inexpensive, plentiful oil, and if that foundation were removed, the global economy would collapse'.[24] The problem, as advisers close to the Bush Administration well know, is that oil production is peaking as global demand has grown owing to depletion and the simultaneous rapid industrial development in China, India and much of the so-called 'Third World'. A report commissioned by Vice President Cheney before 9/11, and undertaken by the Council on Foreign Relations and former Secretary of State James Baker, states categorically that 'The world is currently precariously close to utilizing all of its available global oil production capacity, raising the chances of an oil supply crisis with more substantial consequences than seen in three decades.'[25] The chairman of ExxonMobil declares flatly that 'About half the oil and gas volume needed to meet demand 10 years from now is not in production today.'[26] Yet US oil reserves are expected to be exhausted in 25 years while oil consumption will increase by 33 per cent, natural gas by 50 per cent and demand for electricity by 45 per cent.[27] Oil analyst Daniel Yergin asks, 'And where will that oil come from?' He answers:

One can already see the beginning of a larger contest. On one side are Russian and the Caspian countries, primarily Kazakhstan and Azerbaijan, and on the other side, the Middle East, including

Iraq...the prize of this larger race to meet growing world demand is very tangible.[28]

Thus, the US not only wants to keep Persian Gulf oil flowing but also wants to ensure that no other power or nation within the Middle East can manipulate that flow or alter its price against American interests. Cheney has stated that the country that controls Middle East oil can exercise a 'stranglehold' over the global economy.[29] Democrats do not differ. Former National Security chief Zbigniew Brzezinski has written an entire book calling for US domination of what he terms the 'chief geo-political prize':

Eurasia is the globe's largest continent and is geopolitically axial. A power that dominates Eurasia would dominate two of the three most advanced and economically productive regions. A mere glance at the map also suggests that control over Eurasia would almost automatically entail Africa's subordination...About 75 percent of the world's people live in Eurasia and most of the world's physical wealth is there as well...Eurasia accounts for about three-fourths of the world's known energy resources.[30]

The most serious competitor for access to oil is China, for decades now the most rapidly growing economy in the world, with increasing need for the same fuels required by the American economy. Analysts expect that China will match US oil imports of 10 million barrels per day by 2030.[31] Since the US has embargoed imports from countries it has labeled 'rogue states', like Iran, Syria, Sudan, Libya and Iraq, because they aid or aided groups Washington has dubbed 'terrorist', like Hamas in Palestine and Hezbollah in Lebanon, China has cut special deals with these nations for oil. When Saddam Hussein was still in power, the Chinese also brokered petroleum agreements with Iraq. Around the same time the Chinese also began negotiations with the newly independent states of Central Asia that had formerly been Soviet vassals to build oil and gas pipelines that would bring oil back to China. One of the first measures Washington took after the fall of Saddam was to nullify all previous agreements with foreign nations made by his regime, including the contract with China.

CO-OPTING THE RUSSIAN AND CHINESE BACKYARDS

A principal aim of the US is to 'check' the Chinese and Russians. When the Taliban were overthrown in 2002 the US quickly made agreements with Uzbekistan and Kyrgyzstan to station American aircraft in those nations. The Chinese interpreted these moves as sabotaging their initiative with the newly independent states of Central Asia. As one Chinese official in Xinjiang, the far western province bordering Central Asia, said:

> Our situation has much deteriorated recently. The Americans are driving us out of the region…the US troops are here in order to control the oil reserves in Central Asia…the United States has bases in Japan, the Philippines, in South Korea and Taiwan, and now here – China is going to be encircled.[32]

China's President Jiang Zemin declared that 'Beijing's policy is against strategies of force, and the US presence in Central Asia and the Middle East region…'.[33]

Many Americans remain unaware of the degree to which the US cooperated with the Taliban prior to driving them from power. One primary reason was the growing desire to build oil and gas pipelines from Central Asia through Afghanistan and Pakistan under American control from the very sources of oil the Chinese desired to tap.[34] The American oil corporation, Unocal, working with the State Department and CIA, wooed the Islamists. In the late 1990s the US government knew that the Taliban had granted haven to Osama Bin Laden and al Qaeda, and was also under great pressure from human rights and women's groups to cut all ties with the Taliban owing to their brutal treatment of women and all opponents. But these issues were not what bothered Washington. Though the Clinton Administration had winked at supplies of arms to the Taliban through Pakistan's ISI, blowback was at work again. By this time Islamic fundamentalism was threatening to overwhelm the stability of Pakistan putting the security of any pipeline more at risk. So in 1997 the US altered course and threw its support to a pipeline from the Caspian Sea region through Turkey. This ended any desire to cooperate with the Taliban. Nevertheless, when the Taliban were overthrown the US insisted on its own candidate, Hamid Karzai, who had been a consultant to Unocal, to be Afghanistan's president. Then when Karzai took office Bush appointed Zalmay Khalilzad, also a Unocal employee, as US ambassador.

So such a pipeline is still a possibility, though the overriding goal of US policy is to foster a regime in Afghanistan that will stifle the Taliban and the growing surge of Islamic fundamentalism throughout the entire region. The inherent contradiction in such a policy is clear: the deployment of more and more American and NATO forces in Muslim nations fosters the very threat to stability the US wishes to achieve.

By limiting China's access to oil the US also seeks to prevent it from becoming the superpower it is on track to become. However, with five times as many people to employ, feed and house as the US, any stifling of China by American unilateral actions is bound to produce conflict. Given that there is simply not enough oil to go around that would allow development in China, India and other nations comparable to that of the US, the logical option would be international cooperation in the creation of and investment in alternative forms of energy, rather than the kind of international competition that has brought on two terribly destructive global wars in the last century. In the current context of global economic meltdown the contest for supremacy in Eurasia, the new and deadly 'Great Game' is heating dangerously.

By supporting the Turkish route for a Caspian pipeline the US is also stepping up tension with Russia. As the second largest producer of crude oil and Europe's single source of natural gas, Russia has its own interests at stake. National security remains its highest priority. Although the US promised Russia it would not use NATO to threaten its security after the breakdown of the Soviet system, Washington has enabled former Soviet republics like the Baltic States, Poland and the Czech Republic to join the Atlantic alliance, thereby putting western arms virtually on Russia's border. Russian officials see this as an American encirclement tighter than the one during the communist era. The US has also announced a plan to station a 'missile defense system' in Poland and the Czech Republic, aimed at 'protecting' Europe from a claimed threat from Iran. Russians see this as a ploy to weaken their own defenses, since the so-called menace from Iran is not credible. Simultaneously Washington has cultivated close military ties with the former Soviet republic of Georgia in order to use Georgian territory for the planned oil pipeline to Turkey. The Russians claim (with considerable evidence[35]) that the US tacitly approved a recent military attempt by the newly independent nation of Georgia to permanently annex a region, South Ossetia, disputed between itself and Russia. Thus a new Cold War is brewing.

Though the Russians and Chinese have long had their own mutual disputes, they both have moved closer to each other to counter the increasingly aggressive moves by the US quite literally in their own backyards. As global recession deepens into depression many conditions similar to those that spawned World War II are making an ominous re-appearance.

12
Conclusion

Every American schoolchild is taught that the United States represents principles and values that are the only hope of a rational, orderly, just and peaceful society. As such the American political and moral code is supposed to be an advance over the atavistic regimes of the past and the 'rogue states' of the present, and the model for others to emulate. These values are among the most important ever articulated by humans. Although the American commitment to these principles has been honored as much in the breach of them as their fulfillment, youngsters rarely learn why or how. By and large the nation's students imbibe what the American historian James W. Loewen calls the 'Disney version' of the nation's past which propagates a collective hallucination that the US is the primary source of human progress.[1]

All are taught that one of the nation's, and all humanity's, basic rights is 'self determination' yet their education elides the true and gruesome details of how native peoples of the nation were systematically and ruthlessly deprived of their way of life. Such a fundamental entitlement, it appears, belongs only to Americans. 'Freedom' is another, yet slavery set the stage for the nation's later prosperity and is not presented as a mainstay of the economy for 250 years before it was finally abolished. Surely the descendants of slaves do not share in the bounty their forebears had made possible. Nor is much emphasis placed on the fact that although key amendments to the US Constitution ostensibly guaranteed freedmen full rights or that blacks remained second-class citizens and victims of terrible crimes for a full century after the Civil War while most white Americans pretended not to notice. Despite many advances since the Civil Rights era the majority of black Americans, Hispanics and Native Americans remain in the lowest economic strata of the country, as do a significant proportion of whites. Because the nation's vast wealth is deliberately mal-distributed, the conditions of life for those Americans who dwell on the bottom of society are violent crime, malnutrition, poor health and education, unemployment and despondency, while those at the opposite pole luxuriate in a narcissistic and bloated lifestyle. The term 'democracy' is employed constantly to imply that it actually exists, yet the republican form of government allows only the merest voice for most citizens, while ensuring that real power is concentrated in the hands of insider elites drawn primarily from corporate America who maneuver the levers of rule to serve their own interests first.

None of this is to suggest that vaunted American values are inconsequential. They can only be realized by the deliberate and courageous will to stand up for them, and we must not allow ourselves the luxury of self-deception that they are already attained. The United States is not Nazi Germany, though racism and militarism remain embedded in the culture. It is not a totalitarian dictatorship, though there are many who would foster a command society if they could. The 'American creed' did not emerge full blown from the head of George Washington or Thomas Jefferson but from the constant struggles of those Americans who took the language of the Declaration of Independence at face value and demanded that the Bill of Rights apply to them. This conviction explains the limited extent to which the United States has achieved, at least for the middle classes, the semblance of a humane and comfortable society, though the actual workings of the economy are steadily eroding that.

Visitors to the nation's capital in Washington, DC cannot fail to see the Capitol District's physical resemblance to ancient Rome at the height of its glory (the slums of the city also parallel those of Rome). Those who imagined the capital at the time of its planning envisioned the Roman Republic as their model but the architecture is that of imperial Rome. Perhaps, unconsciously, planners understood what Benjamin Franklin had warned about – that republics up to his time had always degenerated into empire or dictatorship.

The Roman style temple that is the public face of the National Archives on the Washington mall houses the nation's founding documents: original copies of the Declaration of Independence and the Constitution. One enters through gilded portals to a chamber consciously designed to evoke a semi-sacral atmosphere. Along the walls are murals depicting the Founders engaged in the formative acts that gave birth to the nation. Both the Constitution and Declaration hold center stage and are housed in glass tabernacles atop what can only be called altars. Inside are the sacred texts which, in order to get close enough to read, a pilgrim must kneel. All of this was carefully designed to foster what amounts to a quasi-religious experience to drive home the sanctity of the founding of the republic.

It is fitting that we regard the documents and the sanctuary that enshrines them as symbols of indispensable principles. But at bottom the texts remain mere scraps of paper in the absence of a genuine commitment to the values they assert as the birthright of all peoples, not only Americans.

If millions of fellow Americans are still ill-housed or ill-fed, if lies are the medium by which presidents manipulate the citizenry into war against peoples who have done us no harm and our policies rain death, desolation and despair upon innocents in foreign lands, to what degree can we really claim adherence to the creed we profess?

The prosperity and freedoms of favored American citizens has always required that others be deprived, and has always been premised on exploitation in the forms of land grabs, slavery, low wages, the repression of labor rights, currency and interest rate manipulations and direct corporate and military involvement in other nations. Resistance to these measures, at home or overseas, has always been met with violence or war.

Americans delude themselves when they insist that we are a peace-loving people who will go to any extreme to avoid violence. War is the American way of life. The American project began in violence, the nation was born amidst blood and the growth of the American republic is matched by a corresponding chain of carnage from the Pequot Massacre to Wounded Knee to My Lai and to the wars in Afghanistan and Iraq; all alleged to be the fault of others. When the events of 9/11 killed 3,000 people the nation was profoundly traumatized, primarily because Americans could not understand how such outrages could happen to them. Yet the American people, through their government's policies, have been visiting horror throughout the world since the US attained the pinnacle of the global power hierarchy in 1945. These are facts well remembered where they took place, yet all but unknown, or forgotten, in America.

Few voices are raised in condemnation of the suffering we have brought literally to millions. At every turn the bloodbaths were carried out in the name of 'freedom and democracy' over the forces of darkness, led by the only people capable of defending such principles. Yet, ulterior motives lay behind every American war, primarily to enhance the license and material plenty of some Americans, never all, at the expense of those whose land, resources, self-determination or very lives were taken, including the Americans who constituted the armed forces. Thus we delude ourselves that ravaging countries like Vietnam or Iraq is really delivering them from evil; that inscribing the names of tens of thousands upon our own cenotaphs makes the sacrifice holy and acceptable.

Although the United States participated in the creation of international law, now, under the pose of a war on terror, it has flouted the very norms it previously endorsed, all but formally repudiating the Geneva Convention. Should it surprise us that the lawlessness of the American invasion of Iraq, support for corrupt princes, sheiks and emirs, secret torture bases and many other direct or covert interventions in the Muslim world, find their rejoinder in the lawless violence of Islamic extremism? Having fomented Islamic terror by its own coups, assassinations, military forays and support for Israel's continued settlement of land that is supposed to belong to the nation of Palestine, the US government still pretends, in keeping with hallowed ritual, that America is an innocent victim beset by a new set of evildoers. The refrain is always the same: official rhetoric intones that only more armed violence can resolve the problem.

American culture, as the heir of imperial Europe, pretends to a moral superiority but the truth stands naked in the neo-colonies, and as the American economy unravels after decades of being managed as a gargantuan Ponzi[2] scheme, and our collective self-deceptions come undone, we arrive at a critical crossroads.

As this volume reaches its editors the American people have elected a new president whose central campaign guarantee is 'change'. He had been the only presidential hopeful roundly to condemn the march to war in Iraq and he promised that, if elected, he would end it. Declaring, however, that the Iraq War had diverted resources and attention from the real danger, terrorism, he also said that he would increase forces in Afghanistan, thereby ominously foreshadowing an intensification of that conflict. The vast majority of Americans who voted for him did so on the strength of his anti-war credentials. Just as all his predecessors have pledged, Barack Obama vows to sweep 'insiders' from their perches and sinecures and appoint as his advisers those whose commitment is to a fundamental national re-orientation and renewal of the American promise. As his inaugural address declared, 'Those who see war must imagine peace.'

Yet Obama's retention of Robert Gates as Secretary of Defense, his appointment of a prominent lobbyist for a major military contractor as Gates' deputy and his selections of Hillary Clinton as Secretary of State and of retired General James Jones as National Security Adviser is disconcerting at best. In fact all of his major cabinet appointments are pillars of the Washington establishment.

His defenders would undoubtedly argue that Obama must make such appointments or risk the ire of his political opposition, and then see his initiatives grind to a halt. This is the all-too-familiar refrain after every American election.

Gates is a career CIA insider who subsequently became head of CIA himself. Another well-respected career CIA analyst who has condemned both the invasion of Iraq and Afghanistan has called Gates a 'panderer' for his proclivity to tell his superiors what they want to hear, or to keep their secrets.[3] During the Iran–Contra Affair of the mid-1980s he was deputy director and, according to the special prosecutor appointed by Congress to investigate the egregious violation of law involved, was close enough to participants to know a great deal about what really transpired. Yet his claim that he could not remember key incidents served to hide the truth of the many violations of law that transpired and to protect the most prominent malefactors from prosecution.[4]

The Iran–Contra scandal involved secret and illegal transfers of arms to the same Iranian leaders who had held 52 Americans hostage for over a year and who were subsequently cut off from American diplomatic recognition. Money paid by the Iranians for the weapons was then funneled to the Contras (*contrarevolutionarios*) who were attempting the overthrow of the Sandinista government in Nicaragua in violation of stipulations from Congress that barred such aid. Numerous members of the Reagan Administration, including vice president George H.W. Bush, were involved but only a few were punished and most of them subsequently received pardons. Gates' silence clearly made him an accomplice to the full extent of conspiracy and lawbreaking.

Gates must also be counted among the bellicose faithful who believe that the US rightfully employs armed violence against the weak. He has never urged that major powers should be the target of American military strikes, only those who cannot fight back. He condemned the 'half-measures' that he said had led to defeat in Vietnam, although the US dropped about 12 million tons of bombs on that beleaguered nation; and he advocated that the US bomb the tiny nation of Nicaragua in the 1980s to dislodge the Sandinistas, as the Nicaraguan government was known, despite the fact that it had won fair election as the choice of a large majority of Nicaraguans. When he was named to replace Donald Rumsfeld as Defense Secretary in 2005 Gates immediately asserted that the increase of 30,000 troops in Iraq had effectively turned the tide in favor of the United States and advocated a similar 'surge' of troops for Afghanistan. Writing recently in the house organ of the American Foreign Policy Establishment, Gates avows that 'the United States needs a military whose ability to kick down the door is matched by its ability to clean up the mess and even rebuild the house afterward'.[5] Clearly he believes that, despite past failures of the British and Soviets to subdue that nation, Afghanistan can be transformed into an American client state, as does his new commander-in-chief.

Gates is also among the hawks who fear the emergence of China and who call for a major buildup of high-tech weapons systems to meet any potential attempt by the Chinese to thwart American goals in Asia. As the most populous nation on earth, China has its own regional aims, but these too often come into conflict with the longstanding aims of US policy in East Asia. The national security priesthood's ritual incantations about an omnipresent threat from China enforces a collective amnesia. The American public too easily forgets that China has experienced American armed violence before, on its territory and on its very doorstep. It never seems to occur to us that China wishes to protect itself from a perceived threat emanating from ourselves. The following is how Gates perceives China's emergence:

> In the case of China, Beijing's investments in cyber-warfare, anti-satellite warfare, antiaircraft and anti-ship weaponry, submarines, and ballistic missiles *could threaten the United States' primary means to project its power* and help its allies in the Pacific: bases, air and sea assets, and the networks that support them. *This will put a premium on the United States' ability to strike from over the horizon* and employ missile defenses and will require shifts from short-range to longer-range systems, such as the next-generation bomber. [author's emphasis][6]

Gates is also among those insiders who are knee-jerk antagonists to Russia's foreign policy and who claim that Russia is fomenting a new Cold War, when it is American policies that frighten a much weaker Russia. Since the Soviet breakup Washington has clearly pursued Brzezinski's prescription to dominate Eurasia. When our presumed enemies build up their arsenals they do so primarily in fear of our own.

The Clinton and Bush Administrations cultivated close military relations with the new Republic of Georgia, primarily to promote the construction of a pipeline to carry Caspian Sea oil and gas to

Western markets, coming directly into competition with Russian desires to control the flow of these critical fuels derived from what they see as their sphere of interest. Both administrations also hoped that Georgia might become a stationary aircraft carrier for the employment of American firepower against 'threats', perhaps like Iran. But the region of Georgia known as South Ossetia is populated by a majority of Russians so the area has been in dispute since the breakup of the Soviet Union in 1991. The ethnic Russians wish to join Russia and see the nearby Russian army as their protector. In August 2008 Georgian forces, undoubtedly with the foreknowledge of their American military advisers, attacked a major Russian enclave and killed many civilians, prompting a Russian incursion in response and a subsequent bloody encounter. The Bush Administration and Gates instantly proclaimed that this was resurgent Russian imperialism and called for a strengthening of NATO, already condemned by Russia for drawing Poland and the Czech Republic into the alliance, and the plan to station anti-missile bases in these two countries.

> The images of Russian tanks rolling into Georgia last August were a reminder that nation-states and their militaries do still matter. Both Russia and China have increased their defense spending and modernization programs to include air defense and fighter capabilities that in some cases approach the United States' own.[7]

Russia could easily have annexed South Ossetia but it seems intent on abiding by international law and recognition of established national boundaries, and seeks diplomatic ways to resolve the issue, unlike the behavior of the US in Iraq. Gates' interpretation implies a determination to meet Russia on armed terms, a very dangerous proposition that echoes the origins of the Cold War when the US deliberately took steps to ensure that the USSR would become an enemy at the very moment that a genuine prospect for peace and international cooperation was present.

Gates' long history as water carrier for covert and violent interventions in the affairs of other nations makes him a curious candidate to wage the peace President Obama says he desires.

Though he declared in his campaign that lobbyists would be banned from his administration, Obama has also nominated William Lynn as Gates' deputy, a lobbyist for the Raytheon Corporation, a major military contractor receiving billions of dollars from the

US Treasury for the Patriot missile system, the Navy's Tomahawk Missile and an Air Force global positioning satellite. Ever since World War I, when the military-industrial complex President Eisenhower warned against in 1961 really came into existence, it has developed a vested interest in a permanent state of tension and preparation for war. As our history demonstrates unambiguously, when the US prepares for war it usually goes to war.

Secretary of State Hillary Clinton's vote in October 2002 to grant Bush the war-making powers he subsequently exercised to invade Iraq is well known. She claimed during her failed presidential campaign that she was misled, as did John Kerry before her in 2004. Both of these senators were well placed to know that the Bush/Cheney/Rumsfeld claims that Iraq possessed weapons of mass destruction and had close ties to al Qaeda were patently false. Yet because both were political opportunists unwilling to make a stand against the growing hysteria induced by Bush's lies, because that might have derailed their ambitions, they helped to enable the crimes that ensued. Clinton also made it clear during the 2008 campaign that she would have no moral qualms about nuking Iran.

The title 'National Security Adviser' implies responsibilities centered on the protection of the United States from threats to that security but from the time the position was created in 1949 as the US embarked on the Cold War it has been a key player in the numerous interventions and wars that have deliberately been pursued. The National Security State requires enemies and it functions to create them and then exploits that manufactured state of affairs to promote further actions in the name of national security. Any criticism that Obama may face that he is soft or naive will be blunted with retired four-star General James Jones at his side.[8]

It is no secret that the United States has overextended itself. For that reason it has long desired that the North Atlantic Treaty Organization follow its lead in Afghanistan. No matter that NATO was established in 1949 to confront a claimed Soviet threat in Europe; no matter that the presumed threat vanished in 1991. NATO has become its own vested interest. NATO receives the bulk of its operational funding from the US and many of its weapons systems are linked to American military corporations. If this vast bureaucracy is to retain the flow of lucrative contracts, if the functionaries are to continue to draw their salaries, then a new and improved mission for it must be drawn up. If the US is to be 'Globocop', so American strategic thinking goes, then NATO should be its deputy.

Member states of the alliance initially provided assistance after 9/11 but the interests of the new European Union are coming into conflict with the American priorities for NATO, so they are now re-thinking their policies. National Security Adviser General James Jones served as the Supreme Allied Commander of the NATO coalition from 2003 to 2006 and knows all the people who need to be re-persuaded that it is in their interest to prevent Afghanistan from again becoming a haven for the Taliban and al Qaeda, and hence a source of jihadists to dwell among the large Muslim populations of the European Union.

If a resurgent and strengthened NATO is to emerge during the Obama Administration then this will alienate Russia even more and cause her to do what it did when first confronted by this alliance. It will intensify its own arms buildup, improve its nuclear arsenal and the world will be back at five minutes to midnight.

As a career military officer Jones has always followed orders. His advice to General Peter Pace when he assumed the post of Chairman of the Joint Chiefs of Staff was 'You're going to face a debacle and be part of the debacle in Iraq.' Reputedly, Jones was 'so worried about Iraq and the way Rumsfeld ran things that he wondered if he himself should not resign in protest'.[9] Yet he did not. Later he served on a commission evaluating military progress in Iraq. Despite deep misgivings he recommended that the US stay the course: 'Understand the fact that regardless how you got there, there is a strategic price of enormous consequence for failure in Iraq.' So there we have the rub. The long term global strategic goals of the US will be jeopardized; the facts of countless deaths and the destruction of an entire society be damned.

The continued military attacks against Islamic peoples, and the threats to engage in others in Pakistan and Iran, which as Obama has said remain 'on the table', do as much for Taliban and al Qaeda recruitment as any preachments in their religious schools or *madrassas*. The so-called progressive wing of the establishment is on exactly the same page as the neo-conservatives when it comes to dealing with the emergence of Islamic fundamentalism and the intent of its most extreme devotees to wage jihad upon the US and the west: war to the death. No one in power is willing to contemplate honestly why this contest has emerged in the first place, and thereby to remove that cause. Muslims lived side by side with the godless communists for 60 years without jihad. It was not until the Soviets invaded Afghanistan that Islamists coalesced in militant opposition to the communists, with the full encouragement of the US. They turned their guns around against their American sponsors after the Soviet withdrawal only because the US deployed troops on the soil held most sacred to Muslims. Yet, even despite the American support for the Shah in Iran, attempted assassinations of Nasser in Egypt, intervention in Lebanon in 1958 and 1983, support for the corrupt regimes in Saudi Arabia and Kuwait and the all but formal alliance with Israel, it took that fateful foray into Saudi Arabia to mobilize the Islamists against the US. George W. Bush threw down the gauntlet when he employed the term 'crusade' to call Americans to war after 9/11.

Terrorism is not an existential threat to the United States though another global war will be and the continued US armed intervention in the Muslim world shows every indication of promoting just that.

As this book goes to press President Barack Obama has stated that American combat forces will be withdrawn from Iraq by August 2011. Yet, the military has also made it clear that at least 50,000 other troops, not classified as 'combat' will remain. This figure does not include the enormous number of civilian contractors, probably around 100,000 in both Iraq and Afghanistan, who will also serve the empire's needs. Many of these can only be described as paramilitary mercenaries. Obama has also ordered a substantial increase of American forces in Afghanistan, appointed a specialist in counterinsurgency to direct the escalation of the war there and stepped up the employment of predator aircraft, or pilotless drones to attack the Taliban and al Qaeda. While the US military claims that these efforts are weakening the jihadists, the intensified warfare is also killing many more civilians, thereby undermining any claim that the US is winning the hearts and minds of ordinary Afghanis. Indeed, just as American actions in Vietnam did much for Vietcong recruitment, so American war efforts have driven the Taliban into neighboring Pakistan, where consequences similar to the civilian casualties in Afghanistan, are fostering jihadist recruits in that country as well. Thus, what can only be characterized as President Obama's war is inexorably being widened and deepened. Many observers warn that the new president is falling into a trap similar to the one in Vietnam that undid President Lyndon Johnson's presidency.

Obama seems to believe he can do what every other nation attempting a similar goal has failed ignominiously to accomplish in that part of the world. He cannot be oblivious to the parallel dangers his policies may incur with respect to Russia and China, or how Pakistan's devolution into chaos may affect its already tense relations with nuclear armed India, yet he is wading into the slough full speed ahead. Meanwhile, America's albatross-like ally, Israel, has elected an extreme right-wing government that is obsessed with Iran's nuclear program and threatens constantly to destroy its nuclear facilities. Should such an attack come to pass, cataclysmic violence throughout the entire region will be the result, and at the very least will cause the utter collapse of the global economy, dependent as it is on access to Gulf oil. That in turn would foster conditions worse than those that generated World War II.

Notes

CHAPTER 2

1. David E. Stannard, *American Holocaust: The Conquest of the Americas* (New York, Oxford University Press, 1992) x.
2. Stannard, x.
3. Charles C. Mann, *1491: New Revelations of the Americas Before Columbus* (New York, Vintage, 2006) 14.
4. Theodore Roosevelt, *The Winning of the West, Vol. IV* (Lincoln, University of Nebraska Press, 1995) 44.
5. Mann, 16.
6. Stannard, 10–11, 262.
7. Stannard, 69.
8. Stannard, 72.
9. Howard Zinn, 'Columbus and Western Civilization', in Russ Kick (ed.) *You Are Being Lied To* (New York, The Disinformation Company, Ltd., 2005) 212.
10. Zinn, 205.
11. Stannard, 75.
12. Stannard, 33.
13. Mann, 143.
14. Stannard, 8.
15. Jared Diamond, *Guns, Germs, and Steel: The Fates of Human Societies* (New York, W.W. Norton, 1999).
16. American Social History Project, *Who Built America* (New York, Pantheon, 1989) 15–16.
17. Mann, 143.
18. Mann, 144.
19. *Apocalypto* (Directed and produced by Mel Gibson, Touchstone films, 2006).
20. Mann, 134.
21. Mann, 90.
22. Stannard, 89.
23. John Wood Sweet, 'Sea Changes', in Robert Applebaum and John Wood Sweet (eds) *Envisioning an English Empire: Jamestown and the Making of the North Atlantic World* (Philadelphia, University of Pennsylvania Press, 2005) 3.
24. James Horn, 'The Conquest of Eden: Possession and Dominion in Early Virginia', in Applebaum and Sweet, 43.
25. Applebaum and Sweet, 10.
26. Applebaum and Sweet, 41–2.
27. American Social History Project, 36.
28. Applebaum and Sweet, 42.
29. Applebaum and Sweet, 43.
30. Stannard, 106.
31. Applebaum and Sweet, 47.
32. Applebaum and Sweet, 47.

33. Edmund S. Morgan, *American Slavery–American Freedom: The Ordeal of Colonial Virginia* (New York, W.W. Norton, 1975) 99.
34. Stannard, 106.
35. Morgan, 233.
36. Stannard, 107.
37. Stannard, 107.
38. Applebaum and Sweet, 44.
39. Mann, 40.
40. Mann, 37.
41. Mann, 37. While 'Squanto' is celebrated as the native who taught the Pilgrims, this may well be myth. There is no evidence that Indians planted fish with their maize. Such practices existed in Europe. Tisquantum may well have learned this technique there.
42. Richard Drinnon, *Facing West: The Metaphysics of Indian Hating and Empire Building* (New York, Schocken Books, 1990), 60.
43. Drinnon, 61.
44. Drinnon, 43.
45. Jill Lepore, *The Name of War: King Philip's War and the Origins of American Identity* (New York, Knopf, 1998) 93.
46. Eric B. Schultze and Michael J. Tougias, *King Philip's War: The History and Legacy of America's Forgotten Conflict* (Woodstock, Vermont, The Countryman Press, 1999) 4.
47. Lepore, 150–70. Also, Schultze and Tougias.
48. Lepore, 44.

CHAPTER 3

1. By the time of British colonization in North America the term 'Anglo-Saxon' had become commonplace in British usage. In reality there was no such 'ethnic' purity in the British Isles. The population there was an admixture of Picts, Celts, Angles, Saxon, Normans and many others. The British upper classes fastened on to the myth that Englishmen were free before the Norman conquest of 1066 and hearkened back to a golden age of Anglo-Saxon racial superiority and imagined themselves as its inheritor. Colonists under British rule were even more 'mongrelized' since many came from Germany, France, the Netherlands, Spain etc. But those of direct English ancestry adopted this myth and overlaid it on their ideology of divine mission. After the American Revolution the term came to apply to all white Americans. I will use the term they adopted for themselves and which many historians employ as well – Anglo-Americans. See, Reginald Horsman, *Race and Manifest Destiny: The Origins of American Racial Anglo-Saxonism* (Cambridge, Mass., Harvard University Press, 1981).
2. Robert Kagan, *Dangerous Nation: America's Place in the World from Its Earliest Days to the Dawn of the Twentieth Century* (New York, Knopf, 2006) 13. The term is Kagan's. He is among the 'neo-Conservative' intellectuals who have shaped American foreign policy in the George W. Bush Administration. He argues with great approval what to him is the obvious fact of American superiority and its derivation from its British parent. Civilizationism, according to Kagan, is not 'simple' racism. The British then, and, by implication Americans today, bestow liberties and benefits and act as civilizing agents for backward, or barbarous, people, even if this is done by violence.

3. Kagan, 18.
4. Edmund S. Morgan, *The Birth of the Republic, 1763–1789* (Chicago, University of Chicago Press, 1992) 108.
5. In the middle of the eighteenth century the population of New France was 75,000. Anglo-Americans numbered 1.5 million.
6. Kagan, 23.
7. Kagan, 29–30.
8. Gary B. Nash, et al., *The American People: Creating a Nation and a Society*, 2nd Edition (New York, Harper Collins, 1990) 99.
9. Nash, 139.
10. Fred Anderson, *The Crucible of War: The Seven Years' War and the Fate of Empire in British North America, 1754–1766* (New York, Alfred E. Knopf, 2000) 571.
11. Kagan, 31.
12. Kagan, 37.
13. Ray Raphael, *A Peoples' History of the American Revolution* (New York, HarperPerennial, 2002) 129.
14. Raphael, 320–30.
15. Howard Zinn, *A People's History of the United States* (New York: HarperPerennial, 1995) 90.
16. Zinn, 93–4.
17. Zinn, 95.
18. Zinn, 96.
19. William Earl Weeks, *Building the Continental Empire: From the American Revolution to the Civil War* (Chicago, Ivan R. Dee, 1996) 19.
20. Zinn. 97.
21. Charles Beard, *An Economic Interpretation of the Constitution of the United States* (New York, Macmillan, 1935).
22. Samuel Elliot Morrison, *The Oxford History of the United States 1778–1917* (New York, Oxford University Press, 1927) 182.
23. Michael J. Graetz and Deborah H. Schenk, *Federal Income Taxation: Principles and Policies* (New York: Foundation Press, 2005) 4.

CHAPTER 4

1. Sidney Lens, *The Forging of the American Empire: A History of American Imperialism from the Revolution to Vietnam* (New York, Thomas Y. Crowell Co., 1974) 23–4.
2. Lens, 27.
3. William Earl Weeks, *Building the Continental Empire: American Expansion from the Revolution to the Civil War* (Chicago, Ivan R. Dee, 1996) 24–5.
4. Robert Kagan, *Dangerous Nation: America's Place in the World from its Earliest Days to the Dawn of the Twentieth Century* (New York, Alfred A. Knopf, 2006) 93.
5. Kagan, 100.
6. Anders Stephanson, *Manifest Destiny: American Expansion and the Empire of Right* (New York, Hill and Wang, 1995) 24.
7. Richard Drinnon, *Facing West: The Metaphysics of Indian Hating and Empire Building* (New York, Schocken Books, 1990) 90–103.
8. Weeks, 33.

9. Lens, 80–6.
10. Kagan, 153.
11. Lens, 90.
12. Lens, 97.
13. Stephanson, 26.
14. Stephanson, 27.
15. Weeks, 80.
16. Howard Zinn, *A People's History of the United States* (New York, HarperPerennial, 1980) 133.
17. James Wilson, *The Earth Shall Weep: A History of Native America* (New York, Grove Press, 2000) 170.
18. Measurements of skulls and bone structure were still being propagated as evidence of racial hierarchy by the Nazis, but they originated among British and American scientists and medical theorists in the 1840s and gained wide acceptance as proof and justification of both nations' 'right' or destiny to supersede inferior races. These ideas later undergirded the equally pseudo-scientific of Social Darwinism. See, Reginald Horsman, *Race and Manifest Destiny: The Origins of American Racial Anglo-Saxonism* (Cambridge, MA, Harvard University Press, 1981).
19. Horsman, 227.
20. Horsman, 243.
21. Horsman, 212.
22. Frederick Merck, *Manifest Destiny and Mission in American History* (Cambridge, MA, Harvard University Press, 1995) 88.
23. Zinn, 149.
24. Weeks, 121.
25. Zinn, 152.
26. Stephanson, 53.
27. Stephanson, 54.
28. Zinn, 152.
29. Zinn, 163.
30. Weeks, 124.
31. Zinn, 162, 165.
32. Weeks, 124.
33. Weeks, 126.
34. Weeks, 125–8.
35. Weeks, 35.

CHAPTER 5

1. Drew Gilpin Faust, *This Republic of Suffering: Death and the American Civil War* (New York, Vintage, 2009).
2. W. E.B. Dubois, *Black Reconstruction in America: An Essay Toward A History of the Part That Black Folk Played in the Attempt to Reconstruct Democracy in America* (New York, Russell and Russell, 1935) 671.
3. Dee Brown, *Bury My Heart at Wounded Knee: An Indian History of the American West* (New York, Bantam, 1970) 88–91; Stan Hoig, *The Sand Creek Massacre* (Norman, OK, University of Oklahoma Press, 1977) 61–3; Derrick Jensen, *A Language Older Than Words* (New York, Context Books, 2000) 27–9.

4. David E. Stannard, *American Holocaust: The Conquest of the New World* (New York, Oxford University Press, 1992) 126.

5. Walter LaFeber, *The New Empire: An Interpretation of American Expansion, 1860–1898* (Ithaca, Cornell University Press, 1980) 12.

6. LaFeber, 17.

7. LaFeber, 17.

8. Robert V. Bruce, *1877: Year of Violence* (New York, Quadrangle, 1959) 320.

9. Thomas J. McCormick, *China Market: America's Quest for Informal Empire, 1893–1901* (Chicago, Ivan R. Dee, 1967) 25.

10. Richard O. Boyer and Herbert M. Morais, *Labor's Untold Story* (New York, United Electrical Radio and Machine Workers of America, 1979) 65.

11. In 1914 National Guard forces in Colorado attacked mine workers at the Rockefeller-owned Colorado Fuel and Iron Company, who were on strike to join the United Mine Workers Union. The militia set fire to a tent encampment while the miners and their families slept. One man, five women and 13 children were killed. See Boyer and Morais, 190.

12. For a comprehensive analysis of the process that led to consensus among elites for 'reform' that was intended to preserve the economic and political power of the elites see, Gabriel Kolko, *The Triumph of Conservatism: A New Interpretation of American History* (New York, The Free Press, 1963).

13. McCormick, 30.

14. Imperial rivals had similar problems and envisioned similar solutions. Cecil Rhodes declared that:

> My cherished idea is a solution for the social problem, i.e. in order to save the 40,000,000 inhabitants of the United Kingdom from a bloody civil war, we colonial statesmen must acquire new lands to settle the surplus population, to provide new markets for the goods produced by them in the factories and mines.

Quoted in Lloyd C. Gardner, *Imperial America: American Foreign Policy since 1898* (New York, Harcourt Brace Jovanovich, 1976) 18.

15. LaFeber, 27.

16. Robert Kagan, *Dangerous Nation: America's Place in the World From Its Earliest Days to the Dawn of the Twentieth Century* (New York, Alfred A. Knopf, 2006) 249–50.

17. Kagan, 250.

18. LaFeber, 29.

19. LaFeber, 36.

20. LaFeber, 55.

21. LaFeber, 54.

22. Gardner, 34.

23. Howard Beale, *Theodore Roosevelt and the Rise of America to World Power* (New York, Collier, 1956) 57.

24. William Appleman Williams, *The Tragedy of American Diplomacy* (New York, Dell, 1972) 34.

25. Julius William Pratt, *Expansionists of 1898: The Acquisition of Hawaii and the Spanish Islands* (Chicago, Quadrangle Books, 1964) 34–5.

26. LaFeber, 268.

27. LaFeber, 262.
28. Beale, 59.
29. Beale, 61–6.
30. LaFeber, 70.
31. LaFeber, 85–95.
32. LaFeber, 80–5.
33. Richard Hofstadter, *Social Darwinism in American Thought* (Boston, Beacon Press, 1955).
34. LaFeber, 72–80.
35. Gardner, 25.
36. Beale, 49–50.
37. LaFeber, 410–11.
38. LaFeber, 84.
39. Senator Albert J. Beveridge, *Speech: In Support of an American Empire,* January 9, 1899. *Congressional Record,* 56th Congress, Sess. I., 704–12.

CHAPTER 6

1. Howard K. Beale, *Theodore Roosevelt and the Rise of America to World Power* (New York, Collier, 1973) 69–72.
2. Walter Karp, *The Politics of War: The Story of How Two Wars Altered Forever the Political Life of the American Republic* (New York, Franklin Square Press, 2003) 70.
3. Karp, 80.
4. Howard Zinn, *A People's History of the United States* (New York, Harper Collins, 1980) 292.
5. Zinn, 296.
6. Zinn, 296.
7. Zinn, 299–301.
8. Karp, 96.

CHAPTER 7

1. Walter Karp, *The Politics of War: The Story of Two Wars Which Altered Forever the Political Life of the American Republic* (1890–1920) (New York, Franklin Square Press, 2003). In an exchange between Robert Lansing and Wilson on August 4, 1915, the Secretary of State told the president that a state of war with Germany would increase our 'usefulness in the restoration of peace'. Wilson answered that Lansing's view 'runs along very much the same lines as my own thoughts'. Karp, 209.
2. William R. Keylor, *The Twentieth Century World: An International History* (New York, Oxford University Press, 1984) 54.
3. Thomas J. McCormick, *America's Half-Century: United States Foreign Policy in the Cold War* (Baltimore, The Johns Hopkins University Press, 1989) 21.
4. Gordon S. Levin, *Woodrow Wilson and World Politics: America's Response to Revolution* (New York, Oxford University Press, 1968) 1.
5. Howard Zinn, *A People's History of the United States* (New York, Harper Perennial, 1980) 353.
6. Levin, 22.

7. Sidney Lens, *The Forging of the American Empire: A History of American Imperialism From the Revolution to Vietnam* (New York, Thomas Crowell Co., 1974) 239.
8. William Appleman Williams, *The Contours of American History* (Chicago, Quadrangle Books, 1966) 410.
9. Levin, 22.
10. Levin, 34.
11. Levin, 25.
12. Lens, 240.
13. Karp, 181–3.
14. Lens, 240.
15. Keylor, 70–1.
16. Lens, 253.
17. Karp, 224.
18. Lens, 250.
19. Lens, 256.
20. Karp, 213.
21. Lens, 260.
22. Karp, 227.
23. Lens, 259.
24. Karp, 197.
25. Lens, 260.
26. Lens, 261.
27. Keylor, 72.
28. Zinn, 358.
29. Zinn, 363.
30. Keylor, 73.
31. Daniel Yergin, *The Prize: The Epic Quest For Oil, Money, and Power* (New York, Simon and Schuster, 1991) 155–7.

CHAPTER 8

1. Bruce Russett, *No Clear and Present Danger: A Skeptical View of US Entry Into World War II* (New York, Harper and Row, 1972) 44–62.
2. Historians have long debated whether the ten-point message delivered by Secretary Hull to the Japanese on November 26, 1941 was an ultimatum or roadmap for a peaceful outcome of the US–Japanese dispute. Hull himself said 'You cannot give an ultimatum to a proud people and not expect them to react violently.' See, United States Congress, *Report of the Joint Committee on the Investigation of the Pearl Harbor Attack, 79th Congress, 2nd Session, 1946, Part 5* (Washington, DC, US Government Printing Office, 1946) 2175.
3. Stephen R. Shalom, 'VJ Day: Remembering the Pacific War', *Z Magazine*, July–August, 1995.
4. Lloyd C. Gardner, *Imperial America: American Foreign Policy Since 1989* (New York, Harcourt Brace Jovanovich, 1976) 144.
5. Shalom.
6. Russett, 78–9.
7. Nicholson Baker, *Human Smoke: The Beginnings of World War II, The End of Civilization* (New York, Simon and Schuster, 2008) 55.

8. James O. Richardson, *On the Treadmill to Pearl Harbor: The Memoirs of Admiral James O. Richardson, USN* (Washington, DC, Naval History Division, Department of the Navy, 1973) 427.

9. Henry Lewis Stimson, *On Active Service in Peace and War* (New York, Harper and Row, 1948).

10. John Toland, *Infamy: Pearl Harbor and Its Aftermath* (New York, Berkeley Books, 1982) 264; David M. Kennedy, *Freedom From Fear: The American People in Depression and War, 1929–1945* (New York, Oxford University Press, 1999) 526.

11. Edward S. Miller, *War Plan Orange: The US Strategy to Defeat Japan 1897–1945* (Washington, DC, Naval Institute Press, 1991).

12. Herbert Feis, *The Road To Pearl Harbor* (Princeton, Princeton University Press, 1971) 127n.

13. Toland, 262.

14. Toland, 261–2.

15. MAGIC was the generic code-name for the overall program of decoding Japanese transcripts. See, Robert B. Stinnett, *Day of Deceit: The Truth About FDR and Pearl Harbor* (New York, The Free Press, 2000).

16. Michael S. Sherry, *The Rise of American Air Power: The Creation of Armageddon* (New Haven, Yale University Press, 1991) 109.

17. Henry L. Stimson, *Diary*, November 25, 1941. Quoted in Patrick J. Heardon, *Roosevelt Confronts Hitler: America's Entry Into World War II* (DeKalb, Illinois, Northern Illinois University Press, 1987) 218.

18. Stinnett, 171–2; Toland, 6–7.

19. Stinnett, 189–98; Toland, 284–317. A BBC television broadcast in 1989 presented an interview with one of the Americans who plotted the course of the Japanese fleet. See *Sacrifice at Pearl Harbor* (British Broadcasting Corporation, 1989).

20. Toland, 316.

21. One of the most stunning and dramatic examples of this advantage was the ability to lure the main Japanese carrier fleet into the trap set by the US Navy at Midway in June 1942 where Nippon's most important vessels were sunk. After this defeat Japan's grand strategy to encompass and defend the western Pacific was effectively negated, thereby signaling all but certain Japanese defeat. Another was MAGIC's ability to know Admiral Yamamoto's tactical travel plans. American aircraft ambushed his plane, killing him and decapitating the Japanese high command.

22. Stinnett, 98–118; Toland, 314–15.

23. Kennedy, 535–44.

24. Many sources deal with these issues. See, John Jacob Beck, *MacArthur and Wainwright: Sacrifice of the Philippines* (Albuquerque, University of New Mexico Press, 1974); Lewis Brereton, *The Brereton Diaries: The War in the Pacific, Middle East and Europe, October 1941–8 May 1945* (New York, Morrow, 1946); William Manchester, *American Caesar, Douglas MacArthur, 1880–1964* (Boston, Little Brown, 1978); Louis Morton, *United States Army in World War II: The War in the Pacific: The Fall of the Philippines* (Washington, DC Office of the Chief of Military History, Department of the Army, 1953).

25. *Why We Fight!* This remarkable eight-part documentary sponsored by the Department of War, and shown in every movie theater in the US, employed the

latest propaganda techniques and even borrowed footage from Nazi propaganda to stand it on its head.

26. Thomas J. McCormick, *America's Half-Century: United States Foreign Policy in the Cold War* (Baltimore, Johns Hopkins University Press, 1989) 17–36.

27. This was false. Churchill had already pledged to send the Royal Navy to Canada and the Caribbean in the event that England should have fallen to a Nazi invasion. See Robert A. Divine, *Roosevelt and World War II* (New York, Penguin Books, 1970) 34.

28. Warren S. Kimball, *The Most Unsordid Act: Lend-Lease, 1939–1941* (Baltimore, Johns Hopkins University Press, 1969) 236.

29. Russett, 79.

30. Patrick J. Heardon, *Roosevelt Confronts Hitler: America's Entry Into World War II* (Northern Illinois University Press, 1987) 184.

31. William L. Neumann, *America Encounters Japan: From Perry to MacArthur* (New York, Harper and Row, 1965) 229–30.

32. *Fortune*, April 1941.

33. Heardon, 184–5.

34. Richard B. Frank, *Downfall: The End of the Imperial Japanese Empire* (New York, Random House, 1999) 20–2.

35. Shalom.

36. Heardon, 72.

37. Heardon, 69.

38. Antony C. Sutton, *Wall Street and the Rise of Hitler* (Seal Beach, CA, '76 Press, 1976) 21–32; Charles Higham, *Trading With the Enemy: The Nazi-American Money Plot* (New York, Barnes and Noble, 1983) 1–31.

39. Heardon, 183–4.

40. Heardon, 187.

41. Heardon, 159.

42. Heardon, 185.

43. *Barron's*, January 6, 1941.

44. Heardon, 160.

45. Heardon, 185.

46. Charles A. Beard, *President Roosevelt and the Coming of the War 1941: A Study in Appearances and Realities* (New Haven, Yale University Press, 1946) 784–7.

47. Gardner, 144.

48. *Fortune*, May 1941.

49. *Life*, February 7, 1941.

50. Many solid studies support this summary. See David S. Wyman, *The Abandonment of the Jews: America and the Holocaust 1941–1945* (New York, Pantheon, 1984) 42–58; 243–51. Haskell Lookstein, *Were We Our Brothers' Keepers: The Public Response of American Jews to the Holocaust, 1938–1944* (New York, Vintage, 1985).

51. This discussion is based on the following researches: Gar Alperovitz, *The Decision to Use the Atomic Bomb* (New York, Vintage, 1996); Samuel Walker, *Prompt and Utter Destruction: Truman and the Use of Atomic Bombs Against Japan* (Chapel Hill, University of North Carolina Press, 2004); Martin Sherwin, *A World Destroyed: Hiroshima and its Legacies* (Palo Alto, Stanford University Press, 2003).

52. General George Marshall estimated that the Japanese would meet any American invasion of the southern island of Kyushu with more than 300,000 troops and the Japanese were duly building up forces to meet such an eventuality. The opportunity existed to kill hundreds of thousands of soldiers, not civilians, but this option was not taken. See Frank, *Downfall: The End of the Imperial Japanese Empire* (New York, Random House, 1999) 194–8.

53. Tsuyoshi Hasegawa, *Racing the Enemy: Stalin, Truman, and the Surrender of Japan* (Cambridge, The Belknap Press of Harvard University, 2005).

54. Hasegawa, 271–5.

55. Merlin Chockwanyun, 'The Savage Extreme of a Narrow Policy Spectrum: Five Questions with Noam Chomsky', in *Counterpunch,* July 31, 2004. See also, Richard Polenberg, *War and Society: The United States, 1941–1954* (Philadelphia, J.B. Lippincott, 1972) 215–37.

CHAPTER 9

1. Vojteck Mastny, *Russia's Road to the Cold War* (New York, Columbia University Press, 1979) 51–5.

2. William Taubman, *Stalin's American Policy: From Entente to Détente to Cold War* (New York, W.W. Norton, 1982) 24–30.

3. Some examples are: 'We Can Lose the Next War in Seven Days', *Look,* July 8, 1947; 'The Reds Have a Standard Plan for Taking Over a Country', *Life,* June 7, 1948; 'Could the Reds Seize Detroit?' *Look,* August 3, 1948.

4. Edward Pessen, *Losing Our Souls: The American Experience in the Cold War* (Chicago, Ivan R. Dee, 1995) 53, 56.

5. Melvyn P. Leffler, *A Preponderance of Power: National Security, The Truman Administration and the Cold War* (Stanford, CA, Stanford University Press, 1992) 5. Until Soviet archives were opened after the fall of the communist regime in 1991 western analysts estimated Soviet deaths at 20 million. We now know they were far greater.

6. Daniel Yergin, *Shattered Peace: The Origins of the Cold War and the National Security State* (Boston, Houghton Mifflin Co., 1977) 213.

7. For an excellent examination of how the media and Hollywood portrayed Stalin and the Soviets in the most heroic and noble light during the war and how this was exactly reversed, see Michael Barson and Stephen Heller, *Red Scared: The Commie Menace in Propaganda and Popular Culture* (San Francisco, Chronicle Books, 2001).

8. The term was coined by Henry R. Luce, the publisher of *Life, Time,* and *Fortune* magazines. See, Henry R. Luce, 'The American Century', *Life,* February 7, 1941.

9. Pessen, 59; Thomas J. McCormick, *America's Half-Century: United States Foreign Policy in the Cold War* (Baltimore, Johns Hopkins University Press, 1989) 57; Leffler, 115.

10. At the close of World War II Churchill was defeated for re-election as prime minister of the United Kingdom. Seeking to keep his profile before the public he made this speech in the US in which he condemned the USSR for occupying much of Eastern Europe. But Churchill was a hypocrite. He had made a secret deal, known to historians as the 'Churchill–Stalin Percentage Deal'. If Stalin would not aid Greek communists attempting to overthrow the British-backed monarchy, the British would accede to his domination of much of Eastern

Europe. This deal was arranged informally and the details were written on a paper napkin that is now housed in the British Museum.

11. 'The Stalin–Churchill Percentage Deal,' in Thomas G. Patterson (ed.) *Major Problems in American Foreign Policy: Volume II: Since 1914* (Lexington, Massachusetts, D.C. Heath and Co., 1984) 241. See also, Walter LaFeber, *America, Russia and the Cold War* (New York, John Wiley and Sons, 1972) 10; Leffler, 72.

12. LaFeber, 28.

13. McCormick, 235.

14. The term is the title of a book by one of the neo-conservative intellectuals closely aligned with the George W. Bush Administration and is a glorification of American empire and the many forays and interventions the US carried out against much less powerful foes over its entire history. See Max Boot, *The Savage Wars of Peace: Small Wars and the Rise of American Power* (New York, Basic Books, 2002).

15. McCormick, 72–98.

16. Patrick J. Heardon, *Architects of Globalism: Building a New World Order During World War II* (Fayetteville, University of Arkansas Press, 2002) 39.

17. Robert A. Pollard, *Economic Security and the Origins of the Cold War, 1945–1950* (New York, Columbia University Press, 1985) 2.

18. McCormick, 79.

19. McCormick, 77.

20. Carl Soberg, *Oil Power: The Rise and Imminent Fall of an American Empire* (New York, New American Library, 1976) 200.

21. Larry Everest, *Oil, Power, and Empire: Iraq and the U.S. Global Agenda* (Monroe, ME, Common Courage Press, 2004) 57.

22. *Foreign Relations of the United States* (Washington, DC, US Government Printing Office, 1945, Vol.VIII) 54.

23. The phrase is from Paul Kennedy, *The Rise and Fall of the Great Powers* (New York, Vintage, 1989).

24. McCormick, 78.

25. McCormick, 83.

26. Richard J. Walton, *Henry Wallace, Harry Truman and the Cold War* (New York, Viking Press, 1976) 274–7.

27. William R. Keylor, *The Twentieth Century World: An International History* (New York, Oxford University Press, 1984) 283.

28. Leffler, 218.

29. LaFeber, 70; Keylor, 282.

30. McCormick, 87.

31. World War II had fostered conditions for full-scale corporate management of the economy to serve industrial-financial interests. Continuation of this state of affairs would be contingent on the perpetuation of wartime conditions and organization around permanent production for permanent war. Of course, this would also have the effect of minimizing investment and growth in civilian sectors and would deny 'free enterprise' to large proportions of the public. See Seymour Melman, *Pentagon Capitalism: The Political Economy of War* (New York, McGraw-Hill, 1971).

32. Barbara Tuchman, *Stillwell and the American Experience in China, 1911–1945* (New York, Bantam Books, 1980) 187–8, 513–14.

33. Leffler, 83; LaFeber, 24–5.

34. Leffler, 83.
35. Leffler, 85.
36. LaFeber, 26.

CHAPTER 10

1. Randall B. Wood and Howard Jones, *Dawning of the Cold War: The United States Quest For Order* (Chicago, Ivan R. Dee, 1991) 251–4; Melvyn P. Leffler, *A Preponderance of Power: National Security, The Truman Administration and the Cold War* (Stanford, Stanford University Press, 1992) 355–60; Walter LaFeber, *America, Russia, and the Cold War* (New York, John Wiley and Sons, 1972) 90–1.
2. Leffler, 357.
3. Thomas G. Patterson, *On Every Front: The Making and Unmaking of the Cold War* (New York, W.W. Norton & Company, 1992) 93.
4. Leffler, 88.
5. Bruce Cumings, *The Origins of the Korean War,* Vol.I (Princeton, Princeton University Press, 1990) 3–100.
6. Leffler, 89.
7. Bruce Cumings, *Korea: The Unknown War* (London, UK, Penguin Books, 1988) 24.
8. Cumings, *Korea*, 38.
9. Leffler, 252.
10. Leffler, 366–7.
11. Howard Jones, *Crucible of Power: A History of American Foreign Relations Since 1897* (Lanham, MD, Rowman and Littlefield, 2008) 285; James A. Nathan and James K. Oliver, *United States Foreign Policy and World Order* (Boston, Little, Brown and Co., 1981) 120–1.
12. John W. Spanier, *The Truman–MacArthur Controversy and the Korean War* (New York, W.W. Norton, 1965) 17.
13. Leffler, 367.
14. Jones, 287.
15. Jones, 288.
16. Cumings, *Korea*, 88.
17. Cumings, *Korea*, 92.
18. Cumings, 88–90.
19. Cumings, 96.
20. Cumings, *Korea*, 115.
21. Cumings, 112.
22. Nathan and Oliver, 139.
23. Jones, 289.
24. Cumings, 121.
25. Jones, 290.
26. Cumings, 126, 130.
27. Cumings, 123.
28. Cumings, 128.
29. Spanier, 138.
30. Thomas J. McCormick, *America's Half-Century: American Foreign Policy in the Cold War* (Baltimore, Johns Hopkins University Press, 1989) 104.

31. I.F. Stone, *The Hidden History of the Korean War* (New York, Monthly Review Press, 1952) 235.

32. Cumings, 163.

33. Spanier, 146.

34. Cumings, 172.

35. Cumings, 165.

36. Cumings, 182–6.

37. Cumings, 179, 181.

38. Cumings, 178.

39. Cumings, 174–82.

40. Cumings, 194–7.

41. Archimedes Patti, *Why Vietnam: Prelude to America's Albatross* (Berkeley, University of California Press, 1980) 274–80.

42. Marilyn Young, *The Vietnam Wars, 1945–1990* (New York, HarperCollins, 1991) 18.

43. Young, 29.

44. *The Pentagon Papers, as published by the New York Times* (New York, Quadrangle Books, 1971) 262.

45. Young, 113.

46. Young, 118.

47. Young, 106.

48. Young, 184.

49. Young, 191.

50. Young, 192.

51. A new study based on recently declassified documents on the Vietnam War and on interviews with veterans shows clearly that deliberate mass killing of civilians was widespread. My Lai was no aberration. See, Deborah Nelson, *The War Behind Me: Vietnam Veterans Confront the Truth About U.S. War Crimes* (New York, Basic Books, 2008). See also Nick Turse, 'A My Lai a Month', *The Nation,* December 1, 2008; and the film made by Vietnam Veterans Against the War in 1972 based on the testimony of hundreds of veterans, *Winter Soldier* (Winterfilm, 1972).

52. Paul Joseph, *Cracks in the Empire: State Politics in the Vietnam War* (New York, Columbia University Press, 1987) Chapter VI.

53. Myron Allukian and Paul L. Atwood, 'Public Health and the Vietnam War', in Barry S. Levy and Victor W. Sidel (eds) *War and Public Health* (New York, Oxford University Press, 1997) 215–37.

54. William Shawcross, *Sideshow: Kissinger, Nixon and the Destruction of Cambodia* (New York, Simon and Schuster, 179) 150, 209–10.

55. Daniel Ellsberg, *Papers on the War* (New York, Simon and Schuster, 1972).

56. Michael Klare, *Blood and Oil: The Dangers and Consequences of America's Growing Dependency On Imported Petroleum* (New York, Henry Holt and Co., 2004) 26–55.

57. William R. Keylor, *The Twentieth Century World: An International History* (New York, Oxford University Press, 1984) 312.

58. Mike Davis, 'The Poor Man's Airforce', in *Harper's* Magazine, October 2006. The first car bomb (actually a horse-drawn wagon) was detonated by an American anarchist in 1920 in Manhattan. Davis has written a book-length study of the car bomb. See, *Buda's Wagon: A Brief History of the Car Bomb* (London, Verso Books, 2008).

59. David S. Wyman, *The Abandonment of the Jews: America and the Holocaust 1941–1945* (New York, Pantheon, 1984).

60. Andrew Cockburn and Leslie Cockburn, *Dangerous Liaison: The Inside Story of the U.S.–Israeli Covert Relationship* (New York, HarperCollins, 1991) 17.

61. Leffler, 240–5; Cockburn, 26.

62. Cockburn, 27.

63. Cockburn, Chapter 6.

64. Cockburn, Chapter 12; Jane Hunter, *Israeli Foreign Policy: South Africa and Central America* (Boston, South End Press, 1987).

65. The case of Jonathan Pollard is the most notorious example. Pollard was a civilian analyst for the US navy's counterterrorism center who passed secrets to Israel over a period of 20 years. The case was so sensitive that the US government refused to have him tried publicly. See Ronald Olive, *Capturing Jonathan Pollard: How One of the Most Notorious Spies in American History Was Brought to Justice* (Washington, DC, US Naval Institute Press, 2006).

66. Memorandum, from James Bamford to the Federation of American Scientists, June 25, 2001. In this memo Bamford, author of *Body of Secrets: Anatomy of the Ultra-Secret National Security Agency* (New York, Anchor, 2003) quotes at length from numerous press sources that many Israeli officers admit to these mass executions.

67. James M. Ennes et al., *Assault on the Liberty* (New York, Random House, 1993); Peter Hounan, *Operation Cyanide: How the Bombing of the U.S.S. Liberty Nearly Caused World War III* (Vision Press, 2007).

68. Seymour Hersh, *The Samson Option: Israel's Nuclear Arsenal and American Foreign Policy* (New York, Random House, 1991) 137.

69. *New York Times*, 'Iran-Contra Report: Arms, Hostages and Contra: how a Secret Foreign Policy Unraveled', March 16, 1984.

70. David Kaiser, *The Road to Dallas: The Assassination of John F. Kennedy* (Cambridge, Mass., Harvard University Press, 2008) 143–69.

71. The declassified document is reproduced in full in Michael C. Ruppert, *Crossing the Rubicon: The Decline of the American Empire at the End of the Age of Oil* (New Society Publishers, British Columbia, Canada, 2004) Appendix A, 595–608.

72. Kaiser, 53–74; 143–68; Lamar Waldron, *Ultimate Sacrifice: John and Robert Kennedy, the Plan for a Coup in Cuba, and the Murder of JFK* (New York, Carroll and Graf Publishers, 2006) 335–45.

73. 'Soviets Knew Date of Cuba Attack', *Washington Post*, April 29, 2000.

74. Even the president's brother, Attorney General Robert Kennedy, called for a pretext to attack. He advocated that the US 'sink the *Maine*', a clear reference to destroying an American ship and blaming it on Castro. See Michael Dobbs, *One Minute to Midnight: Kennedy, Khruschev and Castro on the Brink of Nuclear War* (New York, Alfred A. Knopf, 2008) 343.

75. John Newman, *JFK and Vietnam: Deception, Intrigue and the Struggle for Power* (New York, Time-Warner books, 1992).

76. Fletcher Prouty, *The Secret Team: The CIA and its Allies in Control of the United States and the World* (Skyline Press, 2008). The author, as chief of Special Operations for the Joint Chiefs of Staff, oversaw the Pentagon's covert operations in league with the CIA, and is the highest ranking insider ever to reveal what he knows about the shadow government.

77. Waldron, 1–23.

CHAPTER 11

1. *New York Times*, May 24, 1992. For the Bush Doctrine see *The National Security Strategy of the United States*, The National Security Council (Washington, DC, the White House, 2002).

2. From a series of interviews Brzezinski gave to the French newspaper *Le Nouvelle Observateur* from 15–21 January 2001, quoted in the *New York Review of Books*, November 15, 2001, 4.

3. John Prados, *Presidents' Secret Wars: CIA and Pentagon Covert Operations From World War II Through the Persian Gulf* (Chicago, Ivan R. Dee, 1996) 363.

4. George Crile, *Charlie Wilson's War: The Extraordinary Story of the Largest Covert Operation in History* (New York, The Atlantic Monthly Press, 2003); Steve Coll, *Ghost Wars: The Secret History of the CIA, Afghanistan, and Bin Laden, From the Soviet Invasion to September 10, 2001* (New York, Penguin Books, 2004) 337–52.

5. The former ambassador to Saudi Arabia, James Akins, attributes a spate of articles appearing in the mid-1970s to background briefing by figures such as Henry Kissinger and Edward Luttwak. One was titled 'Seizing Arab Oil' and was published in *Harpers* Magazine. A similar piece appeared in *Commentary*. See Robert Dreyfuss, *Devil's Game: How the United States Helped Unleash Fundamentalist Islam* (New York, Metropolitan Books, 2005) 247–8.

6. One US government economist put matters this way: 'The Federal Reserve's greatest nightmare is that OPEC will switch its international transactions from a dollar standard to a euro standard.' See Nafeez Mossadeq Ahmed, *Behind the War on Terror: Western Secret Strategy and the Struggle for Iraq* (British Columbia, New Society Publishers, 2003) 232.

7. The Geneva Conventions of 1977 clearly prohibit every action the US took. Ahmed, 142–3.

8. Ahmed, 88.

9. Thomas J. Nagy, 'The Secret Behind the Sanctions: How the U.S. Intentionally Destroyed Iraq's Water Supply', *The Progressive*, September 2001. The information is no longer published on the DOD website. It was available at www.gulflink.osd.mil.

10. The word 'terrorize' was used by former US Attorney General Ramsey Clark as part of the charges he levied against his own country at the United Nations International Criminal Court on Crimes Against Humanity, 1996. See Ramsey Clark et al., *War Crimes: A Report on United States War Crimes Against Iraq* (Commission of Inquiry for the International War Crimes Tribunal, New York).

11. *Philadelphia Enquirer*, April 1, 1999.

12. Quoted in Ahmed, 134–5.

13. Michael Scheur, *Imperial Hubris: Why the West is Losing the War on Terror* (Washington, DC, Brassey's, Inc., 2004) 1–19. Scheur was a career CIA analyst whose principal responsibility was tracking al Qaeda and Osama Bin Laden. He notes the real outrages committed against Muslims and emphasizes that we ignore the roots of Muslim hatred at our peril.

14. The US connection to the global drug trade is well documented and ignored by Congress and the US media. See Peter Dale Scott, *Drugs, Oil and War: The United States in Afghanistan, Colombia and Indochina* (New York, Rowman

and Littlefield, 2003); Alfred McCoy, *The Politics of Heroin: CIA Complicity in the Global Drug Trade* (Lawrence Hill Books, 2003).

15. The CIA has long used the term 'blowback'. Originally it referred to the recruitment of Nazis after World War II for employment against the US's new enemy, the Soviets, and the corrosive effect this had on the intelligence services and American policies. See Christopher Simpson, *Blowback: The First Full Account of America's Recruitment of Nazis and its Disastrous Effect on the Cold War and Our Domestic and Foreign Policy* (New York, Collier Books, 1989). For an up-to-date account of the blowback involved in current policies, see Chalmers Johnson, *Blowback: The Costs and Consequences of American Empire* (New York, Henry Holt and Sons, 2004).

16. Richard Clarke was the counterterrorism adviser for Bush I, Clinton and Bush II. He was aghast at the intent of the Bush Administration to attack Iraq and thereby ignore the real source of attacks while also inflaming anti-Americanism in the Muslim world. He told his superiors in the White House that 'Having been attacked by Al Qaeda, for us to now go bombing Iraq in response would be like invading Mexico after the Japanese attacked us at Pearl Harbor.' See, Richard A. Clarke, *Against All Enemies: Inside America's War on Terror* (New York, Free Press, 2004).

17. Elizabeth Rubin, 'The Cult of Rajavi', *New York Times*, July 13, 2003. The MEK originated in Iran in opposition to the Shah. Its ideology was a mixture of Marxism, nationalism and Islamism. It later assisted the Islamists to overthrow the Shah but the new theocratic regime condemned the MEK for its secular socialist ideas. Subsequently the MEK moved into Iraq where it conducted terrorist raids on Iran in hopes of overthrowing the ayatollahs. They became *de facto* allies of Saddam, aiding his suppression of Iraqi resistance to his rule. After the Gulf War the MEK's bases remained in northern Iraq which was under the protection of US forces. From these bases they continued their attacks on Iran with the full knowledge of the US government. It was not until 1997 that they were added to the list of nations sponsoring terrorism.

18. Ahmed, 180.

19. Ahmed, 167.

20. Alfred W. McCoy, *A Question of Torture: CIA Interrogation From the Cold War to the War on Terror* (New York, Metropolitan Books, 2006) 118–19.

21. Frances Fitzgerald, 'George Bush and the World', *New York Review of Books*, September 26, 2002.

22. The Project for a New American Century, *Rebuilding America's Defenses: Strategy, Forces and Resources for a New American Century*, available at www.newamericancentury.org/RebuildingAmericasDefenses.pdf.

23. Michael Klare, *Blood and Oil: The Dangers and Consequences of America's Growing Dependency on Imported Petroleum* (New York, Henry Holt, 2004) 34–5.

24. Kenneth Pollack, *Foreign Affairs*, July/August 2003, 2–4.

25. Quoted in, Larry Everest, *Oil, Power and Empire: Iraq and the U.S. Global Agenda* (Monroe, ME, Common Courage Press, 2004) 252.

26. Everest, 254.

27. From the 'National Energy Policy, 2002', quoted in Everest, 255.

28. Daniel Yergin, *Washington Post*, December 8, 2002.

29. Everest, 256.

30. Zbigniew Brzezinski, *The Grand Chessboard: American Primacy and its Geostrategic Imperatives* (New York, Basic Books, 1997) 30–1.
31. Research Unit for Political Economy, *Behind the Invasion of Iraq* (New York, Monthly Review Press, 2003) 99.
32. Lutz Kleveman, *The New Great Game: Blood and Oil in Central Asia* (New York, The Atlantic Monthly Press, 2003) 115.
33. Research Unit for Political Economy, 99.
34. Ahmed Rashid, *Taliban: Militant Islam, Oil and Fundamentalism in Central Asia* (New Haven, Yale University Press, 2001) 157–82.
35. GlobalSecurity.org/military/world/southossetia, July 1, 2009. South Ossetia and Abkhazia are provinces of the republic of Georgia but the population is composed mainly of ethnic Russians who wish to secede from Georgia and join Russia. On July 29, 2008 Georgia began bombing villages in South Ossetia. On August 1 Georgia bombed the capital of South Ossetia, Tskhinvali. Many civilian casualties were reported.

CHAPTER 12

1. James W. Loewen, *Lies My Teacher Told Me: Everything Your American History Textbook Got Wrong* (revised and updated) (New York, The New Press, 2008).
2. A Ponzi scheme is a fraudulent investment operation that pays returns to investors from their own money or money paid by subsequent investors rather than from any actual profit earned. Charles Ponzi, an Italian immigrant was the first to use it to his immense gain (until he was caught) in America in the 1920s. A recent scheme was parlayed by Bernard Madoff in the US: he bilked about $65 billion in exactly this way and caused the collapse of many charitable foundations and took the retirement savings of tens of thousands.
3. Ray McGovern, *Robert Gates' Urge to Surge*, www.antiwar.com, November 24, 2008.
4. Lawrence E. Walsh, *Final Report of the Independent Counsel for Iran/Contra Matters* (Washington, DC, US Government Printing Office, 1993) Chapter 16.
5. Robert Gates, 'A Balanced Strategy: Reprogramming the Pentagon For a New Age', *Foreign Affairs*, January/February 2009.
6. Ibid.
7. Ibid.
8. See 'Who Is Jim Jones?', *The New Republic*, November 21, 2008.
9. Jamie McIntyre, 'Jim Jones and Barack Obama have more in common than meets the eye', December 1, 2008, http://ac360.blogs.cnn.com (last accessed December 2008).

Bibliography

BOOKS

Adams, Brooks, *The Law of Civilization and Decay: An Essay on History* (Whitefish, Montana, Kessenger Publishing, 2007).
— *America's Economic Supremacy* (New York, Macmillan Co., 1900).
Ahmed, Nafeez Mossadeq, *Behind the War on Terror: Western Secret Strategy and the Struggle for Iraq* (British Columbia, New Society Publishers, 2003).
Alperovitz, Gar, *The Decision to Use the Atomic Bomb* (New York, Vintage, 1996).
American Social History Project, *Who Built America* (New York, Pantheon, 1989).
Ames, Fisher, Ames, Seth and Thornton Kirkland, John (edited by Seth Ames) *Works of Fisher Ames: With a Selection from his Speeches and Correspondence, Volume 1* (Little, Brown and Company, 1854).
Anderson, Fred, *The Crucible of War: The Seven Years' War and the Fate of Empire in British North America, 1754–1766* (New York, Alfred E. Knopf, 2000).
Applebaum, Robert and Wood, John Sweet (eds) *Envisioning an English Empire: Jamestown and the Making of the North Atlantic World* (Philadelphia, University of Pennsylvania Press, 2005).
Baker, Nicholson, *Human Smoke: The Beginnings of World War II, The End of Civilization* (New York, Simon and Schuster, 2008).
Bamford, James, *Body of Secrets: Anatomy of the Ultra-Secret National Security Agency* (New York, Anchor, 2003).
Barson, Michael and Heller, Stephen, *Red Scared: The Commie Menace in Propaganda and Popular Culture* (San Francisco, Chronicle Books, 2001).
Beale, Howard, *Theodore Roosevelt and the Rise of America to World Power* (New York, Collier, 1956).
Beard, Charles, *An Economic Interpretation of the Constitution of the United States* (New York, Macmillan, 1935).
— *President Roosevelt and the Coming of the War 1941: A Study in Appearances and Realities* (New Haven, Yale University Press, 1946).
Beck, John Jacob, *MacArthur and Wainwright: Sacrifice of the Philippines* (Albuquerque, University of New Mexico Press, 1974).
Beveridge, Sen. Albert J., 'Speech: In Support of An American Empire', January 9, 1899, Congressional Record, 56th Congress, Sess.I, 704–12.
Boot, Max, *The Savage Wars of Peace: Small Wars and the Rise of American Power* (New York, Basic Books, 2002).
Boyer, Richard O. and Morais, Herbert M., *Labor's Untold Story* (New York, United Electrical Radio and Machine Workers of America, 1979).
Brereton, Lewis, *The Brereton Diaries: The War in the Pacific, Middle East and Europe, October 1941 – 8 May 1945* (New York, Morrow, 1946).
Brown, Dee, *Bury My Heart at Wounded Knee: An Indian History of the American West* (New York, Bantam, 1970).

Bruce, Robert V., *1877: Year of Violence* (New York, Quadrangle, 1959).

Brzezinski, Zbigniew, *The Grand Chessboard: American Primacy and its Geostrategic Imperatives* (New York, Basic Books, 1997).

Clark, Ramsey et al., *War Crimes: A Report on United States War Crimes Against Iraq* (Commission of Inquiry for the International War Crimes Tribunal, New York, 1997).

Clarke, Richard A., *Against All Enemies: Inside America's War on Terror* (New York, Free Press, 2004).

Cockburn, Andrew and Cockburn, Patrick, *Out of the Ashes: The Resurrection of Saddam Hussein* (HarperCollins, 1999).

Cockburn, Andrew and Cockburn, Leslie, *Dangerous Liaison: The Inside Story of the U.S.–Israeli Covert Relationship* (New York, HarperCollins, 1991).

Coll, Steve, *Ghost Wars: The Secret History of the CIA, Afghanistan, and Bin Laden, From the Soviet Invasion to September 10, 2001* (New York, Penguin Books, 2004).

Crile, George, *Charlie Wilson's War: The Extraordinary Story of the Largest Covert Operation in History* (New York, The Atlantic Monthly Press, 2003).

Cumings, Bruce, *Korea: The Unknown War* (London, UK, Penguin Books, 1988).

— *The Origins of the Korean War,* Vol. I (Princeton, Princeton University Press, 1990).

Davis, Mike, *Buda's Wagon: A Brief History of the Car Bomb* (London, Verso Books, 2008).

Diamond, Jared, *Guns, Germs, and Steel: The Fates of Human Societies* (New York, W.W. Norton, 1999).

Divine, Robert A., *Roosevelt and World War II* (New York, Penguin Books, 1970).

Dobbs, Michael, *One Minute to Midnight: Kennedy, Khruschev and Castro on the Brink of Nuclear War* (New York, Alfred A. Knopf, 2008).

Dreyfuss, Robert, *Devil's Game: How the United States Helped Unleash Fundamentalist Islam* (New York, Metropolitan Books, 2005).

Drinnon, Richard, *Facing West: The Metaphysics of Indian Hating and Empire Building* (New York, Schocken Books, 1990).

DuBois, W.E.B., *Black Reconstruction in America: An Essay Toward A History of the Part That Black Folk Played in the Attempt to Reconstruct Democracy in America* (New York, Russell and Russell, 1935).

Ellsberg, Daniel, *Papers on the War* (New York, Simon and Schuster, 1972).

Ennes, James M., Loomis, Robert and Carlisle, Sheila, *Assault on the Liberty* (New York, Random House, 1993).

Everest, Larry, *Oil, Power, and Empire: Iraq and the U.S. Global Agenda* (Monroe, ME, Common Courage Press, 2004).

Faust, Drew Gilpin, *This Republic of Suffering: Death and the American Civil War* (New York, Vintage, 2009).

Ford, Glyn with Soyoung, Kwon, *Struggle for Survival: Changing Regime or Regime Change North Korea in the Twenty-First Century* (London, Pluto Press, 2007).

Frank, Richard B., *Downfall: The End of the Imperial Japanese Empire* (New York, Random House, 1999).

Gardner, Lloyd C., *Imperial America: American Foreign Policy since 1898* (New York, Harcourt Brace Jovanovich, 1976).

Goodwin, Doris Kearns, *No Ordinary Time: Franklin and Eleanor Roosevelt: The Home Front in World War II* (New York, Simon and Schuster, 1994) 239.

Graetz, Michael J. and Schenk, Deborah, *Federal Income Taxation: Principles and Policies* (New York: Foundation Press, 2005).

Hasegawa, Tsuyoshi, *Racing the Enemy: Stalin, Truman, and the Surrender of Japan* (Cambridge, The Belknap Press of Harvard University, 2005).

Heardon, Patrick J., *Roosevelt Confronts Hitler: America's Entry Into World War II* (DeKalb, Illinois, Northern Illinois University Press, 1987).

— *Architects of Globalism: Building a New World Order During World War II* (Fayetteville, University of Arkansas Press, 2002).

Hersh, Seymour, *The Samson Option: Israel's Nuclear Arsenal and American Foreign Policy* (New York, Random House, 1991).

Higham, Charles, *Trading With the Enemy: The Nazi-American Money Plot* (New York, Barnes and Noble, 1983).

Hitler, Adolf, *Mein Kampf* (Boston, Houghton-Miflin, 1971) (translated by Ralph Manheim).

Hofstadter, Richard, *Social Darwinism in American Thought* (Boston, Beacon Press, 1955).

Hoig, Stan, *The Sand Creek Massacre* (Norman, OK, University of Oklahoma Press, 1977).

Horsman, Reginald, *Race and Manifest Destiny: The Origins of American Racial Anglo-Saxonism* (Cambridge, Mass., Harvard University Press, 1981).

Hounan, Peter, *Operation Cyanide: How the Bombing of the U.S.S. Liberty Nearly Caused World War III* (Vision Press, 2007).

Hunter, Jane, *Israeli Foreign Policy: South Africa and Central America* (Boston, South End Press, 1987).

Jensen, Derrick, *A Language Older Than Words* (New York, Context Books, 2000).

Johnson, Chalmers, *Blowback: The Costs and Consequences of American Empire* (New York, Henry Holt and Sons, 2004).

Jones, Howard, *Crucible of Power: A History of American Foreign Relations Since 1897* (Lanham, MD, Rowman and Littlefield, 2008).

Joseph, Paul, *Cracks in the Empire: State Politics in the Vietnam War* (New York, Columbia University Press, 1987).

Kagan, Robert, *Dangerous Nation: America's Place in the World from Its Earliest Days to the Dawn of the Twentieth Century* (New York, Knopf, 2006).

Kaiser, David, *The Road to Dallas: The Assassination of John F. Kennedy* (Cambridge, Mass., Harvard University Press, 2008).

Karp, Walter, *The Politics of War: The Story of How Two Wars Altered Forever the Political Life of the American Republic* (New York, Franklin Square Press, 2003).

Kennedy, David M., *Freedom From Fear: The American People in Depression and War, 1929–1945* (New York, Oxford University Press, 1999).

Kennedy, Paul, *The Rise and Fall of the Great Powers* (New York, Vintage, 1989).

Keylor, William R., *The Twentieth Century World: An International History* (New York, Oxford University Press, 1984).

Kimball, Warren S., *The Most Unsordid Act: Lend-Lease, 1939–1941* (Baltimore, Johns Hopkins University Press, 1969).

Kissinger, Henry (using the pseudonym 'Miles Ignotus') 'Seizing Arab Oil', *Harper's*, March 1975.

Klare, Michael, *Blood and Oil: The Dangers and Consequences of America's Growing Dependency On Imported Petroleum* (New York, Henry Holt and Co., 2004).

Kleveman, Lutz, *The New Great Game: Blood and Oil in Central Asia* (New York, The Atlantic Monthly Press, 2003).

Kolko, Gabriel, *The Triumph of Conservatism: A New Interpretation of American History* (New York, The Free Press, 1963).

LaFeber, Walter, *America, Russia and the Cold War* (New York, John Wiley and Sons, 1972).

— *The New Empire: An Interpretation of American Expansion, 1860–1898* (Ithaca, NY, Cornell University Press, 1980).

Layne, Christopher, *The Peace of Illusions: American Grand Strategy from 1940 to the Present* (Ithaca, NY, Cornell University Press, 2006) 50.

Leffler, Melvyn P., *A Preponderance of Power: National Security, The Truman Administration and the Cold War* (Stanford, CA, Stanford University Press, 1992).

Lens, Sidney, *The Forging of the American Empire: A History of American Imperialism from the Revolution to Vietnam* (New York, Thomas Y. Crowell Co., 1974). New edition published in 2003 by Pluto Press with a foreword by Howard Zinn.

Lepore, Jill, *The Name of War: King Philip's War and the Origins of American Identity* (New York, Knopf, 1998).

Levin, Gordon S., *Woodrow Wilson and World Politics: America's Response to Revolution* (New York, Oxford University Press, 1968).

Levy, Barry S. and Sidel, Victor W. (eds) *War and Public Health* (New York, Oxford University Press, 1997).

Lookstein, Haskell, *Were We Our Brothers' Keepers: The Public Response of American Jews to the Holocaust, 1938–1944* (New York, Vintage, 1985).

Mahan, Alfred Thayer, *The Influence of Sea Power Upon History, 1660–1783* (Whitefish, Montana, Kessenger Publishing, 2006).

Manchester, William, *American Caesar, Douglas MacArthur, 1880–1964* (Boston, Little Brown, 1978).

Mann, Charles C., *1491: New Revelations of the Americas Before Columbus* (New York, Vintage, 2006).

Mastny, Vojteck, *Russia's Road to the Cold War* (New York, Columbia University Press, 1979).

McCormick, Thomas J., *China Market: America's Quest for Informal Empire, 1893–1901* (Chicago, Ivan R. Dee, 1967).

— *America's Half-Century: United States Foreign Policy in the Cold War* (Baltimore, The Johns Hopkins University Press, 1989).

McCoy, Alfred, *The Politics of Heroin: CIA Complicity in the Global Drug Trade* (Lawrence Hill Books, 2003).

— *A Question of Torture: CIA Interrogation From the Cold War to the War on Terror* (New York, Metropolitan Books, 2006).

Melman, Seymour, *Pentagon Capitalism: The Political Economy of War* (New York, McGraw-Hill, 1971).

Merck, Frederick, *Manifest Destiny and Mission in American History* (Cambridge, MA, Harvard University Press, 1995).

Miller, Edward S., *War Plan Orange: The U.S. Strategy to Defeat Japan 1897–1945* (Washington, DC, Naval Institute Press, 1991).

Morgan, Edmund S., *American Slavery–American Freedom: The Ordeal of Colonial Virginia* (New York, W.W. Norton, 1975).

— *The Birth of the Republic, 1763–1789* (Chicago, University of Chicago Press, 1992).

Morrison, Samuel Elliot, *The Oxford History of the United States 1778–1917* (New York, Oxford University Press, 1927).

Morton, Louis, *United States Army in World War II: The War in the Pacific: The Fall of the Philippines* (Washington, DC Office of the Chief of Military History, Department of the Army, 1953).

Nash, Gary B., Jeffrey, Julie Roy, Howe, John R., Frederick, Peter J., Davis, Allen F., Winkler, Allan M. (eds), *The American People: Creating a Nation and a Society*, 2nd Edition (New York, HarperCollins, 1990).

Nathan, James A. and Oliver, James K., *United States Foreign Policy and World Order* (Boston, Little, Brown and Co., 1981).

Nelson, Deborah, *The War Behind Me: Vietnam Veterans Confront the Truth About U.S. War Crimes* (New York, Basic Books, 2008).

Neumann, William L., *America Encounters Japan: From Perry to MacArthur* (New York, Harper and Row, 1965).

Newman, John, *JFK and Vietnam: Deception, Intrigue and the Struggle for Power* (New York, Time-Warner books, 1992).

Olive, Ronald, *Capturing Jonathan Pollard: How One of the Most Notorious Spies in American History Was Brought to Justice* (Washington, DC, US Naval Institute Press, 2006).

Patterson, Thomas G. (ed.) *Major Problems in American Foreign Policy: Volume II: Since 1914* (Lexington, Massachusetts, D.C. Heath and Co., 1984).

— *On Every Front: The Making and Unmaking of the Cold War* (New York, W.W. Norton & Company, 1992).

Patti, Archimedes, *Why Vietnam: Prelude to America's Albatross* (Berkeley, University of California Press, 1980).

Pessen, Edward, *Losing Our Souls: The American Experience in the Cold War* (Chicago, Ivan R. Dee, 1995).

Polenberg, Richard, *War and Society: The United States, 1941–1954* (Philadelphia, J.B. Lippincott, 1972).

Pollard, Robert A., *Economic Security and the Origins of the Cold War, 1945–1950* (New York, Columbia University Press, 1985).

Powaski, Ronald E., *Toward an Entangling Alliance: American Isolationism, Internationalism, and Europe* in Denson, John V., *Reassessing the Presidency* (Greenwood, 1991).

Prados, John, *President's Secret Wars: CIA and Pentagon Covert Operations From World War II Through the Persian Gulf* (Chicago, Ivan R. Dee, 1996).

Pratt, Julius William, *Expansionists of 1898: The Acquisition of Hawaii and the Spanish Islands* (Chicago, Quadrangle Books, 1964).

The Project for a New American Century (PNAC), *Rebuilding America's Defenses: Strategy, Forces and Resources for a New American Century* (2000).

Prouty, Fletcher, *The Secret Team: The CIA and its Allies in Control of the United States and the World* (Skyline Press, 2008).

Raphael, Ray, *A Peoples' History of the American Revolution* (New York, Harper Perennial, 2002).

Rashid, Ahmed, *Taliban: Militant Islam, Oil and Fundamentalism in Central Asia* (New Haven, Yale University Press, 2001).

Research Unit for Political Economy, *Behind the Invasion of Iraq* (New York, Monthly Review Press, 2003).

Richardson, James O., *On the Treadmill to Pearl Harbor: The Memoirs of Admiral James O. Richardson, USN* (Washington, DC, Naval History Division, Department of the Navy, 1973).

Roosevelt, Theodore, *The Winning of the West, Vol. IV* (Lincoln, University of Nebraska Press, 1995).

Ruppert, Michael C., *Crossing the Rubicon: The Decline of the American Empire at the End of the Age of Oil* (New Society Publishers, British Columbia, Canada, 2004).

Russett, Bruce, *No Clear and Present Danger: A Skeptical View of U.S. Entry Into World War II* (New York, Harper and Row, 1972).

Scheur, Michael, *Imperial Hubris: Why the West is Losing the War on Terror* (Washington, DC, Brassey's, Inc., 2004).

Schultze, Eric B. and Tougias, Michael J., *King Philip's War: The History and Legacy of America's Forgotten Conflict* (Woodstock, Vermont, The Countryman Press, 1999).

Scott, Peter Dale, *Drugs, Oil and War: The United States in Afghanistan, Colombia and Indochina* (New York, Rowman and Littlefield, 2003).

Shawcross, William, *Sideshow: Kissinger, Nixon and the Destruction of Cambodia* (New York, Simon and Schuster, 1979).

Sherry, Michael S., *The Rise of American Air Power: The Creation of Armageddon* (New Haven, Yale University Press, 1991).

Sherwin, Martin, *A World Destroyed: Hiroshima and its Legacies* (Palo Alto, Stanford University Press, 2003).

Simpson, Christopher, *Blowback: The First Full Account of America's Recruitment of Nazis and its Disastrous Effect on the Cold War and Our Domestic and Foreign Policy* (New York, Collier Books, 1989).

Soberg, Carl, *Oil Power: The Rise and Imminent Fall of an American Empire* (New York, New American Library, 1976).

Spanier, John W., *The Truman–MacArthur Controversy and the Korean War* (New York, W.W. Norton, 1965).

Stannard, David E., *American Holocaust: The Conquest of the Americas* (New York, Oxford University Press, 1992).

Stephanson, Anders, *Manifest Destiny: American Expansion and the Empire of Right* (New York, Hill and Wang, 1995).

Stimson, Henry Lewis, *On Active Service in Peace and War* (New York, Harper and Row, 1948).

Stinnett, Robert B., *Day of Deceit: The Truth about FDR and Pearl Harbor* (New York, The Free Press, 2000).

Stone, I.F., *The Hidden History of the Korean War* (New York, Monthly Review Press, 1952).

Strong, Josiah, *Our Country: Its Possible Future and Its Present Crisis* (Bibliolife, 2009).

Sutton, Antony C., *Wall Street and the Rise of Hitler* (Seal Beach, CA., '76 Press, 1976).

Takaki, Ronald, *Why America Dropped the Atomic Bomb* (Boston, Little, Brown and Co., 1995) 7.

Taubman, William, *Stalin's American Policy: From Entente to Détente to Cold War* (New York, W.W. Norton, 1982).

Toland, John, *Infamy: Pearl Harbor and Its Aftermath* (New York, Berkeley Books, 1982).

Tuchman, Barbara, *Stillwell and the American Experience in China, 1911–1945* (New York, Bantam Books, 1980).

Turner, Frederick Jackson, *The Significance of the Frontier in American History* (Ann Arbor, Michigan, Scholarly Publishing Office, University of Michigan, 2005).

Vidal, Gore, *Washington, D.C.* (New York, Random House, 1967) 242–3.

Waldron, Lamar, *Ultimate Sacrifice: John and Robert Kennedy, the Plan for a Coup in Cuba, and the Murder of JFK* (New York, Carroll and Graf Publishers, 2006).

Walker, Samuel, *Prompt and Utter Destruction: Truman and the Use of Atomic Bombs Against Japan* (Chapel Hill, University of North Carolina Press, 2004).

Weeks, William Earl, *Building the Continental Empire: From the American Revolution to the Civil War* (Chicago, Ivan R. Dee, 1996).

Williams, William Appleman, *The Tragedy of American Diplomacy* (New York, Dell, 1972).

— *The Contours of American History* (Chicago, Quadrangle Books, 1966).

Wilson, James, *The Earth Shall Weep: A History of Native America* (New York, Grove Press, 2000).

Wood, Randall B. and Jones, Howard, *Dawning of the Cold War: The United States Quest For Order* (Chicago, Ivan R. Dee, 1991).

Wyman, David S., *The Abandonment of the Jews: America and the Holocaust 1941–1945* (New York, Pantheon, 1984).

Yergin, Daniel, *Shattered Peace: The Origins of the Cold War and the National Security State* (Boston, Houghton Mifflin Co., 1977).

— *The Prize: The Epic Quest For Oil, Money, and Power* (New York, Simon and Schuster, 1991).

Young, Marilyn, *The Vietnam Wars, 1945–1990* (New York, HarperCollins, 1991).

Zinn, Howard, *A People's History of the United States* (New York: HarperPerennial, 1995).

US GOVERNMENT DOCUMENTS

Foreign Relations of the United States (Washington, DC, US Government Printing Office, 1945, Vol. VIII) 54.

The National Security Council, *The National Security Strategy of the United States* (Washington, DC, the White House, 2002).

United States Congress, *Report of the Joint Committee on the Investigation of the Pearl Harbor Attack, 79th Congress, 2nd Session, 1946, Part 5* (Washington, DC, US Government Printing Office, 1946).

US Government, *Inaugural Addresses of the Presidents of the United States* (Washington, DC, US Government Printing Office, 2001).

ARTICLES

Allukian, Myron and Atwood, Paul L., 'Public Health and the Vietnam War', in Levy, Barry S. and Sidel Victor W. (eds) *War and Public Health* (New York, Oxford University Press, 1997).

Bamford, James, 'Memorandum to Federation of American Scientists', in James Bamford, *Body of Secrets: Anatomy of the Ultra-Secret National Security Agency* (New York, Anchor, 2003).

Chockwanyun, Merlin, 'The Savage Extreme of a Narrow Policy Spectrum: Five Questions with Noam Chomsky', *Counterpunch*, July 31, 2004.

Davis, Mike, 'The Poor Man's Airforce', *Harper's* Magazine, October 2006.

Fitzgerald, Frances, 'George Bush and the World', *New York Review of Books*, September 26, 2002.

Horn, James, 'The Conquest of Eden: Possession and Dominion in Early Virginia', in Applebaum, Robert and Wood, John Sweet (eds) *Envisioning an English Empire: Jamestown and the Making of the North Atlantic World* (Philadelphia, University of Pennsylvania Press, 2005) 43.

Luce, Henry R., 'The American Century', *Life*, February 7, 1941.

Nagy, Thomas J., 'The Secret Behind the Sanctions: How the U.S. Intentionally Destroyed Iraq's Water Supply', *The Progressive*, September 2001.

Pollack, Kenneth, *Foreign Affairs*, July/August 2003, 2–4.

Rubin, Elizabeth, 'The Cult of Rajavi', *New York Times*, July 13, 2003.

Shalom, Stephen R., 'VJ Day: Remembering the Pacific War', *Critical Asian Studies, Bulletin of Concerned Asian Scholars*, Volume 39, Number 2, June 1995.

Sweet, John Wood, 'Sea Changes', in Applebaum, Robert and Wood, John Sweet (eds) *Envisioning an English Empire: Jamestown and the Making of the North Atlantic World* (Philadelphia, University of Pennsylvania Press, 2005).

Turse, Nick, 'A My Lai a Month', *The Nation*, December 1, 2008.

Yergin, Daniel, *Washington Post*, December 8, 2002.

Zinn, Howard, 'Columbus and Western Civilization', in Kick, Russ (ed.) *You Are Being Lied To* (New York, The Disinformation Company, Ltd., 2005) 212.

NEWSPAPERS AND MAGAZINES

Barron's, January 6, 1941.

Fortune, April 1941.

Fortune, May 1941.

Life, February 7, 1941.

'The Reds Have a Standard Plan for Taking Over a Country', *Life*, June 7, 1948.

'We Can Lose the Next War in Seven Days', *Look*, July 8, 1947.

'Could the Reds Seize Detroit?', *Look*, August 3, 1948.

New York Review of Books, November 15, 2001.

New York Times, May 24, 1992.

Philadelphia Enquirer, April 1, 1999.

'Soviets Knew Date of Cuba Attack', *Washington Post*, April 29, 2000.

FILMS CITED

Apocalypto (Directed and produced by Mel Gibson, Touchstone Films, 2006).

Sacrifice at Pearl Harbor (British Broadcasting Corporation, 1989).

Why We Fight, Episode I (Directed by Frank Capra, Timeless Media Group, 2007).

Winter Soldier (Winterfilm, 1972).

Index

Acheson, Dean 157, 177, 181–2, 184, 202
Adams, Brooks 92
Adams, John 61–2, 92
Adams, John Quincy 64, 66–7, 72, 92
Adams, Samuel 54
Afghanistan 2, 3, 14, 15, 175, 177, 216–19, 220–1, 226, 231–4, 236–8
Al Qaeda 220–2, 226, 236–8, 254n, 255n
Alien Act 61
Albright, Madeleine 5
American Century 15, 91, 143, 156, see also Luce, Henry R.
American Civil War 9, 41, 72, 74, 75–9, 81, 83, 88, 93, 98, 100, 121, 129, 229
American Revolution 6, 45, 50, 53, 60, 70, 241, 242, 261, 263
Anglo-Saxonism 69, 70
Anglo-Saxon Christianity 93
Arawak 20–2
Army of the Republic of Vietnam (ARVN) 189, 192, 19
Atahualpa 25

Beveridge, Albert 95
Baker, James 224
Baruch, Bernard 141, 157
Baruch Plan 157
Battle of Britain 138, 140
Battle of Dien Bien Phu 191
Battle of New Orleans 64
Baum, L. Frank 81
Berlin Crisis 1948, 169
Bill of Rights 7, 53, 56, 59, 61, 120, 230
Black Elk 69
Bolsheviks 116–18, 122
Bretton Woods 161
Bryan, William Jennings 106, 109, 112, 113

Byrnes, James 147–8
Brzezinski, Zbigniew 215, 217, 224, 234
Bush, Doctrine 216
Bush, George H.W. 219, 220, 255n
Bush, George W. 3, 15, 204, 209, 216, 222–4, 226, 233–6, 238, 241, 250n, 255n

Carter Doctrine 217
Carter, Jimmy 208–9, 217
Caspian Sea region 216, 227–34
Central Intelligence Agency (CIA) 14, 15, 159, 168, 175, 189
Cheney, Richard 221, 224–5, 236
China 2, 10, 12, 14, 16, 25, 61, 62, 96, 98, 103, 108, 122, 126–7, 129, 132, 134, 139, 142–3, 147–8, 166, 171–3, 175, 177–9, 181–6, 188, 191, 197, 216–17, 219, 224, 227, 234–5, 238
China market 98
Chivington, John 80–1
'Christmas' bombing 197
Churchill, Winston 101, 137, 147, 157–9, 164, 174, 201, 248n, 249n
Clay, Henry 65–6
Clay, Lucius 169
Cleveland, Grover 88, 90, 100
Clifford, Clark 154, 195, 203
Clinton, Hillary 232, 236
Clinton, William J. 220, 226, 234, 255n
Columbus, Christopher 20–2, 26, 26–7
Committee for the Marshall Plan 167
Common Sense 53
Compromise of 1877, 77–8
Confederacy, the 63, 65, 75, 77
Cortez, Hernando 22–7
Cuba 10, 14, 21, 67, 94–102, 177, 210–13

Declaration of Independence 8, 51, 230
Domino theory 191, 199
Dresden 1
Dulles, Allen 213
Dulles, John Foster 151, 162, 189

Eisenhower, Dwight 14, 146, 168, 186–7, 203, 211, 236
Emancipation Proclamation 77
Emerson, Ralph Waldo 72
English Civil War 28–30
Espionage Act 120

Federalists 57–61, 65
Final Solution 16, 125
Forrestal, James 163
Fourteen points 118, 123
French and Indian War 43, 49, *see also* Seven Years War
Franklin, Benjamin 6, 43, 47, 55, 230
Full spectrum dominance 3

Gates, Robert 232–5
Geneva Accords 1954, 189, 191–2
Geneva Convention 187, 189, 205, 232, 254
Glorious Revolution 44, 46
Grant, Ulysses S. 88
Great China Market 9, 61, 108, 142
Great Depression 13, 139–41, 143, 150, 161
Greater East Asia Co-Prosperity Sphere 136, 139, 142
Greek civil war 158
Guantanamo Bay 10, 212

Hamilton, Alexander 50, 54, 56–7, 59–60, 62
Hay, John 75, 85, 92
Hayes, Rutherford 78
Hitler, Adolph 12, 13, 15, 22, 125, 137–8, 140–2, 144, 149, 152–3, 166, 174, 202
Hiroshima 1, 2, 125, 145, 147–8, 157, 169, 188, 220
Ho Chi Minh 160, 189–90, 194–6
Holocaust 18–19, 201, 203
Hoover, J. Edgar 131
House–Grey Memorandum 114

Iran 3, 15, 105, 123, 158, 166, 177, 200, 206, 207–10, 216, 219, 222, 225, 227, 233, 235–9, 253, 255–6
Iran–*Contra* Scandal 209
Iraq 2, 3, 15, 177, 202, 206, 208–9, 216–20, 222, 224–5, 232–6, 238
'Iron Curtain' speech 157
Israel 3, 36, 145, 200–6, 232, 238–9

Jackson, Andrew 59, 63–4, 68–9
Jamestown 27, 30–2, 35
Jay, John 60
Jeffersonian Democrats 57–8
Jefferson, Thomas 3, 8, 50, 51, 53, 57–63, 65, 68, 69, 190, 230
Jiang Jieshi 171–2, 181
Jiang Zemin 226
Johnson, Andrew 79
Johnson, Lyndon 193, 195, 205, 238
Jones, James J. 236

Kennan, George F. 159, 163, 174
Kennedy, John F. 193, 212–14
Kennedy, Robert 212–13
Khmer Rouge 198
Kim Il-Sung 181
Kimmel, Husband 128, 132–4
King Philip's War 40, 42, 47
Korean War 178–88
Ku Klux Klan 78–9, 100, 121

Laissez-faire, ideology of 83–5, 170
Las Casas, Bartolomeo 21, 32
League of Nations 118–19, 139
Lebensraum 153
LeMay, Curtis 2, 146
Lend-Lease programme 137, 149, 152, 201
Liliuokalani, Queen 89
Lincoln, Abraham 5, 72, 75, 80, 85
Locke, John 44, 51
Lodge, Henry Cabot 89–90, 92, 95, 99, 102, 119
Louisiana Purchase 63, 67, 70
Luce, Henry R, 143

MacArthur, Douglas 133–4, 180–1, 183–5, 188
Madison, James 55, 62, 65–6

Mahan, Alfred Thayer 92
MAGIC 130, 132–3, 145–6, 218,
        247n15, 247n21
Manhattan Project 147, 151
Manifest Destiny 5, 66, 70, 96, 109
Mao Jedong 173
Marshall, George C. 129–30, 146,
        173, 202, 249n
Marshall Plan 165–7, 170
'Martial Plan' 166, see also Wallace,
        Henry
Massachusett 17, 34–6, 42
Massasoit 34–5, 39–40
McCarthy, Joseph 175
McKinley, William 85, 95, 97–8, 102
McNamara, Robert 2, 194
Mein Kampf 153
Metacomet ('King Philip') 40–1
Mexican War 74, 115
Military–Industrial Complex 13, 168,
        171, 236
Mitteleuropa 106
Monroe Doctrine 67, 88–91, 98, 139,
        155, 162, 212, 217
'Monroe Doctrine for Asia' 139
Monroe, James 64, 66
More, Thomas 28
Morgenthau, Henry 127
Mossadegh, Mohammed 209
My Lai massacre 195–6

Nagasaki 2, 125, 145, 147–8, 157,
        169, 188
National Front for the Liberation of
        Vietnam (NLF) 192
National Security Act 1949, 175
National Security Council (NSC)
        175–7, 185, 188, 224
NSC-68, 176–7, 185, 188
National Security State 168, 176, 211,
        236
Nazi (Nazis) 11, 30, 18, 20, 70, 79,
        105, 118, 122, 124–6, 135–8,
        144, 147, 149, 151–6, 158, 166,
        177, 180, 186–7, 201, 230
Neutrality Act 12, 137, 141
New American Century 215, 223
Nixon, Richard M. 181, 185, 195–7,
        199

North Atlantic Treaty Organization
        (NATO) 169–70, 227, 235–7

Obama, Barack H. 232–8
Olney, Richard 90
Open Door Policy 10, 12, 96, 103,
        106, 108, 112, 116, 123, 125,
        128, 136, 139, 150, 152–3, 172,
        173, 178–80

Paine, Tom 53
Palestine 2, 201–3, 205, 225, 232
Patriot Act 7
Pearl Harbor 12, 15, 89, 124–35,
        137–9, 141–3, 145, 147, 149,
        171, 224
Pentagon Papers 199
Peoples' Liberation Army of Vietnam
        194
Permanent War Economy 14, 150,
        155, 168–70
Pequot tribe 38–9
Pequot massacre 39, 63, 231
Philippine War 10
Pizarro, Francisco 23, 25–7
Polk, James 63, 69–74
Post Traumatic Stress Disorder 76, 198
Powell, Colin 222
Powhatan 27, 31–4, see also
        Wahunsonacock
Proclamation of 1763, 49
Project for A New American Century
        (PNAC) 223–4
Puritans 29–30, 34, 36–40, 42, 44, 94
Puritan Revolution 29, 46

Quosco (Cuzco) 22, 25

'Rebuilding America's Defenses' 15,
        176, 223
Red Scare 121
Red Army 13, 147–9, 152, 155–6,
        158–9, 166, 172, 179, 216–17
Revolutionary War 3, see also
        American Revolution
Rice, Condoleezza 223
Richardson, James O. 128–9
RMS Lusitania 113

Roosevelt, Franklin D. 1, 12, 105, 124, 126, 135–7, 139–40, 142, 144, 154, 200, 202, 224
Roosevelt, Theodore 19, 62, 89, 92, 107
Rumsfeld, Donald 221, 233, 236–7

Saddam Hussein 3, 15, 206, 209, 218, 220–3
Sand Creek massacre 63, 80
Saudi Arabia 200, 209, 215, 217–20, 224, 238, 254n
Sedition,
 Act of (1798) 61
 Act of (1918) 120
Seven Years War 43, 48, 6, *see also* French and Indian War
Seward, William 87
Shays Rebellion 54, 57
Short, Walter 132–4
Smith, Adam 45
Smith, John 27, 30–2
Smith, Walter Bedell 183
Social Darwinism 93, 96
Soviet Union 2, 12–14, 122, 125, 129, 140, 147, 149, 151–3, 155, 159–60, 165–6, 172, 174, 184–5, 210, 212, 215–17
Stalin, Josef 122, 125, 147–9, 153–6, 158, 162, 164, 166–7, 171–3, 179, 186, 207
Stimson, Henry 127–9, 130, 145, 147, 155, 172
Strong, Josiah 93
Sumner, William Graham 92
Syngman Rhee 180–1

Taliban 220–1, 225–6, 237–8
Trail of Tears 69
Tenochtitlan 22–3, 25
Tet Offensive 195
Tisquantum (Squanto) 35, 241n

Tokyo 1, 2, 12, 121, 139, 146
Tonkin Gulf Resolution 193
Treaty of Versailles 118–19, 122–3
Triple Alliance 105
Triple Entente 105
Truman Doctrine 162, 164, 180
Truman, Harry S. 124, 145–7, 154–8, 162–4, 166–9, 172, 175–6, 178–80, 182, 184–5, 191, 202–3
Turner, Frederick Jackson 91

USS *Maine* 99

Viet Minh 190
Vietnam 2, 10, 17, 123, 125, 160, 175, 189–92, 195–6, 199
Vietnam, North, 188, 193
Vietnam, South, 189–90, 193, 195
Vietnam War 166–99
Viet Minh 189–92

Wahunsonacock 27, 31–3, 35
Wallace, Henry 141, 166–7
Wampanoag 27, 34–5, 39–41
War of 1812 2, 3, 64
War Plan Orange 129, 139
Washington, George 3, 6, 48, 50, 53, 55, 57, 60, 64, 211, 230
Whiskey Rebellion 56
Wilson Woodrow 11, 103, 104, 110, 112–21, 123, 150, 245n.
Wolfowitz, Paul 215, 223
World War II 1
Wounded Knee massacre 63, 81, 231

Yalta 155, 159, 168, 172, 179
Yamamoto, Isoruko 128–9, 131–2, 247n

Zimmerman Note 107, 115–17
Zionist Movement 201
Zhou En-Lai 184